Digital Security in Corporate World by Ratnesh Dwivedi

Create Space ,Am Amazon Company

Books may be purchased by contacting the publisher and author.

Cover Design: Ratnesh Dwivedi

Interior Design: Ratnesh Dwivedi

Publisher: Create Space,An Amazon Company

Editor: Ratnesh Dwivedi

ISBN(10) :1985679698

ISBN(13) :978-1985679696

1. AI 2. API 3. Digital Security 4.Digital Commerce

First Edition: Feb 2018

Printed in USA

Digital Security in Corporate World

Vol-1

Ratnesh Dwivedi

'To My Friends in Corporate World,Who Wants to Do Digitally Secure Business'

Index

The Blueprint to Becoming a Customet Centric Company:How to bring Salesforce's vision of Customer Centric Company to Life

Building a Digital Platform to Lead in the API Economy

Building Transactions to Relationships : Building The Connected Retail Experience

Business Process Management : Best practices for integrating BPM with Anypoint Platform

Closing The IT Delivery Gap:Make Your IT Team More Productive and Innovative

Connectivity Benchmark Report

Deliver zero message loss   environments that scale :A guide   to   cloud messaging   with Anypoint MQ and Anypoint Platform

Digital Transformation in Higher Education:How to increase the clock speed of IT delivery

Foreward

Facebook Inc has recently launched a feature by using which,one can track any photograph posted by his friend or any one not in his/her friend's list, but using Facebook.The feature is based on API and Computational Intelligence System.Similary 'Vahna' a drone flying car is completey digitally operated based on Artificial Intelligence,API and Computational Intelligence System.Its been almost 30 years world has been doing business on digital platforms.From fundamental services like e-mailing and accounting now digital landescape has covered entire corporate world upto minutest and deepest part. From Banking and Finance,Insurance,IT and Software,Aviation and Automobile,Defence,Intelligence and Security,Mining,Oil and Gas,Energy,Media,Government,Academia,Basic Sciences,Medical Sciences,Engineering and Technology and so on.

Above sectors and rest of those which are not mentioned here can not move a bit withot digital intervention.But the more these sectors are dependent on digital lansescape more is the danger of security lapses,data theft,and data protection from wrong doings and wrong hands.

The Volume -1 of book 'Digital Security in Corporate World' deal with many major and minor areas as under

5 Proven Steps for Retail Survival:How to Transform for a Digital World

7 ways APIs, microservices, and DevOps can transform your business

The 7 Habbits of Highly Effective API and Service Management

10 lessons every product executive should know 10 about their API program

Anypoint Platform Performance

Anypoint Platform Cloud Security and Compliance

API Led Connectivity for Australian Government

API-led Connectivity for other Governments

API-led Connectivity : The Next Step in the Evolution of SOA

APIs and Devops) Great Alone,Better Together

Architecting the Composable Enterprise IT for the 21st century

Software may be eating the world but APIs are giving it teeth

Best Practices for Microservices Implementing a foundation for continuous innovation

The Blueprint to Becoming a Customet Centric Company:How to bring Salesforce's vision of Customer Centric Company to Life

Building a Digital Platform to Lead in the API Economy

Building Transactions to Relationships : Building The Connected Retail Experience

Business Process Management : Best practices for integrating BPM with Anypoint Platform

Closing The IT Delivery Gap:Make Your IT Team More Productive and Innovative

Connectivity Benchmark Report

Deliver zero message loss   environments that scale :A guide   to cloud messaging   with Anypoint MQ   and Anypoint Platform

Digital Transformation in Higher Education:How to increase the clock speed of IT delivery

The Vol 1 of book has tried to touch upon all sectors which use digital technology for minute to minute business.

In this great and lengthy work Author expresses his thanks to his close friend in The Langley - Christopher Daemon for being of tremendous help in providing materials.Author spent 15 sleepless nights to proof read,edit and design the book.

My parents at such stage of 78 and 70 respectively,when they should be taking rest, are still worrying and supporting his son with all thier might.I have no words to thank both of them.My wife Suman and 9 year old Son Pragun are now habitual of my cynicism for global neteorking and research and I must thank both of them for all the adjustments both are doing in thier life.Last a word of thanks to Amazon for providing platform for publishing this worthwhile work.

Ratnesh Dwived

Feb 16,2018

5 Proven Steps for Retail Survival: How to Transform for a Digital World

Introduction

In recent years, much of the retail press has been centered on new channels to market: e-commerce, m-commerce, and omni-channel commerce. Thanks to the high-profile bankruptcies of Borders Books and Tower Records, industry analysts rung the death knell for brick-and-mortar retail. They claimed it was simply not possible to compete with the choice, convenience, and cost benefits that e-commerce vendors like Amazon provided.

But, as brick-and-mortar stores continue to flourish, that prediction has proven to be premature. Apple's retail stores have proven to be enormously successful, and pure play e-commerce vendors such as Bonobos, Warby Parker and even Amazon itself have all opened physical stores.

This success reflects a new point of competition: customer experience. Customers' purchasing decisions are based on more than just price and product. Customers are placing increasing value on their relationship with the brand, a personalized shopping experience and seamless service across channels, irrespective of whether they are online or offline. In this context, retailers with physical locations, who are able to deliver human interactions that are empathetic to customers' needs, have an inherent advantage in delivering a superior experience.

However, this change reflects a much deeper shift. As customer purchasing decisions focus less on product and price, so too is the market moving away from the traditional competitive paradigms of scale and scope. In a world in which the customer experience trumps all, the point of competition now becomes speed of execution. How quickly can retailers meet customers' needs? How quickly can they respond to changing preferences? And how quickly can they respond to volatile economic and market conditions? In a world where once the large dominated the small, it is now the fast that are out-competing the slow.

Amazon's success is not because it is an e-commerce retailer. Amazon's success is based on its maniacal focus on moving faster than any of its competitors. As Jeff Bezos, Amazon's founder and CEO, said in his 2015 letter to shareholders, "We want to combine extraordinary customer-serving capabilities with speed of movement, and nimbleness."

IT is central to this change. IT has emerged as the key enabler of business strategy and business execution. And so, in a world in which the key point of competition is speed, the speed at which an organization can operate is in large part determined by the speed at which the IT function can deliver.

How then can IT leaders deliver the speed necessary to win against a backdrop of narrowing margins and growing resource constraints? How can they free up teams from "keep the lights on" IT to projects that will deliver growth? Existing responses, such as agile development approaches, are necessary but not sufficient to deliver the exponential increases in speed that customers are demanding.

MuleSoft's experience shows that winning retailers - both brick-and-mortar and e-commerce retailers alike - are making a deliberate shift to change their IT operating models. Rather than viewing IT as a delivery function, they choose to frame IT as an enablement function. By delivering technology assets, captured as reusable API building blocks, Central IT can act as a platform that allows Line of Business (LoB) teams to self-serve. And by driving reuse of these assets across teams, these organizations can then realize a 2-5x increase in productivity, and ultimately, speed of execution.

Distilling learnings from working leaders in this space - including 2 of the top 5 global retailers, and 4 of the top 7 global CPG firms - read on to discover 5 principles that will help retailers reach their digital transformation goals and thrive in today's competitive environment.

> "The new IT operating model was necessary to make sure that we build the foundation to drive agility and speed. The big benefit to the business of becoming more agile is the opportunity to innovate everywhere, not only in central IT."
>
> — Frank Brandes, Director, Global Enterprise
>
> Business Integration, Unilever

5 Architectural Principles for Success

01 Deliver central API assets to enable innovation "at the edge"

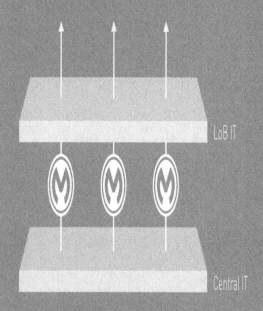

LoB IT

Central IT

Retail organizations often operate in multiple geographic markets and multiple product segments, each with their own idiosyncrasies. To reflect customers' needs, it's critical that local teams are able to drive innovation in their local markets.

Yet many IT teams are unable to do this because of day-to-day, business-as-usual IT demands. In fact, consensus estimates from analyst firms such as Gartner and Forrester put "keep the lights on" IT spend at 70-85 percent.

By providing a central backbone of services, Central IT can provide the platform for growth that allows LoB teams to focus on innovation and growth.

| Proof point | A global quick service restaurant with locations in more than 100 countries wanted to consolidate best practices and accelerate innovation at scale. Central IT built out a set of reusable services that allowed in-country teams to self-serve and drive local innovation. For example, a mobile application is now launching in multiple countries that is built on a common core, yet allows each region to differentiate.

02 Drive reuse of API assets to increase agility

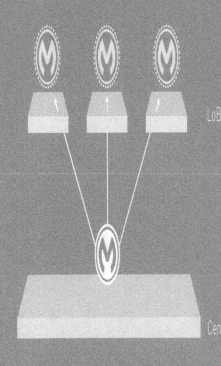

LoB IT

Central IT

In an omni-channel world, customers demand the same shopping experience across in-store, web and mobile channels. This presents a complex connectivity challenge as retail IT teams must work across different business units and bring together disparate technology solutions combining POS, on-premises ERP and SaaS e-commerce solutions.

As the number of sales channels or markets grows, this work is often needlessly duplicated through custom code. This results in additional effort and cost, and opens the door for inconsistent processes.

Delivering this connectivity logic through API building blocks that can then be reused across channels, can provide 2-5x increases in implementation speed.

| Proof point | America's leading rent-to-own retailer drives sales through in-store, web, and franchisees, as well as more recently building a new sales channel through kiosks installed at third party retailers. By reusing core business services, this retailer is able to launch new channels 2x faster than before.

3

03 Ensure API assets are discoverable

In organizations where central assets do exist, they are often hidden or difficult to find.

As a result, LoB teams find that it is easier to (re)create their own assets, rather than invest the time in looking further.

For developers to leverage the API-led building blocks, it's critical to remove as much friction as possible. This should include ensuring that APIs are easy for developers to find and incorporate into their workflow, as well as considering internal evangelism and education efforts to promote awareness.

| **Proof point** | Coca-Cola works with an international network of bottling subsidiaries and wanted to drive consistent processes across the entire network. Therefore, Coca-Cola developed a set of reusable integration assets that are shared through MuleSoft's Anypoint Exchange, a centralized, easy-to-use platform which all groups can access to discover and consume what's been built.

04 Build API assets to enable self-service

Even if API assets are discoverable, they will not be leveraged by developers if they are not easy to consume.

Developers invariably search for the most efficient way to solve the problem that is in front of them. If the developer onboarding experience is poor - for example, if the API is not well documented - API assets will ultimately not be adopted and developers will turn to lower friction alternatives to meet their needs.

Therefore, just like the end-to-end customer experience in retail, thinking about the end-to-end developer experience is critical for success.

| **Proof point** | GANT, a leading lifestyle and apparel retailer with 750 stores in 70 markets, has partnered with MuleSoft to build a set of reusable API assets that can be leveraged across geographies. To support adoption, GANT has leveraged MuleSoft's Anypoint Platform to build API portals to help developers understand how to use the APIs, as well as "API notebooks" that include interactive API examples.

5

05 Think beyond technology

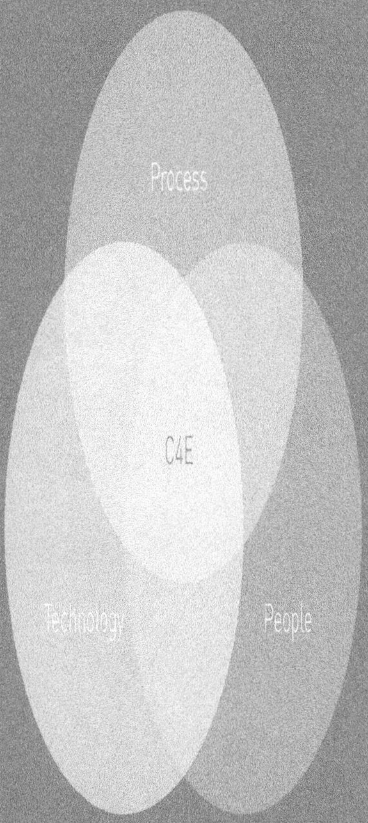

Successfully implementing these architectural approaches demands more than just technology. It requires a change in organizational mindset, and may also require new roles to be created or redistributed across team members. For example, in a world where services are more prevalent, greater resourcing must be devoted to DevOps.

Without such a holistic consideration of the end-to-end lifecycle, the impact of such architectural approaches will at best be limited, and at worst, nonexistent, as IT teams revert to existing approaches.

In this context, organizations should consider building a cross-functional Center for Enablement (C4E team that helps to catalyze, lead, and role model such change.

Process

C4E

Technology   People

| **Proof point** | Unilever, one of the world's leading consumer packaged goods companies, partnered with MuleSoft to set up an in-house adaptive integration capability, which operates in a DevOps framework, focused on self-service oriented API connectivity and supported by a Center for Enablement approach.

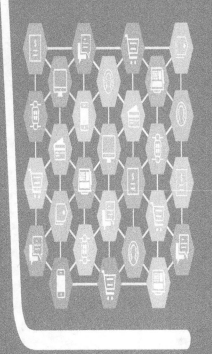

So, now what?

Here are some questions we recommend asking yourself:

-- Is there a gap between the needs of the business and the ability of IT to deliver?

-- Will existing approaches be sufficient to close that gap?

-- Would the principles discussed be relevant to your organization?

How do I start? Where do I start? What's my roadmap for success?

Contact MuleSoft to figure out the best way to get started.

 MuleSoft®

MuleSoft's mission is to connect the world's applications, data and devices. MuleSoft makes connecting anything easy with Anypoint Platform™, the only complete integration platform for SaaS, SOA and APIs. Thousands of organizations in 60 countries, from emerging brands to Global 500 enterprises, use MuleSoft to innovate faster and gain competitive advantage.

7 ways APIs, microservices, and DevOps can transform your business

Co-edited by
Ross Mason

CONTENTS

FOREWORD

Ross Mason

We've all heard the phrase, "Change is the only constant." It has never been more true than now, where nothing stands still and digital disruptors are changing the pace of business at an alarming rate. As a result, organizations are increasingly looking for ways to become more agile. This has left us with a variety of technology buzzwords, from microservices to DevOps to digital platforms to APIs, all promising great gain.

In a buzzword-laden landscape, it's worth asking which are worth the cost and time to implement. Which actually provide enterprise value? The answer is that they all could—or none could.

The type of transformation enterprises are looking for isn't a simple matter of buying software and optimistically hoping that it will magically transform the issues in a business. To get good at constant change and thrive in today's hyper-competitive business environment, organizations need to be deterministic and create an organizational capacity for change.

This means leadership needs to set and frequently reinforce the expectation that roles and processes need to change too, in order to support a new way of operating. It also means leadership and their teams need to define how the changes will be measured so that everyone is on the same page around what is working and what is not.

In this book, we will present several points of view on DevOps, microservices, and APIs, all of which are designed to help you create that organizational capacity for change. The pieces in this book will serve as thought starters to help you reach your digital transformation goals.

It's time to look beyond the buzzwords and make the tech trends serve the larger enterprise. Don't let fear of missing out get the best of your judgement; make these trends and technologies uniquely work for you.

APIs, microservices, and the changing role of IT

BY ROSS MASON

To succeed in today's digital economy, organizations need to drive at a very different clock speed and embrace change in their customer's market, competitive landscape and products. Below are five technology trends that I predict will have a major impact on businesses.

1. The changing role of IT

With new digital disruptors knocking down the door and competition growing fierce across all industries, I predict we will see an uptick in organizations making an effort to change the way they operate internally to innovate more quickly at the edges. The role of IT is fundamental to this organizational change, as it starts with IT unlocking core systems with APIs and then working cross-functionally with development teams to encourage and empower them to build some of their own solutions using IT-provided, self-service assets like APIs and templates. The broader development team is also encouraged to add new assets or improve existing assets, scaling the network effect of these assets.

Aligning the broader business around the same mindset fosters a collaborative environment, where teams will automatically inquire into what assets exist that can accelerate their current projects, or what assets don't exist that they can create for others to reuse in future projects. As the asset base grows, more teams become self-reliant and can drive new products to market faster. With consumer expectations changing frequently, organizations require a new IT operating model to build and iterate faster to stay competitive. Taking five months to build a mobile API that adds a customer-expected service and then another five months to implement the change won't cut it any longer.

2. The rise of internal API economies

I predict we'll see more organizations participate in the external API economy by opening up services to third parties via APIs in an effort to drive revenue by joining as many value chains as possible. According to a Harvard Business Review article, Salesforce generates 50 percent of its revenue through APIs, Expedia generates 90 percent and eBay generates 60 percent, showing that APIs are real revenue drivers if leveraged properly. Many banks, for instance, are starting to leverage APIs to not only unlock data from core systems but also to build whole ecosystems around their product offerings. With ProgrammableWeb's directory now surpassing 16,500 open APIs, the opportunities to participate in the external API economy are only growing.

However, in order to participate in the external API economy, organizations first need to establish an internal API economy. This is accomplished by using APIs to help remove the limitations of legacy systems and empower the broader organization to be self-reliant. As a result, organizations can move faster, be more agile, deliver products and services more cheaply and quickly and react to changing market conditions.

3. API security is now a top-level concern

The role of APIs in securing enterprise data is hugely important, yet undervalued. Imagine a house with many closed doors and windows that represent access to enterprise data. Over the years, people have likely opened up most of the windows, the back door and even dug tunnels to gain access. With all these visible and hidden points of entry, it's extremely difficult to lock down the data, understand who uses it, where they use it and where it goes when it leaves the four walls of the enterprise.

The internal value of APIs is to provide a single entry point for all data sources, removing any unwanted back doors, windows and tunnels. IT can make sure access is only gained through the front door, or the API, which is secured by design. Secured by design means an API would never be released that doesn't have credentials that are signed and regulated. While it's beneficial to have data move around the enterprise freely to speed up efficiency, IT needs to govern and control it and even shut it down if the information has been syphoned out without proper authority. I believe more companies will start to mitigate data risk internally with APIs.

4. Microservices architecture keeps gaining traction

The challenge for organizations is understanding how they will build and leverage their microservice architecture. Do individuals build the exact services they need every time they need them (e.g., Netflix)? Do organizations form small teams around bits of code that operate independently (e.g., Spotify)? Or some other variation that mixes-and-matches microservices with other architectures?

Microservices are great at early-stage implementation. However, as teams build microservices that could be beneficial if leveraged by a broader set of people, those microservices should graduate into APIs, which have interfaces and are discoverable. A microservice is not meant to have an interface but rather serves a piece of functionality in an application. If teams open that microservice up to a broader audience internally or externally, they should put an API on top of it and start managing that as a reusable capability. I believe more companies will start to bridge the gap between microservices and traditional systems with APIs to promote development speed and agility.

5. Chatbots for customer service

We will see a lot of experiments focused on figuring out how best to fuse automation and human control to provide better customer service and support. How much can organizations actually automate without driving the customer away? What's the right balance between automating something through software versus getting humans involved? How do organizations change the interaction model between their customers and partners to help them find information quicker without pointing to a representative?

In the near term, chatbots need to quickly understand intonation to determine if the caller should go to a representative or stay on the line to answer a few more questions. If the caller gets frustrated because too many questions are being asked by the chatbot, the system should recognize the frustrated tone and push the caller through to a representative. The representative should then be equipped with all the caller's information so the caller doesn't get more frustrated at having to repeat everything (we've all been through this). Balancing chatbot automation with human interaction won't be successful if the two worlds don't hand off well to each other, and APIs are at the core of accomplishing this.

What do you think? Are these five trends impacting your organization? And what other trends should we watch out for?[1]

---

1   This article first appeared on InfoWorld.

Thinking outside the microservices box

BY PAUL CRERAND

Microservices are on the rise, with almost half (44%) of IT professionals now deploying applications as a set of independent, modular assets that support individual business processes. There's plenty of reasons why there's so much buzz around this approach right now.

Microservices are essentially a way of breaking large, monolithic applications down into a set of loosely coupled functions that are clearly defined to support a specific business process. This enables organizations to roll-out new digital capabilities much faster and reduce the risk of disruption during updates, making them well-suited for customer-facing processes.

Searching for a microservices blueprint

While there's widespread acceptance of these benefits, many IT teams are still in the dark as to how best to make the shift to microservices. All too often, organizations will simply look to others that have pioneered a successful approach; especially the trendy digital natives such as Netflix or Spotify. Given some organizations, particularly in highly regulated industries, have different security and compliance needs, trying to emulate a singular approach might not be feasible.

For example, larger organizations with more legacy systems and siloed applications will have different needs than younger, smaller firms. Every organization is unique, so what works for one won't necessarily work for another. 130-year-old Unilever, for example, created over 80 microservices to support its continued growth, allowing the company to connect its eCommerce applications to the various legacy systems that support its core operations across a global portfolio of brands. Unilever is pairing its microservices architecture with API-led connectivity to drastically reduce development time for new eCommerce applications.

As a result, Unilever is able to deploy three to four times faster, proving that organizations with aging legacy IT and established cultures can gain major advantages from reengineering their applications around a microservices architecture if they use the right approach.

Creating a pragmatic tailor-made architecture

Organizations with diverse circumstances and requirements can all benefit from microservices. So, what should organizations consider when looking to build out their own pragmatic blueprint for a microservices architecture?

→ **Identifying the right tool for the job:** It's important to remember that a microservices architecture might not be the best fit for every application. If an organization, for instance, relies heavily on a legacy ERP application that has supported critical business processes for decades, then it should make sure the rewards of switching to a microservices approach outweigh the risks of keeping the legacy application in place.

Just as organizations get the most from the cloud by identifying which workloads will benefit most from moving out of an internal data center, they must ask the right questions to determine whether the benefits outweigh the risks of reengineering established applications.

➡ **Managing microservices with APIs:** By their nature, microservices proliferate. So at a large scale, organizations could find them just as, or even more, unwieldy as the monolithic applications they're designed to replace. As a result, it's vital to consider how microservices will be managed as large numbers of small teams build apps and access business critical systems and data on a regular basis.

One way to manage microservices effectively is through well-managed APIs, given each microservice exposes a managed API endpoint. The end result: Developers and lines of business users can innovate quickly while central IT maintains the right SLA, governance and security.

➡ **Connecting to legacy and SaaS apps:** For larger organizations with more legacy systems and SaaS applications in place, it's also critical to identify how these systems can be integrated with microservices. Again, API-led connectivity provides an ideal solution to avoiding the astronomical costs that would result from building point-to-point integrations. Unilever took this approach to create an eCommerce platform that unified its portfolio of more than 400 brands on a common operating model.

Using API-led connectivity, Unilever created an application network to connect the platform's multiple tools–including NetSuite, Demandware and Google Analytics, among others–and provide access to key on-premises systems such as SAP, which holds its product and customer master data.

Seeing the bigger picture

Ultimately, microservices will be an essential tool in meeting an accelerated pace of customer demand. Yet, organizations should be careful not to get caught up in the hype and embark on a microservices deployment without first understanding what the right approach is.

'One-size-fits-all' is rarely true in IT, and microservices are no different. By taking their own unique circumstances into account, organizations will find it much easier to understand how to get the most from a microservices architecture.[2]

2   This article first appeared on Information Age.

Why DevOps and APIs are a match made in heaven

BY PAUL CRERAND

In our technology-driven world, organizations cannot afford to stand still. They need to deliver software at high velocity without sacrificing stability, which is why DevOps has become such a popular approach.

As the name suggests, DevOps is an attempt to combine software development and IT operations in order to effectively get the best of both worlds: the rapid iteration favored by the former and the stability, reliability and security favored by the latter. Ultimately, DevOps helps to ensure that IT can more effectively support the needs of the business.

But it isn't just DevOps practices that improve the bottom line for companies. Alongside the move to DevOps, companies are also recognizing the need for API strategies to accelerate innovation.

According to MuleSoft's 2017 Connectivity Benchmark Report, 94 percent of IT leaders say they can deliver new products and services to market faster with APIs. Together, DevOps and APIs deliver greater business value than what they can deliver individually.

When Dev met Ops

The DevOps movement has exploded over the past few years. Gartner pegged 2016 as the year when it finally broke through into the mainstream, employed by 25 percent of Global 2000 organizations. Furthermore, of the 50 enterprises ECS Digital surveyed, only 11 percent said they aren't planning to adopt DevOps.

Modern, "fail fast", cloud-centric organizations powered by automated and agile development processes like Amazon are leading the DevOps charge. For those more reliant on legacy technology and operating in highly regulated industries, such as financial services, adoption o this relatively new approach has been slower.

After all, DevOps requires a significant cultural change. However, many are starting the journey by adopting new tools to strip out inefficiencies from the development lifecycle. It's all about accelerating time-to-market to meet customer demand, while reducing failure rates and inefficiency.

An unexpected bump

There are challenges associated with this new approach to software development and delivery. For example, if organizations become too focused on the production model, it can become all-too-easy to keep on pushing out software assets without thinking about whether they offer real value to the business.

Or worse, those assets live in a silo and aren't discoverable and reusable by the rest of the business. Just because it is much easier to produce in this environment, it doesn't mean the code production treadmill should keep on turning unfettered.

Organizations therefore need to balance the highly efficient DevOps production model with an efficient consumption and reuse model via APIs. Consider a DevOps project designed to expose customer data from a legacy platform onto a mobile app.

With a well-designed API, that legacy data can be discovered inside the organization by other teams so that they too can use the information for other projects. The approach is faster, more efficient and cost-effective. Additionally, the more discoverable the assets, the faster they become ready for reuse, potentially to audiences that might otherwise not have known about them, thus driving greater agility and innovation.

DevOps and APIs—the perfect partners

With this API-led connectivity approach, every asset becomes a managed API, discoverable through self-service with no loss of control. Organizations as diverse as Spotify and Siemens are already embracing this approach to become more agile, efficient and innovative.

Like Amazon, Spotify has been at the vanguard of the DevOps movement, benefitting from a slick, seamless pipeline of software production. However, it also found that multiple departments were producing duplicate assets and that these assets were difficult or those outside their specific silo to take advantage of.

Using APIs to build an application network, Spotify has been able to expose the capabilities being moved through the pipeline to third-party partners and internally to speed up time-to-market and create new business opportunities.

Siemens, meanwhile, has been able to expose assets managed by its data management team via APIs, eliminating bottlenecks and ensuring partners and internal teams can self-serve to drive greater business agility.

It did so in part thanks to a cross-functional team spanning central IT, line of business and mobile teams that ensures all assets created through the DevOps pipeline are broadly consumed and fully utilized. The results speak for themselves: Siemens has halved the time taken to get a first release of a new capability out to other teams in the business working on related projects.

The marriage of API-led connectivity with DevOps will not necessarily be easy, requiring a change in mind-set to one where assets are produced with the intent that they will be consumed by others in the business. As such, central IT needs to change culturally to become an enabler of reusable, self-service consumption. However, as the likes of Spotify and Siemens can attest, the rewards speak for themselves.[3]

---

3   This article first appeared on the Computer Business Review.

API-driven microservices will become the norm

BY PAUL CRERAND

Despite being an obsolete term a few years ago, "microservices architecture" is fast becoming one of the most popular ways to design software applications. Widely regarded for the agility it affords organizations in today's fast-changing world, microservices allow organizations to break down large, monolithic applications into a set of loosely coupled services.

Yet, amid microservices' growing popularity, organizations should not do it for fashion. One size doesn't fit all and trying to follow in the footsteps of pioneers like Spotify and Netflix might not be feasible.

For example, one of the major challenges for established companies when adopting microservices is learning how to mix this architecture pattern with the many other architectural patterns already deployed in the enterprise. Additionally, companies need to learn how to manage the speed and flexibility that microservices fuel, as well as the complexity it creates.

To gain true value from microservices, business and IT leaders need to start by assessing business objectives and evaluating if the architecture can coexist with traditional applications, as well as current systems, business processes and operational and compliance imperatives, combined with their DevOps capability and maturity. For most organizations, it will mean complementing microservices with an API strategy.

Why microservices?

The microservices approach is in many ways a modern reincarnation of the decades-old idea of component-based development (CBD, and it also draws upon the principles of Service-oriented Architecture (SOA. Thanks to standardized containers, highly flexible cloud infrastructure and APIs—which tie apps, systems and devices together—microservices allow developers to break down monolithic apps into loosely coupled functions focused on supporting specific business processes. In so doing, organizations can be much more agile in responding to new market requirements, rolling out robust digital capabilities quickly and easily to customers, employees, and partners alike.

From an IT perspective, the benefits are even clearer. Aside from the fact that microservices are faster to build, test and deploy, they also add reliability to the mix. If a fault occurs, for example, it will only affect users of that specific service rather than the entire IT stack.

Microservices are also easy to scale and can be changed, updated and deployed in a simple, automated manner. For developers, microservices mean greater flexibility and productivity, allowing them to independently develop and deploy services in smaller teams, and code in the languages and frameworks they're most comfortable with.

The importance of an API strategy

However, organizations must also be aware that microservices aren't a silver bullet. For one thing, this architectural approach creates an increasing number of services that can result in information barriers and service sprawl.

Additionally, it usually brings additional complexity for developers, who now have to mitigate fault tolerance and network latency, while dealing with a variety of message formats as well as load balancing. There's also a danger of duplication of effort; teams must put extra resources into transparency and communication, especially in use cases spanning more than one service.

To help tame microservices complexity, organizations should implement an API strategy. APIs not only bridge the gap between microservices and traditional systems, they also make microservices easier to build and manage. With an API strategy, organizations can expose the functionality of microservices as products, which can lead to the creation of both internal and external business value.

APIs can also overcome the significant costs associated with building point-to-point integrations between legacy systems and SaaS apps, enabling organizations to quickly plug and unplug microservices into their application networks, which connect digital assets and capabilities across the entire IT stack.

Firms like Spotify are taking this approach, using APIs to manage and connect microservices as part of a DevOps push to streamline business processes and create a more agile and responsive company. For example, SKY has adopted a microservices architecture approach for which it uses

Replaceability, Operability, Accessibility & Maintainability (ROAM as its guiding principles.

It's not all about those at the vanguard of technology in-novation either; 130-year-old Unilever has built over 80 microservices to connect eCommerce applications with legacy systems around the world.

Thanks to an API-led connectivity approach, the global giant has been able to reduce development time and deploy 3-4 times faster to drive success. Other more traditional compa-nies, including high street lending giant Barclays, and airline flydubai, are reaping similar benefits from microservices by taking the same approach.

Looking ahead

It's important not to rush into microservices just because it's what others are doing. Organizations that are heavily reliant on monolithic legacy deployments must do their research first to make sure that switching will be worth the disruption caused by re-engineering these applications. However, if they do, API-led connectivity is the only choice to manage the crucial integration piece effectively and minimize the risk of uncontrollable microservices sprawl.

In today's uncompromising business climate, organizations need to take calculated risks to stand out from the crowd, get closer to customers and work more productively. More and more organizations around the world will look to a combination of microservices and API-led connectivity to do just that.[4]

4   This article first appeared on Information Age.

Splunk's CIO on DevOps, APIs, and the evolving role of IT

BY ROSS MASON

The role of IT has evolved from a centralized delivery model to IT as a service, where IT-owned capabilities are being offered as a service throughout the business to drive new levels of agility. One CIO embracing the changing role is Declan Morris of Splunk, which enables organizations to turn massive streams of data into operational intelligence. (Disclosure: Splunk is a customer of my employer, MuleSoft.)

In this Q&A, Declan explains how Splunk's IT team is driving value across the organization and partnering with the business to deliver on unified vision focused on customers and growth. Recalling his experiences at Splunk and Adobe—where he was on the original team that helped launch Adobe Creative Cloud—Declan shares best practices around how CIOs can take advantage of the technology trends impacting every industry and how CIOs can help pivot to new business models when needed.

The role of the CIO is getting harder. Why on earth do you do it?

Declan Morris: It's a great time to be in IT. I love the rate of innovation that we're seeing in our industry. When I started my career, the typical product rollout was approximately 12 to 18 months. However, the consumerization of IT has accelerated everything. Now, the companies making serious change and thriving are the folks that are excited about what's going on in IT. They realize the power of IT and harness it to drive customer adoption and business growth.

How is Splunk's IT team armed for this fast-paced era?

DM: The typical IT shop will hire business system analysts (BSAs) as a means to engage with their internal clients. However, I believe that the traditional IT model is done and dusted. At Splunk, we strive to hire product managers and product owners. We want people to have a passion for what they own and to really think about IT as a product. That means creating a companywide vision, aligning the rest of the organization around that vision and executing against it. This is the way I truly believe IT is going. It's inevitable.

I'd love to unpack the shift from IT to product more. What role do APIs play in this shift at Splunk?

DM: We are now an API-driven economy. There's no question. APIs allow us to bring disparate sets of services together to create something new, where the whole is greater than the sum of the parts. And, we can do it in record time. For example, when challenged to launch Splunk Cloud trial in 90 days, traditionally that would have been handled exclusively by the product organization. However, our IT team was able to deliver 95 percent of the functionality using an API-based strategy, where our team could easily orchestrate behind the scenes with other SaaS providers like AWS, Ping, Stripe, and Salesforce. We delivered the trial in less than 90 days, contributing to accelerated adoption of our Splunk Cloud solution across the industry. I shudder to think what it would have taken if we attempted this initiative five to seven years ago.

With the right API strategy, IT can truly deliver business value. In return, the value raises the executive leadership team's confidence in the IT organization's ability to deliver, which in turn leads to further investment opportunities. At Splunk, we're in the early stages of truly creating an API marketplace, where we can extract value from reuse and consistency across the board. The building blocks are there. That is absolutely the way we're heading. As noted in a recent McKinsey article, the IT department is "radically reframing." In conjunction with this reframe is the need for CIOs to evolve and partner closer with business leaders.

How do you communicate the value your team is building to your CEO and CFO?

DM: If the executive leadership team doesn't know where they're going, then IT has no way of knowing where it's going. Splunk's CEO Doug Merritt has been crystal clear and consistent in his messaging for what our vision is to get to $2 billion in revenue in the next three years. It makes my job, frankly, a lot easier. As a team, IT can reverse engineer from that viewpoint and can critically look at what the business needs are to drive greater value rather than becoming a choke point—the worst outcome for any CIO.

From one month to the next, our business is never static. CIOs have to be adaptable in this environment and comfortable with ambiguity. If priorities have changed for the right reasons and it's tied to business value, change is good.

However, many CIOs will encounter an executive leadership team that's less open to change or lacks a crystal-clear vision. In these situations, one effective strategy is to gut check your idea with all the major influencers before engaging the CEO. When the CEO seriously questions what is being put forward, the rest of the executive leadership team can jump to your support because they have their fingerprints on the strategy.

How do you approach the adoption and management of SaaS applications in your IT landscape?

DM: This behavior is induced by what the business drivers are. It's not about cherry-picking a SaaS solution. The SaaS solutions we consider have to blend in with our overall corporate strategy, and we hinge our IT strategy off where our CEO is taking the company. Earlier this year, he put down the challenge to the organization to double revenue in the next three years that could double our employee base. That's been a rally call for the company. Our responsibility within IT is to ensure that the additional SaaS applications we introduce on top of our platform actually complement and contribute towards that goal. We take a very critical approach to evaluating what SaaS vendors play well within our ecosystem and to ensuring that they're expansible.

Additionally, I think the SaaS providers have done an amazing job circumventing IT to a certain extent and going straight to the business to sell their technology. While a couple years ago this created a sea of shadow IT within companies, today we're having more constructive and healthy conversations with the wider business on what problems they are trying to solve. At Splunk, we have a Portfolio Working Group with representation from every major part of the business. We meet as a group to come up with ways to solve the business needs.

Furthermore, it's imperative that IT teams understand how to diagnose their SaaS environments. If an error occurs and the CEO asks what happened, you can't simply say, "Well that was SaaS, so we don't have the ability to do an inquiry." There's an expectation. My advice is to pay close attention to the SaaS providers you work with to ensure that you can really tap into their environment and have access to what you need to run your business.

A slightly different topic: How are you implementing DevOps?

DM: If you have a DevOps team, it's probably a red flag. DevOps is a framework, not a team. One way to know you have DevOps is when you look around the table, you are unable to separate the ops people from the engineers because they're working closely together. Also, when you have the inevitable P1, who takes the call? If DevOps is done right, there is truly a joint sense of ownership. It shouldn't be about the ops person restoring service. It's "we" need to restore the service. In today's DevOps world, the mission team should be able to sit around a physical table and collaborate. At Splunk, we're absolutely all in. It's invigorating and exciting. We have a lot of folks to thank, including Spotify and Amazon Web Services (AWS), for being pioneers in the space.

Finally, what advice would you give to CIOs going through major transitions?

DM: When companies go through major transitions as they scale, more often than not CIOs will encounter the corporate antibodies—the naysayers that question why they need to change when they've always done it a certain way. The advice I give to every CIO is as follows: If you're going through a major transition, especially one where there will be corporate antibodies, peel off an energized and motivated team to execute the transition and set them up for success. The team doesn't have to be very large—in my previous job at Adobe, I left behind a product team of 350 to start a team of 12. For me, it was inevitable our industry would go through a seismic shift, and if we didn't embrace it, we were going to be left on the wayside.[5]

5   This article first appeared on CIO.com.

How the API Economy is igniting a cultural shift in businesses

BY ROSS MASON

We are in the middle of a generational shift in technology. The convergence of digital forces—namely mobile, SaaS, cloud, big data, Internet of Things (IoT), and social—is creating a massive disruption in the market and altering consumer expectations. Today, everything needs to be personalized, dynamic, always on, and always mobile.

As a result, there's no shortage of organizations hoping to reinvent themselves for the digital age. Success in today's fast-paced economy relies on continuous innovation and adaptation, leaving no room for disjointed technologies and stagnant processes.

However, most organizations are struggling to adapt to this new, rapid way, which may be one of the reasons why 52 percent of the Fortune 500 have fallen off the list since

2000. It also explains a key reason why the likes of Amazon, which is manically focused on moving faster than competitors, has climbed the ranks in under eight years.

For Amazon, winning is about speed, agility, inventiveness and an ability to try many experiments rapidly and fail fast. Recent experiments by the once-exclusively internet company include opening its first brick-and-mortar retail store and soon opening its first convenience stores.

It's clear the big no longer eat the small; the fast eat the slow. Speed is one of the single most important characteristics that determine a company's success today. It's critical for bringing new products to market, establishing new global presences, changing existing processes, and onboarding new partners—all faster than competition.

However, speed is proving to be a struggle across industries as new digital forces converge. So, how can companies speed up to win in the API economy, which is simply the sum of digital exchanges between two or more parties?

The IT delivery gap

A big barrier for companies looking to achieve speed is the IT delivery gap. IT has a relatively fixed set of resources and a constrained capacity to deliver on new projects. Yet, as new digital forces enter the workplace, the business wants to move faster and continuously evolve to meet new market and consumer needs. All of a sudden, project backlogs build up and overwhelm central IT teams, who then hold back the business.

In this frazzled state, IT teams often resort to creating shortcuts to complete projects on tighter timelines and smaller budgets. These shortcuts often mean creating point-to-point connections between systems, usually with an outsourced workforce. However, each point-to-point connection creates tight dependencies between applications so any future changes require extensive and costly downstream work.

The resulting technical debt compounds the problem with little thought given to long term manageability or reuse. Eventually, business users don't feel a strong partnership with the IT team, leading them to take matters into their own hands and purchase their own technology tools. This is known as shadow IT, and it puts mission critical customer and product data at risk, putting more pressure on central IT.

The reality for established enterprises is that the centralized IT model is no longer working. IT teams can't keep running faster on the project hamster wheel. With today's digital forces knocking down the door, central IT needs to evolve and operate under a new model that caters to ever-changing business needs.

The new IT operating model

To close the IT delivery gap, IT needs to shift away from the traditional project-based approach—where they try to deliver all IT projects themselves—and toward an approach that allows IT to build reusable assets that are consumable by the broader development community within the organization.

The modern API is the core enabler behind this approach. Modern APIs adhere to standards (e.g., HTTP, REST, JSON) that are developer-friendly, language agnostic, and easily accessible and understood broadly by developers. These modern APIs are more than code. They are products; they live beyond any one project; they have a strong discipline for security and governance; and they have their own software development lifecycles (SDLC) of designing, testing, building, managing, and versioning. These new API characteristics completely change the disrupt-or-be-disrupted game.

Now with API-led connectivity, rather than connecting everything point-to-point, key assets become managed APIs that can be discovered by developers in an environment still tightly secured by central IT. Central IT essentially "Lego-ifies" the business, as teams compose, recompose and adapt these building blocks to address changing needs. Then, the speed with which every subsequent project is delivered begins to accelerate because the new operating model eliminates the work needed to build future projects and processes from scratch.

The internal API economy

The web has proven how effective APIs can be in driving speed and innovation on top of self-service capabilities. With approximately 16,000 open APIs on the web, developers can build an idea in days and scale it or kill it just as quickly. Almost all of us use these services every day. Almost every popular mobile app we use leverages building blocks on the web, so app developers don't need to build their own maps, communication services, data services, and more. Developers can focus on building value and innovation on top of these APIs.

To participate in the external API economy, businesses need to drive an internal API economy first. Innovation at the edges doesn't work unless a business can unlock its core, which is often made up of big, monolithic infrastructure. By opening up APIs internally, businesses can free themselves from the limitations of their legacy systems, changing the way they deliver digital products and services to customers, partners and employees.

To drive this innovation, organizations are shifting to an IT-as-a-Service operating model, where IT-owned capabilities are being offered as a service to the business. With this strategy, businesses are creating internal API economies, where assets are consumed and built upon to drive new value internally and externally.

A successful internal API economy requires IT to decentralize and democratize application development and data access to the business as a whole. In addition, central IT needs to invest in enabling a broader set of developers internally to discover, use and self-serve these assets, so the business can deliver more of their own projects. This changes the relationship between IT and the business.

To win in the digital era, companies need to play a larger role in the API economy. We're all used to the instant connectivity that puts the world at our fingertips. Today, it's difficult to imagine standing in a long line at the bank to cash a check, or waiting more than 10 minutes for our taxi to arrive. Whereas a mere five years ago that would have been a normal part of our daily lives.

The unsung hero of our connected world is the modern API. It's what makes possible all the interactivity that we've come to expect and rely upon. It helps drive the speed with which new technology products can be brought to market faster than the competition, establish new market presences quickly, and change processes and workflows to fit evolving consumer tastes.[6]

6   This article first appeared on CIO.com.

Physical, virtual, social: Is the application network next?

BY ROSS MASON

Networks have always been at the heart of our society, defining our relationships, creating our experiences and ultimately shaping our lives. From the steam railways that enabled commerce between cities and towns, to the cables that paved the way for global communication over telephones and then the internet, networks have a history of redefining our way of life.

More recently, the internet has given rise to virtual networks that allow us to connect to vast computing resources, and social networks that allow us to cultivate our own global communities. Recent estimates suggest that by next year, 2.44 billion people will be connected via social networks, illustrating the scale of influence these platforms have on our society. Facebook alone already boasts 1.86 billion active users, with 1.26 billion people signing in every day to connect with their network.

The dawn of a new network

In the new digital era these networks have collectively ushered in, connectivity has become the foundation of every consumer experience, business model, process, product and service. In this world, the more connections that organizations make, the more value they will be able to get out of their digital assets.

Connectivity is critical to new technology advances in areas like the Internet of Things (IoT), artificial intelligence (AI) and augmented reality (AR). None of these technologies work if you can't connect to data and assets. However, given the number of applications, data sources, and devices that companies now rely on, the old way of connecting these assets has broken down; it is too heavy, costly and resource in-tensive. Gluing everything together into one big, monolithic thing is a recipe for disaster in a world where digital change happens so quickly. So much so that recent research found that half of IT departments now fail to complete digital projects on time.

Ultimately, this has brought us to a tipping point where a new type of network, an application network, is needed to connect everything together to open up new possibilities. This new type of network fundamentally changes the way that organizations think about IT delivery and connectivity.

By allowing IT to connect the business to a catalogue of digital assets and capabilities that enable them to self-serve their own innovation projects, an application network ignites a complete cultural and functional shift. Following the principles of Metcalfe's law, every new asset that is connected to the application network increases its overall value by making its data and capabilities available for others to discover and consume. In this way, IT ceases to be a bottleneck through which innovation must flow and instead becomes an enabler to the rest of the business. Where the current IT model involves having to deliver every project from start to finish, IT's task is to provide just enough enablement to encourage the application network to grow, whilst championing best practices and providing governance to create a trusted ecosystem.

The building blocks of software

The nodes of an application network are APIs, which turn digital capabilities into reusable building blocks. The application network provides the 'digital glue' that enables these building blocks to be composed and recomposed for greater agility, flexibility and speed. Businesses can rapidly compose new services and make them pluggable and reusable for anyone who has access. Additionally, discovery becomes inherent and part of the engagement layer of application networks. Business teams will by default look to see if a capability they need already exists, in the same way that consumers head to the Apple App Store to see if there is 'an app for that'.

With an API-led approach to connectivity, business innovation accelerates rapidly, as new applications, data sources and devices can simply be 'plugged' into the application network, as easily as you might plug in a printer. As such, innovation can be led by anyone who has the potential to add value to the organization's digital ecosystem–from internal development teams to external partners.

Ultimately, this is the beginning of the next era of the web, where APIs and application networks can make any capability available to people and machines. We are already starting to see major global organizations beginning to realize the benefits of this approach. For example, Spotify has created an application network by deploying reusable APIs to improve information sharing across its entire business and to develop applications much faster than others in the market. Unilever has similarly used an application network to remove the barriers to business innovation, by shifting the focus away from individual assignments and towards reusable platform capabilities.

In the same way that physical, virtual, and social networks have shaped society, defined relationships and created new experiences, application networks promise to usher in a new wave of business and technology innovation. Take the automotive industry for example, where software companies and car manufacturers are already vying to own the in-vehicle experience.

In the future, people could be paying for experiences powered by many API-connected services, rather than the car itself. More broadly, industry is fast approaching a point where sponsored adverts are replaced with targeted APIs based on their search criteria that allow consumers to directly buy products and services from a web page.

These examples are just the tip of the iceberg of possibilities being created by API-led connectivity. Like the many connectivity revolutions that have come before, application networks will be the cornerstone upon which the next digital revolution is founded, organizing API economies and shaping the course that our society charts into the future.[7]

7   This article first appeared on ITProportal.

ABOUT MULESOFT

MuleSoft makes it easy to connect the world's applications, data and devices. With our market-leading Anypoint Platform™, companies are building application networks to fundamentally change the pace of innovation. MuleSoft's API-led approach to connectivity gives companies new ways to reach their customers, employees and partners. Organizations in more than 60 countries, from emerging companies to Global 500 corporations, use MuleSoft to transform their businesses.

To find out how, visit www.mulesoft.com.

The **7** Habits of Highly Effective API and Service Management

The 7 Habits of Highly Effective API and Service Management

A New Enterprise challenge has emerged. With the number of APIs growing rapidly, managing them one-off or via Excel or corporate wiki is no longer feasible.

The smartest organizations have discovered a set of best practices to design powerful APIs that leverage existing services, to effectively manage those APIs throughout their lifecycle and to scale their deployment across consumers and devices. This eBook examines the relationship between APIs and services and presents the key elements of a successful API strategy in the form of 7 habits.

In this eBook you will learn:

- How to leverage existing services in the API economy
- Where to get started with your API strategy
- Key criteria for selecting an API Management solution
- Strategies to overcome API security and identity challenges
- How and why to apply the fundamentals of API First Design

Table of contents

Changing the game: A shift in strategy

Service Oriented Architecture sets the stage for API management

Over the last decade, many companies implemented SOA to one degree or another in the name of reuse and consistency. By decomposing functionality into atomic services, SOA promised to deliver streamlined processes, increased efficiency, and lower costs. However, few SOA initiatives delivered on this promise.

SOA had the right ambition but the wrong approach. The original intent of SOA - to enable reuse of services, provide flexibility and scalability and to allow interoperability between services and applications - was exactly what businesses wanted. The problem however, was in execution. Organizations incorrectly structured their SOA projects with a "top-down" approach that caused numerous issues across the enterprise. This top-down approach dictated a rip-and-replace strategy whose aim was to gradually replace aging enterprise systems with modern alternatives. The problem was, these projects often dragged on for years, consuming far more resources and budget than planned, ultimately becoming an expensive burden to the business.

This is one of the main reasons why for many, SOA has become a relic of the past, a word replete with negative connotation. The monolithic, top-down initiatives of the past have failed, costing businesses millions of dollars and ultimately failing to deliver projected business value. SOA was essentially considered dead. Nevertheless, the fundamental principles of SOA are still sound and have been given new life in the form of API management.

Next gen SOA: API management

API management is essentially the next generation of SOA. But how will API management avoid the well-known pitfalls that derailed so many SOA initiatives? While API management shares many commonalities with SOA, there are two key differences. First, rather than a top-down, rip-and-replace approach, API management uses a "bottom-up," wrap-and-renew approach. APIs essentially breathe new life into services by layering accessible and developer-friendly interfaces on top of them, effectively shielding consumers from the underlying technology. Secondly, API initiatives are all about ROI. Projects have defined milestones and rapid implementations, making impact immediate and ROI easy to measure.

This approach delivers on the initial promises of SOA and more:

- Accelerated application development
- Reduced risk of failure
- Improved developer effectiveness
- Agility and flexibility

Often considered two sides of the same coin, API management has emerged to pick up where SOA initiatives left off. API management adopted and improved upon the best of the underlying principles of SOA.

SOA and API management share key core principles:

- Abstraction of business logic
- Solid governance frameworks
- Reuse of services

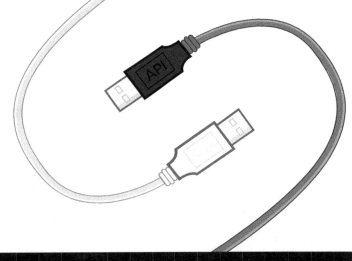

What is an API?

APIs can be defined in multiple ways. In fact, some think that API and Service are interchangeable terms, while others think they're at opposite ends of the spectrum. Before moving on, it's important to establish a common definition of API. In simplified terms, an Application Programming Interface provides a way for developers to interact with and consume a service.

An analogy is useful in illustrating what this really means, so let's consider a service that all of us consume every day - electricity. Electricity is delivered to consumers by a utility company. The utility company provides a service (electricity) to consumers that is accessible through electrical sockets. These sockets vary from one country to another, limiting access to only those consumers with the correct plugs for that socket. The plugs are essentially consumers, only able to make use of the service if they have the appropriate authorization. In this case, the API is the socket itself. APIs are gateways between services and consumers, providing consumers access to services through various interfaces depending on their credentials. In addition, consumers can utilize the services they receive and implement them in their own way. Consider a laptop, which consumes electricity through a socket. Through its own "API," a USB socket, it can provide that same electricity service to charge other devices.

Driving forces behind API adoption

> Gartner predicts 75% of Fortune 500 enterprises will open an API by 2014. In this new API economy, those without an API strategy will be left behind."

Organizations are beginning to understand the importance of APIs and the value they deliver to business. But what exactly is causing all the fuss?

Business agility: Much more effective than creating business logic and exposing it as a website is creating business logic and exposing it as an API. With APIs, it doesn't matter how the logic is used; clients and consumers can consume the API and expose it to their liking, delivering efficiency and enabling innovation for the enterprise.

API economy: Businesses are developing "API products" as new sources of revenue. Expedia generates over $2 billion annually through the data made available through their API. Salesforce generates 75% of their revenue through API activity. The API economy is here and growing fast.

Internet of things: The number of things that can be connected is growing fast; everything from your coffee pot to your thermostat to your car can now be accessed via API. As a result, businesses are finding more and more opportunities to create connectivity in new places.

Now that we've defined what APIs are, their relationship to services and SOA, and the reasons behind their growing importance in the enterprise, it's time to dig into the 7 habits that drive effective API management. If you're starting an API initiative or wondering how to get started, following these best practices will ensure that your APIs are easy to use, fast to deploy, and deliver the business results you expect.

Habit 1:

Apply an API-First design approach

Typically, a business owner starts off by identifying the need for an API. Next, the business owner works with an architect to actually design the API and from that comes the specifications of the API. Once the specifications are complete, they are communicated by the architect to the API development team that will implement the back-end of the API.

With an API-First approach, rather than implementing an application and then building and API on top of it, businesses first create the interface and then put the back-end logic into place - whether it be cloud-based or on-premise.

This method allows organizations to isolate concerns and to focus on clear, well-defined API specifications instead of implementation concerns. API-First development provides a simple framework that enforces better REST API design practices, helping businesses focus on API resources and messaging before undergoing the heavy lifting and back-end implementation.

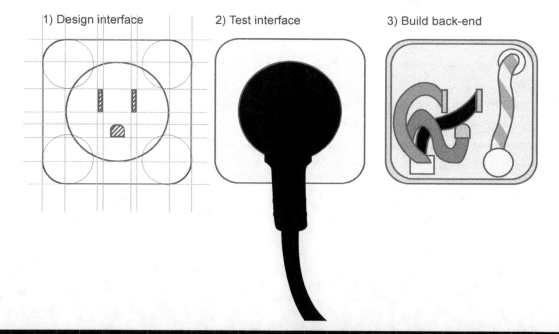

1) Design interface   2) Test interface   3) Build back-end

Habit 2:

Choose a solid API runtime

Once an API is designed, created and its back-end implemented, it's time to find the right runtime. Choosing a runtime is crucial, as it affects how successful your API strategy will be in terms of service, liability, scale and ability to meet future needs. So what key capabilities should you look for in an API runtime?

Hybrid support: As more and more businesses are moving to the cloud, it is important to find a runtime that allows you to deploy applications both in the cloud as well as on-premise without having to modify anything. This allows businesses to burst into the cloud when extra resources are needed or even shift from on-premise to the cloud if and when your business needs require. The ability to develop applications once and deploy them in the cloud or on-premise provides a host of possibilities without complexity.

Scalability, reliability, availability: These "-ilities", along with performance, are crucial when searching for a solid API runtime. The last thing you want is an unstable runtime that crashes or experiences outages. Choosing the right enterprise grade technology for your API runtime is crucial to the success of your API.

Strong Orchestration: A successful runtime should provide strong orchestration and orchestration capabilities. The ability to carry out complex back-end orchestration plays a key role in translation between the API layer and back-end implementation.

Habit 3:

Create a central service repository

After designing, developing, and running the API on a solid platform, exposing the API in a central repository is paramount. Surfacing the API facilitates API discoverability and accessibility by people who need it. A central service repository also makes it easy to categorize and search through services while providing a consolidated view of APIs; it is the place for all design and runtime governance.

Forums and documentation make it easy for developers to assess an API's fit for purpose and to get started quickly with API consumption. Finally, with visibility into key metrics of APIs, business owners and architects know how an API is performing so they can take corrective action and continue to improve the API in future versions.

Habit 4:

Manage services through versions, policies and contracts

Tracking service versions and consumers gives businesses insight into who is using APIs, which versions they're using and how they're using them. This helps with API lifecycle management and allows API publishers to assess the impact of retiring a version. In addition, policies and contracts are crucial to enforcing security and managing SLAs with API consumers. An API solution should offer a way to easily create well-defined policies and contracts and associate them with the right APIs and consumers.

Habit 5:

Promote and socialize your APIs

Creating a developer portal to establish a community around your API is important to its success. By making it easy for users to follow your API, download documentation and ask questions, API publishers can engage with API consumers on an ongoing basis. Providing and promoting content that simplifies API consumption strengthens your user base, ultimately helping your API be successful.

Habit 6:

Monitor and assess API usage

Understanding which parts of your service are being used is important, but it's only part of the picture. You need to see how consumers are using it. With metrics for both overall usage and per consumer usage, businesses can closely monitor API activity and engagement. The ability to monitor API usage over a defined period of time and to understand usage patterns from both technical and business perspectives is valuable as it helps business owners and technical teams better understand their users and ultimately create a better service.

Habit 7:

Continually improve

The ability to refactor your APIs by iterating through habits 1-6 multiple times allows you to optimize your API over time to improve consumer experience and productivity.

Conclusion

With the progression towards a more connected and API-driven world, defining the right API strategy and selecting the right API platform is crucial to supporting innovation and growth. Following the 7 habits outlined above will ensure a winning API strategy. To make that strategy a reality, MuleSoft's Anypoint Platform for APIs delivers an end-to-end solution to design APIs that developers will love; easily connect them with backend services; run them in a secure, scalable environment; and manage them throughout their lifecycle.

Learn more about MuleSoft or contact us
to discuss your API or integration needs today.

[Contact us] [Learn more]

About MuleSoft

MuleSoft provides the most widely used integration platform for connecting SaaS and enterprise applications in the cloud and on-premise. Delivered as a packaged integration experience, CloudHub™ and Mule ESB™ (Enterprise Service Bus) are built on proven open source technology for the fastest, most reliable on-premise and cloud integration without vendor lock-in.

10 lessons every product executive should know about their API program

"MuleSoft's API-led connectivity approach improved productivity by 10x. That's a huge win in a digital world that's changing constantly."

— Simon Post, Group CIO, Dixon's Carphone

Introduction

To get customized solutions to market quickly, many product executives build their own stack and seek tools and processes to help product managers and engineers innovate and collaborate. This approach slows down dramatically when teams spend time doing undifferentiated "donkey work": building connectivity logic to data sources; figuring out how to orchestrate across various backend services and caching mechanisms; or trying to decipher how to accurately map and transform data between two endpoints.

Based on work with customers across many industries and global regions, we have found that the presence of an API-led connectivity program is a critical factor in how quickly teams can innovate in cost-effective ways using sound architectural practices. We have compiled a list of the top ten lessons learned by successful Product Executives in their approach towards becoming an API-led product organization.

10 lessons every product executive should know about their API program

3

01 Build for today while preparing for tomorrow

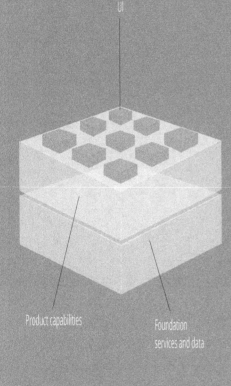

UI

Product capabilities

Foundation
services and data

Today, new UIs and additional product capabilities are requested while existing product features see repeated change, and product strategies shift at an unrelenting pace.

Products should be a dynamic composition of services rather than a inflexible monolith. Creating a highly-modular set of underlying services creates a future-proof network and makes reacting to tomorrow's changes easy.

"It's important to discusss how rapidly technology is evolving and the importance of investing in things like the integration layer and APIs. None of us know what's coming next, we know at the end of the day change is the new constant, but how do you continue to deliver value in that world?"-Yvonne Wassenar, CIO, New Relic

Lesson
Give up the hardwire band-aid.

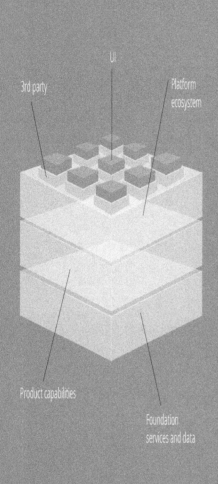

UI

3rd party

Platform
ecosystem

Product capabilities

Foundation
services and data

02 Apply platform strategy as product strategy

Demand surges can be unpredictable.

Even with relatively few APIs exposed, customers and partners will demand new services and continuously updated experiences. As products evolve, demand may grow in unexpected ways: Amazon Web Services is a prime example.

Test and ensure all APIs are ready to meet consumer expectations before publishing. Check the full product architecture is API-enabled from the bottom most foundation of your systems and data all the way to the public UI.

Lesson
Be platform ready today.

5

03 Treat your API like a product

Today, a product's user interface is the main touchpoint, however, API interfaces are set to become the new normal.

Rapidly piecing together components, via APIs, into a new product, or sub-product, requires each piece to be understood and validated through a feedback cycle. Investing in developer on-ramp and API user experience (APX) is therefore essential for product adoption. API storefronts should attract, and make adoption easy for developers.

Lesson

Make APX a priority.

04 Be agile in the right way

Agility to respond to customer feedback is key. Teams must quickly prototype beta releases, gather feedback, pivot and course correct without causing mayhem internally.

Agile product organizations think in terms of building blocks with modules of sub-products and functionality that can be quickly composed, disassembled, changed, and recomposed. For this to be possible, APIs for all foundational, product and ecosystem services must be discoverable and well-documented.

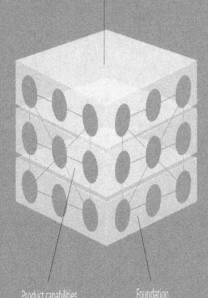

Platform ecosystem

Product capabilities

Foundation
services and data

Lesson
Design the API consumption experience.

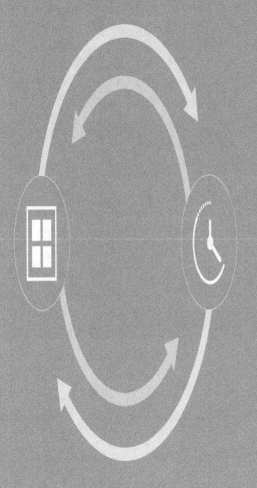

05 Use tools fit for modern delivery

The healthiest product organizations incorporate DevOps best practices for lean requirements, continuous deployment, testing automation and application delivery.

The ability to reduce mean time-to-production by removing latent hand-off and back-and-forth between developers and operators is key. In addition, the cultural aspects of collaboration, process and people management should not be overlooked as delivery is operationalized.

Lesson

Plug into your DevOps infrastructure.

06 Have a connectivity strategy

An API-led connectivity approach has become the new standard. It enables strategic use and re-use of connectivity infrastructure. In contrast, when code is written to quickly "hard-wire" APIs to the back-end or to orchestrate multiple APIs, it generally cannot be adapted for use by multiple teams so additional connections are made and hidden dependencies develop which can threaten product quality, reliability and supportability.

The best way to combat the desire to "hard-wire" is to make it easier to connect to backend infrastructure, APIs and services the right way. Publish connectivity templates that can be easily discovered and leveraged during product development. Empower product teams to utilize existing API interfaces and proven architecture patterns. Don't waste time rebuilding the same connectivity components for every new product release.

Lesson
Make solving for connectivity easy.

07 Collaborate to reduce technical debt

Encourage collaboration throughout the development lifecycle of every component of the API-led connectivity fabric - from API design to business logic orchestration, all the way down to the last database query. Enable product developers to experiment, mock, test and get feedback incrementally and regularly. Involving downstream users early drives product usability, and collaborating with other developers helps ensure best-practices are shared and adopted.

Practicing collaboration at scale will go a long way towards building high quality, reliable, and well architected products.

Lesson

Extract & codify best practices. Share knowledge. Encourage collaboration.

08 Create product architecture transparency

Products powered by an API-connected fabric can have complex interdependencies across hundreds of moving parts. Architecture visibility is the key to understanding critical breakpoints within the product, and for planning management strategies such as how and when to apply rate limits in different areas of the architecture.

Keep a pulse on individual APIs and microservices. Use predictive analytics and preventive maintenance to avoid disasters. If something does break, know how to quickly troubleshoot and respond to issues.

Lesson
Register and monitor every single API.

09 Provide defense in depth

In today's digital world, getting hacked is just a matter of time. Unfortunately, developers often don't prioritize and incorporate security best practices. Instead, downstream teams are called up on to address security after the product is fully developed, resulting in ineffective implementations.

Ensure developers design security in from the beginning by providing them with security best practices in the form of architectural design patterns and runtime policies. Employ controlled governance at the edge, through internal micro-gateways and with global, federated policies.

Lesson
Secure locally, manage and monitor globally.

10 Build a network for your product

The success of an API-enabled product will rely on interconnected exchanges of business data and functional capabilities: A network of microservices. Change is unavoidable, and it will likely require new functionality composed from different entities talking to each other.

A forward-looking product strategy should include an architectural vision of a vast network of business capabilities. Building out the network requires robust strategies for how product services and capabilities are designed, developed, secured, governed and monitored.

"Our growth over the next 10 years will be driven by our ability to take existing capabilities and compose them together in new and interesting ways. MuleSoft is helping us rapidly unlock those capabilities, make them discoverable and enable their controlled reuse when launching new products to the market." Andy Lapin, Cox Automotive

Lesson
Your best moving part will come from the outside. Plan for it now.

So, now what?

Here are some questions we recommend asking yourself:

-- Am I thinking in terms of modular API enabled building blocks?

-- Do I have a responsive organization?

-- Are my engineers sharing best practices amongst each other?

-- Is my product architecture something I can rapidly take a pulse on, and
   have confidence that it is following best (design and runtime) practices?

How do I start? Where do I start? What's my roadmap for success?

Contact MuleSoft to figure out the best way to get started.

 MuleSoft

Anypoint Platform Performance

This document describes highly performant Anypoint Platform production deployments, and explains the architectural features of Mule, the runtime engine of Anypoint Platform, that contribute to its performance.

Introduction

Assessment of performance and scalability is a complex topic because there are many possible types of integration deployments. This whitepaper presents a high level overview of the performance of Mule, the runtime engine of Anypoint Platform, and provides real world scenarios where Anypoint Platform has been deployed successfully in environments where performance was mission critical.

Customer Use Case - Proxying APIs

A global network service provider needed a solution that could expose and manage tens of thousands of internal assets with API-led connectivity. The solution, therefore, needed to be easy to manage, deploy, scale and integrate into their ecosystem with little overhead. It also needed to support customizable SLA-based and access-control policies with authentication systems such as LDAP and PingFederate.

After evaluating multiple options, they chose Anypoint Platform from MuleSoft for it's ability to meet all the functional objectives and for exceeding their performance expectations for

- Scalability
- Out-of-the-box performance
- Stability

Scalability

Scaling is measured in terms of throughput (TPS) as the number of nodes increases. Figure 1 shows the linear scaling from a single node setup to a 2-node cluster, with some policies enabled using a 1KB payload.

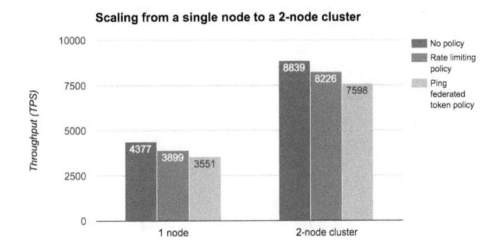

Setup: API Gateway 2.0. EC2 lab, JMeter v2.11 @10 and 20 threads. 1KB payload. Tomcat backend.

Out-of-the-box performance (non-blocking)

With the non-blocking processing strategy enabled by default, getting optimal performance no longer requires special tuning. Figure 2 shows the comparison of non-blocking and blocking processing strategy, tuned and out of the box.

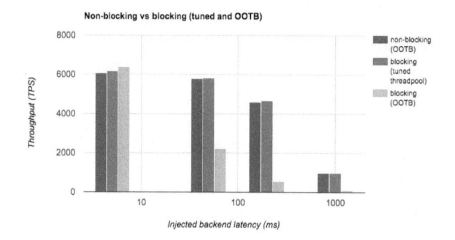

Setup: API Gateway 2.0. EC2 lab. JMeter v2.11 @1000 threads. 1KB payload. Tomcat backend with increasing delay: (5ms, 50ms, 200ms, 1000ms).

Out-of-the-box performance (API Gateway policies)

Enforcing a policy on every incoming request incurs CPU cycles. The benchmark below measures the overhead added to round-trip time on each API request - by applying a specific policy on an existing API measured in milliseconds.

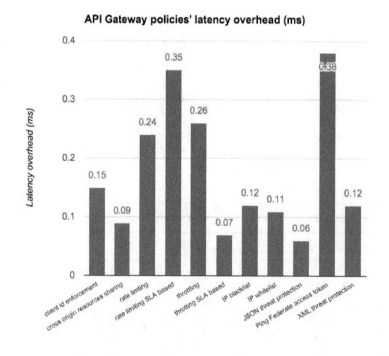

Stability

Stability is often taken for granted under normal circumstances, and only gets noticed when something becomes unstable. Stability can be confirmed by monitoring the trend of throughput and resource utilization under increasing load and external factors like backend latency. Figure 3 below shows API Gateway throughput is stable as the load increases. The response time also increases but at a slower rate than the increase in load threads.

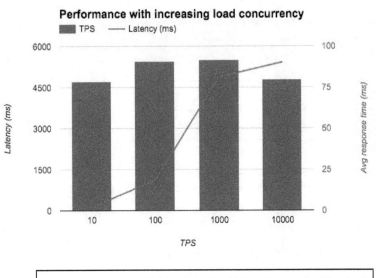

Performance with increasing load concurrency

Setup: API Gateway 2.0. EC2 lab. API Bench, with increasing threads. 1KB payload.

Figure 4 below shows a constant rate of memory utilization under high load with various backend latencies. The memory utilization of API Gateway remains constant, unlike typical thread-based implementations where resource utilization increases as the rate of load increases.

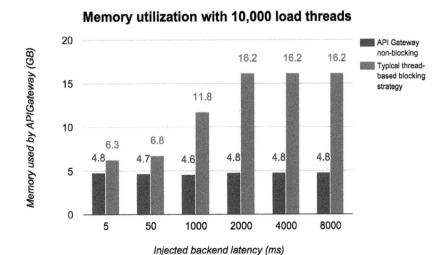

Memory utilization with 10,000 load threads

Setup: API Gateway 2.0. EC2 lab. JMeter v2.11 @10000 threads with increasing backend delay. 1KB payload.

4

Customer Use Case – JMS Connectivity with Message Broker

One of the most common patterns in integration (and Message Oriented Middleware) is asynchronous messaging. There are multiple types of messaging brokers/vendors (MSMQ, IBM MQ, SonicMQ, etc.) and protocols (JMS, AMQP, MQTT, etc). Note that each message broker has pros and cons, including performance. For instance, some hardware based appliances are faster than others.

The most common open messaging standard in the industry is **JMS**. And the most popular open source JMS provider is **ActiveMQ**. In this benchmark, we test the performance of the Mule runtime interfacing with an ActiveMQ message broker.

JMS Benchmark Test Result

Mule with JMS connector <-> ActiveMQ	TPS
Rate of enqueuing	14K
Rate of dequeuing	7.8K
Overall Setup: Mule 3.7. physical lab (24-core). API Bench, 1KB payload. ActiveMQ 5.9.	

Customer Use Case – Batch Processing

Within a Mule application, batch processing stands on its own as an independent block of code. From an external resource, the Batch Module accepts sets of data – perhaps polling for the input – to process data in chunks. Batches handle any record-level failures that occur in processing so as to prevent failure of a complete batch job. Further, you can set or remove variables on individual records so that during batch processing, Mule can route or act upon records in a batch according to a record variable.

In general, batch performance varies based on record size, number of records, and the complexity of the underlying processing and transformation at each step.   The following benchmark shows the performance of a scenario simulating a ETL use case, with input data in a csv file outputting to a database accessed through its REST APIs. The tested batch use case has the following phases:

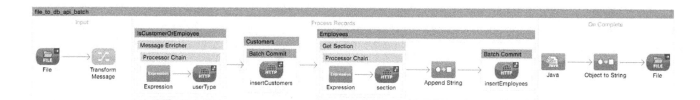

Input phase:
- The input csv file is loaded
- Each record is transformed into an java object using DataWeave

Process phase:
- Entries are divided into two different groups: employees and customers
- If it is a customer record, insert into the customers table
- If it is an employee record, query the department of the employee then insert into the employee table

Complete phase:
- Output the batch summary report to a file

Figure 5 below shows how the batch job processed and moved 1 million records (100 MB in size) from the input csv file to the database desintintation in just under 2 hours. The processing time, the time spent in the Batch "process" phase, and the total time, the time spent in the Batch job end-2-end, both increase linearly with the number of records being processed. When there are few records to process, the actual processing time is short which makes the input phase the dominating contributor to the total time. When there are many input records, the parallel processing of the Batch (default 16 threads) makes its processing overhead negligible.

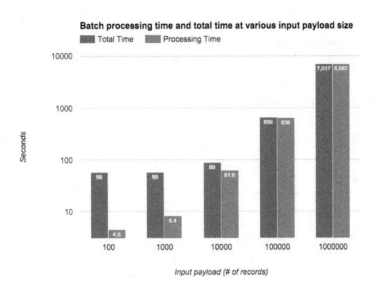

Setup: Mule 3.7. physical lab. JMeter, 100 bytes per record. # of records varies. MySQL backend.

Since Batch is a lightweight construct and is not computing-intensive, the results above can be achieved with a 2-core machine. However, it is important to note that for most batch job scenarios, the system is usually IO-bound because the application is blocked by operations on disks (for persistence), database or other downstream services. The following plot shows the disk utilization % increases as the number of records increases.

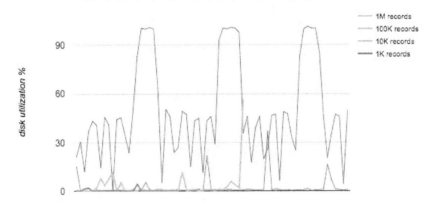

Customer Use Case – Data Transformation

Data transformation is a core requirement for most integrations. Anypoint Platform provides multiple types of transformers, including XSLT, DataWeave and DataMapper. The below benchmark shows transformations performance using DataWeave with payload size of 100KB (1000 records) with simple complexity.

Scenario	TPS with DataWeave
xml2xml	1803
json2json	1017
pojo2pojo	141
xml2pojo	1131
json2pojo	1498
csv2json	1611

DataWeave with 1MB payload on CloudHub

When the input payload size is over 150KB for csv and json input type, DataWeave writes the request objects to disk. Therefore, payload threshold tests were set up to range from 150KB to 1 MB in size. The tests ran in the performance lab and on the CloudHub worker cloud and results validated that higher disk writes resulting from larger payload sizes don't impact performance.

The figure below shows that DataWeave's throughput when deployed to CloudHub is stable.

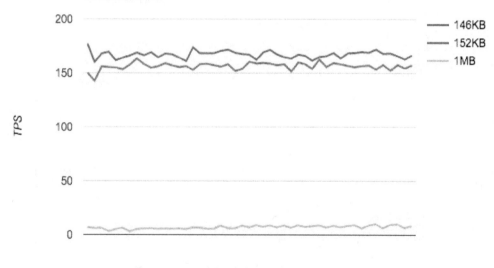

DataWeave Json2Json transformation on CloudHub 4-vcore worker

time (5-min test)

Anypoint Platform - Integration Platform as a Service (iPaaS) solution

A world leader in higher education software serves many universities and students across the globe. They sought to improve their existing integration solution as it was largely home-grown, with numerous parts handled by disparate teams. The company deemed that system slow, fragile, and difficult to maintain. After evaluating various integration solutions, they chose Anypoint Platform - iPaaS solution to handle the following requirements:

- Provide a reliable, highly available environment
- Enable a global customer base with regional cloud support
- Service tens of thousands of transactions per day, irregularly distributed.

Anypoint Platform - iPaaS offers a reliable, zero-downtime global solution. With MuleSoft's iPaaS solution, users can deploy applications to CloudHub, a fully hosted, fully managed worker cloud running on Amazon Web Services. The CloudHub worker cloud, a hosted Mule runtime that inherits the same performance capabilities as the standalone Mule runtime, has distributions available in regions around the world.

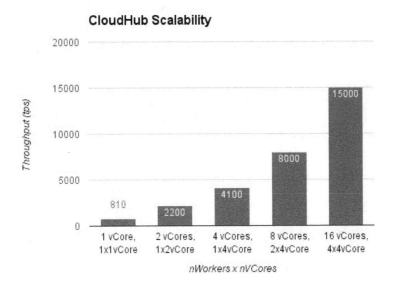

CloudHub scales well both vertically and horizontally. CloudHub offers several different worker sizes and allows users to easily deploy multiple workers of a selected type. The chart above shows scalability by the number of vCores (virtual cores). The first three values are related vertically, in terms of the power of a single worker. The last three values are related horizontally, by the number of 4 vCore workers.

Notes on the testing environment

Where to run the load test is an important consideration in the test setup. If tests were done in a production-like environment, the noises and variables would affect the precision and repeatability of the benchmarks. However, if all tests were done in a dedicated, controlled environment, the gathered data may not reflect reality.

To solve this dilemma, we set up a dynamic performance lab covering both requirements: a dedicated physical lab and an EC2 lab on shared cloud.

	Types	Specifications
Physical lab	Dell R620	24-core, 36GB RAM, standard disks, 10Gbit network.
EC2 lab	c3.xlarge	4-vcore, 7.5GB RAM, standard disks, 1Gbit network.

All machines run Red Hat Linux 4.8.2 and Java HotSpot 1.7.

Anypoint Platform Cloud Security and Compliance

Whitepaper

Overview

Security is a top concern when evaluating cloud services, whether it be physical, network, infrastructure, platform or data security. MuleSoft's Anypoint Platform is designed to be a secure platform for our customers. Anypoint Platform spans SOA, SaaS Integration and APIs. This whitepaper covers the security and compliance of MuleSoft's cloud services, namely CloudHub and API Platform.

MuleSoft's approach to cloud security is two-pronged: (a) we actively and consciously avoid inspecting, storing, manipulating, monitoring, or otherwise directly interacting with sensitive customer data; and (b) we provide a highly secure environment in which customers can perform sensitive data manipulations. MuleSoft's dedicated security team follows industry best practices, runs internal security audits and maintains policies that span operations, data security, passwords and credentials, and secure connectivity.

As all our cloud services are built on the AWS platform, we rely on Amazon's leading physical and network security. MuleSoft also enforces operation controls based on industry standard best practices for public cloud services, including, but not limited to:

* Principle of least privileged access
* Role based access controls
* Data security (not storing sensitive data, encrypting data at rest, and more)
* Regular audits
* Customer advisories and established escalation processes
* Penetration testing

MuleSoft ensures compliance with multiple industry standards and regulations through regular audits. We can provide an SSAE16 SOC2 report, as well as PCI level-1 and HiTrust attestations of compliance, upon request.

Operations

MuleSoft's goal is to provide a secure platform where customers can operate, while giving customers the freedom and confidence to do so without our examination or intervention. In order to do this, MuleSoft follows industry best practices for operational processes to provide a secure environment for customers. These include, but are not limited to:

* Comprehensive security policies
* Least privilege access
* Secure virtual private cloud environments
* Regular application and network penetration testing and vulnerability scanning
* Regular external reviews of our security program and audits of adherence to security compliance standards
* Logging and alerting of platform-level security events
* Strong authentication for administrative sessions

- Secure software development lifecycle (SLDC) methodology and standards
- Security incident response and disaster recovery procedures
- Tight controls and restrictions on administrative rights

Data Security

When the Anypoint Platform is run as a cloud service, MuleSoft transmits data for customers, though we are data agnostic. MuleSoft does not inspect, store, manipulate, monitor or otherwise interact directly with customer data payloads. MuleSoft understands that the data customers are transmitting should be treated carefully to mitigate any security risks. To this end, customers maintain control over their data, configuration and workers.

CloudHub workers serve as a secure instance for transmitting and processing data by giving each application its own independent virtual machine. Each worker is fully isolated from other tenants.

Passwords and Credentials

All account passwords and credentials are stored in a non-reversible secure format in the database. Data encryption as a feature of the platform can also be enabled. Customers can store credentials for their own services inside the Mule Credential Vault. CloudHub customers can also use the Secure Environment Variables feature to ensure that sensitive configuration, such as passwords or keys, are stored in an encrypted form on our servers.

Facilities and Network

Amazon is MuleSoft's cloud provider and the Amazon Web Service (AWS) cloud infrastructure has been architected to be one of the most flexible and secure cloud computing environments available today. AWS's world-class, highly secure data centers utilize state-of-the-art electronic surveillance and multi-factor access control systems. Data centers are staffed 24x7 by trained security guards, and access is authorized strictly on a least-privileged basis. Environmental systems are designed to minimize the impact of disruptions to operations. Multiple geographic regions and availability zones allow you to remain resilient in the face of most failure modes, including natural disasters or system failures.

AWS has achieved ISO 27001 certification and has been validated as a Level 1 service provider under the Payment Card Industry (PCI) Data Security Standard (DSS). AWS undergoes annual SOC 1 audits and has been successfully evaluated at the Moderate level for Federal government systems as well as DIACAP Level 2 for DoD systems. AWS infrastructure is in alignment with the following SOC 1/SSAE 16/ISAE 3402 (formerly SAS 70 Type II), SOC2, PCI DSS Level 1, ISO 27001, and ITAR.

More detail on AWS security can be found here.

Secure Connectivity

MuleSoft's platform includes support for secure protocols and provides tools to build secure services on our platform. MuleSoft recommends that customers use these protocols and tools to secure their services to secure their business. These include, but are not limited to:

- SSL
- PGP payload encryption/decryption
- OAuth2
- WS-Security
- SAML

CloudHub also provides built in security for communication from the cloud to on-premises application, databases, and services using the Virtual Private Cloud (VPC) offering. VPC enables customers to connect to its corporate data centers (whether on-premises or in other clouds) to CloudHub as if they were all part of a single, private network through an IPsec or SSL based VPN.

Data Sovereignty

The Anypoint Platform provides customers with the opportunity to configure their integrations to run in different regions of the world so customers can be compliant with local regulations. When a customer configures an integration to run in a specific region, data is only transmitted and processed within that region. These regions include the US, EU, Asia Pacific, and South America. For example, CloudHub allows MuleSoft customers to transmit their customer's payload data in a manner consistent with the EU Data Protection Directive by using CloudHub's EU region.

For more information, please see the documentation.

Third Party Certification

In order to reassure our customers about our security posture, MuleSoft pursues multiple security and compliance standards, all subject to external validation. By continually auditing our environment, controls and practices against different standards from different industries, we are able to deliver ultimate peace of mind with respect to how we handle and protect our customers' data.

SSAE 16

MuleSoft can provide an SSAE16 SOC2 report upon request.

From the AICPA's website:

"Report on Controls at a Service Organization Relevant to Security, Availability, Processing Integrity, Confidentiality or Privacy

These reports are intended to meet the needs of a broad range of users that need to understand internal control at a service organization as it relates to security, availability, processing integrity, confidentiality and privacy. These reports are performed using the AICPA Guide: Reporting on Controls at a Service Organizations Relevant to Security, Availability, Processing Integrity, Confidentiality, or Privacy and are intended for use by stakeholders (e.g., customers, regulators, business partners, suppliers, directors) of the service organization that have a thorough understanding of the service organization and its internal controls. These reports can form an important part of stakeholders:

- *Oversight of the organization*
- *Vendor management program*
- *Internal corporate governance and risk management processes*
- *Regulatory oversight"*

HiTrust

MuleSoft is a registered compliant HiTrust service provider. The registration letter from the HiTrust council can be provided upon request.

From the HiTrust Alliance website:

"Developed in collaboration with healthcare and information security professionals, the HITRUST CSF rationalizes healthcare-relevant regulations and standards into a single overarching security framework. Because the HITRUST CSF is both risk- and compliance-based, organizations can tailor the security control baselines based on a variety of factors including organization type, size, systems, and regulatory requirements.

By continuing to improve and update the CSF, the HITRUST CSF has become the most widely adopted security framework in the U.S. healthcare industry. This commitment and expertise demonstrated by HITRUST ensures that healthcare organizations leveraging the framework are prepared when new regulations and security risks are introduced."

PCI Compliance

MuleSoft is a level-1 PCI service provider. An Attestation of Compliance (AoC) can be provided upon request.

From the PCI Council's website:

"PCI DSS is the global data security standard that any business of any size must adhere to in order to accept payment cards, and to store, process, and/or transmit cardholder data. It presents common-sense steps that mirror best security practices."

On-premises Security

Anypoint Platform can be deployed in the cloud (CloudHub) or on-premises (Mule ESB). When a customer chooses to run Anypoint Platform on-premises, MuleSoft systems do not interact with customer data at all. Customers configure and run the software and handle all storing, processing and transmitting of data directly, without interference from MuleSoft. As MuleSoft does not process, store or transmit customer data, information security standards are dictated by how the customer's environment is managed. MuleSoft ESB can also be modified to support a FIPS compliant environment. Anypoint Platform on-premises is a solid part of our customers' secure and compliant environments.

More Information

MuleSoft is dedicated to ensuring that customers can meet their security and compliance goals with our platform. For more information or answers to questions about MuleSoft security and compliance, please contact info@mulesoft.com.

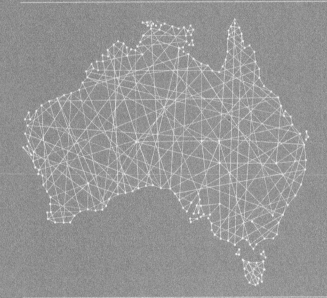

API-LED CONNECTIVITY FOR

AUSTRALIAN GOVERNMENT

EXECUTIVE SUMMARY

KEY CHALLENGES

- Agencies must embrace digital transformation to execute on increasingly complex mission objectives while controlling costs to stay within budget.
- At its core, digital transformation is driving agencies to reframe their relationships with citizens, employees, and other agencies through leveraging new technologies to engage in ways that were not possible before.
- These new technologies - cloud, mobile, big data, and the Internet of Things (IoT) - demand a new level of connectivity that cannot be achieved with yesterday's integration approaches.

RECOMMENDATIONS

- Adopt an API-led connectivity approach that packages underlying connectivity and orchestration services as easily discoverable and reusable building blocks, exposed by APIs.
- Structure these building blocks across distinct data, process and experience layers, to achieve both greater organisational agility and greater control.
- Drive technology change holistically across people, processes and systems in an incremental fashion.

THE DIGITAL TRANSFORMATION IMPERATIVE

Australian Government agencies are not immune to the pressure to digitally transform. Executive and legislative leaders see the massive potential for new technologies used in the private sector to support line of business objectives and lower costs, and are shaping policy to drive digital transformation in government. In 2013, Stephen Conroy, then Labour Communications Minister, announced the National Cloud Computing Strategy, stating that "the adoption of cloud services can assist agencies to reduce costs and improve their service delivery." Later that year, then Liberal Communications Minister and now Prime Minister Malcolm Turnbull, in partnership with Finance Minister Mathias Cormann, signed the Commonwealth's new cloud policy, demanding agencies "must adopt cloud where it is fit for purpose, provides adequate protection of data and delivers value for money". In 2015 Turnbull announced Australia's commitment to an Open Government Partnership, leading to the Open Government National Action Plan submission in December 2016, which committed to "better access to government-held information and data, with release of high-value data sets and reforms to our information access laws." Most recently, the newly formed Digital Transformation Agency announced their digital transformation agenda, noting their vision to make it "simple and fast to get things done with government, through any channel." Taken together, these pieces of legislation provide the catalyst for agencies to embrace and respond to the forces of digital transformation.

For private sector organisations and public sector entities alike, one thing is clear - technology is the critical enabler of digital transformation. Mobile and cloud, for years viewed as trends on the horizon, are now proven drivers for IT-enabled disruption, both inside and outside the enterprise. The API, once seen as a tool for programmers, is providing both a new route to market as well as enabling disintermediation of the value chain that supports that route to market. For example, via its Product Advertising API, Amazon sells its goods through third-parties, thus extending its distribution reach. At the same time, the IT infrastructure on which these APIs run has in turn been made available for other uses through the Amazon Web Services API.

Line of business and IT leaders must act now to ensure their agencies can stay abreast of technological changes. However, digital transformation is not easily realised. It is certainly not the result of implementing a single application or a single technology. Rather, digital transformation can only be achieved when organisations are able to bring multiple technologies together to create truly distinctive and differentiated offerings. To do so, they must bring data from disparate sources to multiple audiences, such as to citizens, employees, and other agencies. It is in this context that connectivity must be viewed as an executive concern and why Deloitte points to the CIO as being more appropriately described as the "Chief Integration Officer". Ultimately, connectivity is not only a critical enabler of digital transformation, it is arguably the biggest differentiator of success.

Traditional methods for integrating applications do not work for digital transformation. These approaches, designed at a time with fewer endpoints and slower delivery expectations, often cannot move at the pace that today's mission objectives require. Just as digital transformation requires Australian government departments and agencies to embrace a new set of technologies, it is imperative they embrace a new level of connectivity across the enterprise. This whitepaper proposes a new approach to integration – API-led connectivity – that extends traditional service oriented approaches to reflect today's connectivity needs. We'll outline the core of this approach and implementation challenges and discuss how IT leaders can realise this vision in their own organisations.

WHY EXISTING CONNECTIVITY APPROACHES WILL FAIL

The technologies underlying digital transformation have enabled organisations to engage with their stakeholders in new and innovative ways. These technologies, notably cloud, mobile and IoT, have dramatically increased the number of endpoints to connect to. Where once an organisation may only have had to consider its internal systems, it must now consider an exponentially larger set of endpoints both inside and outside the agency. For example, creating useful business intelligence and analytics insights may have previously run from a single enterprise data warehouse, or a data cube, whereas today many agencies need to consider a wide range of varying data sources from inside and outside the firewall, like cross-agency sources, social media and IoT. This could extend to building a new data lake, like Hadoop, or utilising open APIs from 3rd party sources which are yet more sources of required connectivity.

Moreover, the frequency with which these new systems change has also increased. For example, whereas the database schema of SAP or a mainframe DB2 system may only change annually, the requirements for systems connecting to new sources, like ServiceNow, Pegasystems, Microsoft Dynamics 365 or Salesforce may change weekly, daily or even hourly. It is this speed of innovation that is a defining characteristic of digital transformation and IT must strive to enable rather than hinder such change.

IT leaders then must meet two seemingly contradictory goals: they must ensure stability and control over core systems of record, while enabling innovation and rapid iteration of the applications that access those systems of record. This is the challenge now variously referred to as bimodal or two-speed IT.

Existing connectivity approaches are not fit for these new challenges. Point-to-point application integration is brittle and expensive to maintain. Service-oriented Architecture (SOA) approaches provide some instruction in theory, but have been poorly implemented in practice. The principles of SOA are sound: well-defined services that are easily discoverable and easily re-usable. In practice, however, these goals were rarely achieved. The desire for well-defined interfaces resulted in top-down, big bang initiatives that were mired in process. Too little thought, if any, was given to discovery and consumption of services. And using SOAP-based Web Services technology to implement SOA proved to be a heavyweight approach that was ill-suited then and even more ill-suited now for today's mobile use cases.

A new approach is required, one that leverages existing investments, and enables IT to seize the moment to drive transformational change; one that enables agility, yet also allows IT to maintain visibility and control. This change is a journey that requires shifting IT's mind-set away from project delivery, to delivering assets as services and enabling project leaders to self-serve and build their own connections, processes and applications, while Central IT governs access, SLAs and data quality. In short, IT must become a platform for the agency.

API-LED CONNECTIVITY: THE EVOLUTION OF SOA

While connectivity demands have changed, the central tenets of SOA have not: that is, the distillation of software into services that are well-defined, re-usable and discoverable.

This vision is perhaps even more important given the proliferation of endpoints. The complexity of providing multiple stakeholders customised views of the same underlying data source, whether it be an Oracle database or an SAP system, increases exponentially with the number of channels through which that data must be provided. It also reinforces the need for data at the point of consumption to be decoupled and independent from the source data in the system of record, becoming variously more coarse-grained or fine-grained as the use case requires.

This problem lends itself to a service oriented approach in which application logic is broken down into individual services, and then re-used across multiple channels. Yet, the heavyweight, top-down implementation approaches previously noted are not a fit for the agility that today's digital transformation initiatives demand.

To meet today's needs we propose a new construct, API-led connectivity, that builds on the central tenets of SOA, yet re-imagines its implementation for today's unique challenges. API-led connectivity is an approach that defines methods for connecting and exposing your assets. The approach shifts the way IT operates and promotes decentralised access to data and capabilities while not compromising on governance. This is a journey that changes the IT operating model and which enables the realisation of the 'composable enterprise', an enterprise in which its assets and services can be leveraged independent of geographic or technical boundaries.

CUSTOMER SPOTLIGHT: ANONYMOUS GOVERNMENT AGENCY

ACCELERATING PROJECT DELIVERY SPEED TO IMPROVE CITIZEN EXPERIENCES

Many government ICT departments lack the resourcing to maintain an effective IT security posture while rapidly delivering on their current project pipeline. Annual strategic ICT plans promise new and more specialised initiatives, yet the endless complexities of agency ICT infrastructures have slowed the adoption of these transformative initiatives. Decades of accumulated point-to-point code, combined with a preponderance of dated legacy systems, has slowed agility. As the executive director of one Australian statutory authority agency explained, "we needed to fix decades worth of point-to-point code with unwieldy links that made adding new features and functions very difficult."

With MuleSoft, this statutory authority agency is transitioning from a point-to-point architecture to one centered around API-led connectivity, enabling them to deliver better citizen experiences by accelerating the speed at which they can deliver IT projects. One of these projects, for example, provides caseworkers with a 360 view of each citizen from a single platform, resulting in the reduction of time required to review cases, as well as a 90% decrease decrease in rework. The same APIs that expose data to caseworkers are re-used to expose case information to a citizen-facing mobile application, as well as to the agency's in-person service centers, providing a superior citizen experience across multiple channels at a reduced cost. As the director explained, "these dramatic improvements have been incredible and would not have been possible without connectivity support provided by Anypoint Platform."

These results are not abnormal; by leveraging MuleSoft to realize API-led connectivity, government agencies across Australia have been able to significantly increase the speed at which they can deliver new projects, reducing ICT expenditure while providing world-class experiences to citizens.

API-led connectivity calls for a distinct 'connectivity building block' that encapsulates three distinct components:

1 **Interface:** Exposing data in a governed and secured form via an API

2 **Orchestration:** Application of logic to that data, such as transformation and enrichment

3 **Connectivity:** Access to source data, whether from physical systems, or from external services

[Figure 1: Anatomy of API-led connectivity]

1. **Interface**: Exposing data in a governed and secured form via an API

2. **Orchestration**: Application of logic to that data, such as transformation and enrichment

3. **Connectivity**: Access to source data, whether from physical systems, or from external services

Designing with the consumption of data top of mind, APIs are the instruments that provide both a consumable and controlled means of accessing connectivity. They serve as a contract between the consumer of data and the provider of that data that acts as both a point of demarcation and a point of abstraction, thus decoupling the two parties and allowing both to work independently of one another (as long as they continue to be bound by the API contract). Finally, APIs also play an important governance role in securing and managing access to that connectivity.

However, the integration application must be more than just an API; the API can only serve as a presentation layer on top of a set of orchestration and connectivity flows. This orchestration and connectivity is critical: without it, API to API connectivity is simply another means of building out point-to-point integration.

"THREE-LAYERED" API-LED CONNECTIVITY ARCHITECTURE

Large enterprises have complex, interwoven connectivity needs that require multiple API-led connectivity building blocks. In this context, putting in a framework for ordering and structuring these building blocks is crucial. Agility and flexibility can only come from a multi-tier architecture containing three distinct layers:

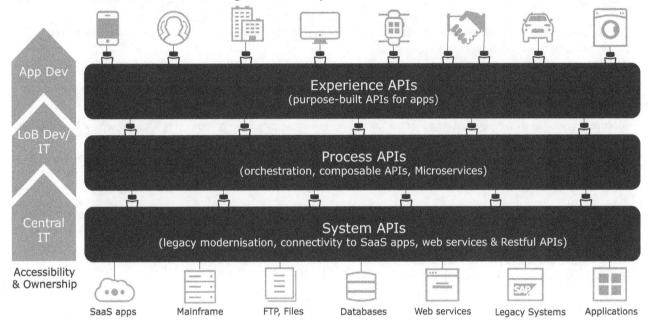

[Figure 2: API-led connectivity]

System Layer: Underlying all IT architectures are core systems of record (e.g. Mainframe, SAP, TechnologyOne Financials, Oracle EBS, Oracle database etc). Often these systems are not easily accessible due to connectivity concerns and APIs provide a means of hiding that complexity from the user. System APIs provide a means of accessing underlying systems of record and exposing that data, often in a canonical format, while providing downstream insulation from any interface changes or rationalisation of those systems. These APIs will also change more infrequently and will be governed by Central IT given the importance of the underlying systems.

Process Layer: The underlying processes that interact and shape this data should be strictly encapsulated independent of the source systems from which that data originates, as well as the target channels through which that data is to be delivered. For example, in a purchase order process, there is some logic that is common across products, geographies and channels that can and should be distilled into a single service that can then be called by product-, geography- or channel-specific parent services. These APIs perform specific functions and provide access to non-central data and may be built by either Central IT or Line of Business / Project teams.

Experience Layer: Data is now consumed across a broad set of channels, each of which want access to the same data but in a variety of different forms. Experience APIs are the means by which data can be reconfigured so that it is most easily consumed by its intended audience, all from a common data source, rather than setting up separate point-to-point integrations for each channel.

The benefits of thinking about connectivity in this way include:

MISSION

- IT as a platform for the agency: By exposing data assets as a service to a broader audience, IT can start to become a platform that allows mission teams to self-serve.
- Increase developer productivity through re-use: Realising an API-led connectivity approach is consistent with a service oriented approach whereby logic is distilled to its constituent parts and re-used across different applications. This prevents duplication of effort and allows developers to build on each other's efforts.
- More predictable change: By ensuring a modularisation of integration logic, and by ensuring a logical separation between modules, IT leaders are able to better estimate and ensure delivery against changes to code. This architecture negates the nightmare scenario of a small database field change having significant downstream impact, and requiring extensive regression testing.

TECHNICAL

- Distributed and tailored approach: An API-led connectivity approach recognises that there is not a one-size-fits-all architecture. This allows connectivity to be addressed in small pieces and for that capability to be exposed through the API or a Microservice.
- Greater agility through loose coupling of systems: Within an organisation's IT architecture, there are different levels of governance that are appropriate. The so-called bi-modal integration or two-speed IT approach makes this dichotomy explicit: the need to carefully manage and gate changes to core systems of record (e.g. annual schema changes to SAP) whilst retaining the flexibility to iterate quickly for user facing edge systems such as web and mobile applications where continuous innovation and rapid time to market are critical. Separate API tiers allow a different level of governance and control to exist at each layer, making possible simultaneous loose-tight coupling.

Each API-led connectivity layer provides context regarding function and ownership

Layer	Ownership	Frequency of Changes
System Layer	Central IT	6-12 months
Process Layer	Central IT and Line of Business IT	3-6 months
Experience Layer	Line of Business IT and Application Developers	4-8 weeks; more frequently for more mature companies

- Deeper operational visibility: Approaching connectivity holistically in this way allows greater operational insight, that goes beyond whether an API or a particular interface is working or not, but provides end-to-end insight from receipt of the initial request call to fulfilment of that request based on an underlying database query. At each step, fine grain analysis is possible, that cannot be easily realised when considering connectivity in a piecemeal fashion.

CUSTOMER SPOTLIGHT:
SERVICE NEW SOUTH WALES

LEVERAGING API-LED CONNECTIVITY FOR LEGACY MODERNIZATION

Many agencies have prioritised legacy modernisation as a means of increasing IT agility and capabilities while reducing costs. APIs provide a highly effective means of doing so, enabling secure access to legacy systems in a way that maintains system integrity and abstracts away the complexity of these systems from their underlying data and services. One organisation with whom MuleSoft partnered, Service New South Wales, leveraged this approach to anchor an initiative that provides access to hundreds of disparate government services from a single platform. MuleSoft powers APIs that expose data and services from legacy systems spanning across over 40 different government departments to a front-end application built on the Salesforce platform. So, for example, if a citizen wants to access a birth certificate, they can now do so via Service NSW's platform of mobile, web, and in-person channels, each of which call a set of reusable APIs exposing the required data and services from the NSW Registry of Births Deaths & Marriages to fulfill the request.

This API-led approach has conferred a number of benefits. In addition to enabling one-stop-shop access to different services, using APIs to unlock data from legacy systems has enabled the agency to digitize and automate services that previously required manual interaction across different state agencies. This resulted in an 50% increase in the number of digitally delivered services. Furthermore, this approach has paved a way towards migrating off of many legacy systems that were approaching end-of-life, leading to further IT cost reductions. Last but not least - governing access to sensitive citizen data through APIs instead of through point-to-point code bolstered the overall security of the platform.

According to Ben McMullen, the IT director responsible for the project, "using MuleSoft and taking an API-led approach to our overall architecture was critical. MuleSoft has provided us with a robust and flexible platform that not only supports our current activities but allows us to extend them over time. Their tools are an integral part of our entire operation." By unlocking these systems with APIs, the director and his team plan on continuing to accelerate digital service delivery, with a goal of increasing the number of digitally delivered services by an additional 40% over the next 3 years.

For further details, see full case study here.

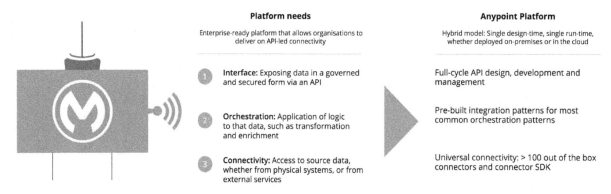

Platform needs

Enterprise-ready platform that allows organisations to deliver on API-led connectivity

Anypoint Platform

Hybrid model: Single design-time, single run-time, whether deployed on-premises or in the cloud

1. **Interface:** Exposing data in a governed and secured form via an API

2. **Orchestration:** Application of logic to that data, such as transformation and enrichment

3. **Connectivity:** Access to source data, whether from physical systems, or from external services

Full-cycle API design, development and management

Pre-built integration patterns for most common orchestration patterns

Universal connectivity: > 100 out of the box connectors and connector SDK

[Figure 3: Anypoint Platform differentiators for API-led Connectivity]

MuleSoft's Anypoint Platform is the only solution that allows enterprises to truly deliver on their digital transformation through realising API-led connectivity. In particular, Anypoint Platform is the only solution that enables end-to-end connectivity across API, service orchestration and application integration needs through a single unified platform. This allows developers to rapidly connect, orchestrate and enable any internal or external endpoint. The result is a 3x to 6x faster time to launch new initiatives, connect systems, and unlock data across the enterprise and a 30% reduction in integration costs.

MuleSoft's solutions are easy to use and understand meaning any developer can quickly become productive without lengthy training in vendor specific technologies. This results in higher employee productivity, and in many cases, we have seen a 70% productivity increase for app development teams.

Finally, MuleSoft's experience in partnering with our customers to drive digital transformation initiatives allows our customer success teams to bring expertise in change management, organisational design and IT development best practices to complement our technology offerings and truly partner to drive success. Anypoint Platform is the world's leading connectivity and integration solution and is trusted by 35% of the Fortune 500 and over 90 government departments globally, including leading agencies in New South Wales, Queensland, Victoria, and the Australian federal government.

Anypoint Platform is trusted by over 1000 enterprises worldwide and MuleSoft is the only vendor to be named a Leader in both the Gartner Magic Quadrant for Full Lifecycle API Management and the Gartner Magic Quadrant for Enterprise Integration Platform as a Service (iPaaS)..

ABOUT MULESOFT

MuleSoft's Anypoint Platform is trusted by over 1000 enterprises worldwide including over 10 US federal civilian and defense agencies, and is the only vendor to be named a Leader in both the Gartner Magic Quadrant for Full Lifecycle API Management and the Gartner Magic Quadrant for Enterprise Integration Platform as a Service (iPaaS).

API-led Connectivity for Government

Executive Summary

Key Challenges

- Agencies must embrace digital transformation to execute on increasingly complex mission objectives while controlling costs to stay within budget.

- At its core, digital transformation is driving agencies to reframe their relationships with citizens, employees, and other agencies through leveraging new technologies to engage in ways that were not possible before.

- These new technologies - SaaS, mobile, and the Internet of Things (IoT) - demand a new level of connectivity that cannot be achieved with yesterday's integration approaches.

Recommendations

- Adopt an API-led connectivity approach that packages underlying connectivity and orchestration services as easily discoverable and reusable building blocks, exposed by APIs.

- Structure these building blocks across distinct data, process and experience layers, to achieve both greater organizational agility and greater control.

- Drive technology change holistically across people, processes and systems in an incremental fashion.

The Digital Transformation Imperative

Government agencies are not immune to the pressure to digitally transform. Executive and legislative leaders see the massive potential for new technologies used in the private sector to support mission objectives and lower costs, and are shaping policy to drive digital transformation in government.

In 2010, Vivek Kundra, then CIO of the US Federal Government, mandated that agencies must "implement cloud-based solutions whenever a secure, reliable, and cost-effective cloud option exists." And while cloud adoption has still been slow, initial successes from agencies such as the GSA and the USDA are increasing the pressure to adopt cloud solutions.

Similarly, there has been an increased push for open government, as signified by President Obama's 2013 executive order making open and machine-readable data the new default for government information. The increasing exposure of data creates opportunities for agencies to leverage that data to improve mission execution.

Most recently, digital transformation has been driven by the GSA, as evidenced by their May 2016 launch of the Technology Transformation Service. According to US CIO Tony Scott, the TTS is intended to "strengthen the way federal agencies develop, buy, and share cutting-edge solutions."

For private sector organizations and public sector entities alike, one thing is clear - technology is *the* critical enabler of digital transformation. Mobile and cloud, for years viewed as trends on the horizon, are now proven drivers for IT-enabled disruption, both inside and outside the enterprise. The API, once seen as a tool for programmers, is providing both a new route to market as well as enabling disintermediation of the value chain that supports that route to market. For example,

via its Product Advertising API, Amazon sells its goods through third-parties, thus extending its distribution reach. At the same time, the IT infrastructure on which these APIs run has in turn been made available for other uses through the Amazon Web Services API.

Mission and IT leaders must act now to ensure their agencies can stay abreast of technological changes. However, digital transformation is not easily realized. It is certainly not the result of implementing a single application or a single technology. Rather, digital transformation can only be achieved when organizations are able to bring multiple technologies together to create truly distinctive and differentiated offerings. In order to do so, they must bring data from disparate sources to multiple audiences, such as to citizens, employees, and other agencies. It is in this context that connectivity must be viewed as an executive concern and why Deloitte points to the CIO as being more appropriately described as the "Chief Integration Officer". Ultimately, connectivity is not only a critical enabler of digital transformation, it is arguably the biggest differentiator of success.

Traditional methods for integration applications do not work for digital transformation. These approaches, designed at a time with fewer endpoints and slower delivery expectations, often cannot move at the pace today's mission objectives require. Just as digital transformation requires agencies to embrace a new set of technologies, so they must embrace a new level of connectivity. This whitepaper proposes a new approach to integration - API-led connectivity - that extends traditional service oriented approaches to reflect today's connectivity needs. We'll outline the core of this approach and implementation challenges and discuss how IT leaders can realize this vision in their own organizations.

Why existing connectivity approaches will fail

The technologies underlying digital transformation have enabled organizations to engage with their stakeholders in new and innovative ways. These technologies, notably SaaS, mobile and IoT, have dramatically increased the number of endpoints to connect to. Where once an organization may only have had to consider its internal systems, it must now consider an exponentially larger set of endpoints both inside and outside the agency. For example, financial payment transactions previously carried out by checks, are now transacted by an expanded set of channels — including telephone, online and mobile banking.

Moreover, the frequency with which these new systems change has also increased. For example, whereas the database schema of a core banking system may change only on an annual basis, the requirements of the online and mobile banking applications connecting to those systems may change weekly, daily or even hourly. It is this speed of innovation that is a defining characteristic of digital transformation and IT must strive to enable rather than hinder such change.

IT leaders then must meet two seemingly contradictory goals: they must ensure stability and control over core systems of record, while enabling innovation and rapid iteration of the applications that access those systems of record. This is the challenge now variously referred to as bi-modal or two-speed IT.

Existing connectivity approaches are not fit for these new challenges. Point-to-point application integration is brittle and expensive to maintain. Service-oriented Architecture (SOA) approaches provide some instruction in theory, but have been poorly implemented in practice. The principles of SOA are sound: well-defined services that are easily discoverable and easily re-usable. In practice, however, these goals were rarely achieved. The desire for well-defined interfaces resulted in top-down, big bang initiatives that were mired in process. Too little thought, if any, was given to discovery and consumption of services. And using SOAP-based WebServices technology to implement SOA proved to be a heavyweight approach that was ill suited then and even more ill suited now for today's mobile use cases.

A new approach is required, one that leverages existing investments, and enables IT to seize the moment to drive transformational change; one that enables agility, yet also allows IT to maintain visibility and control. This change is a journey that requires shifting IT's mindset away from project delivery, to delivering assets as services and enabling project leaders to to self-serve and build their own connections, processes and applications, while Central IT governs access, SLAs and data quality. In short, IT has to become a platform for the the agency.

API-led connectivity: The evolution of SOA

While connectivity demands have changed, the central tenets of SOA have not: that is, the distillation of software into services that are well-defined, re-usable and discoverable.

This vision is perhaps even more important given the proliferation of endpoints. The complexity of providing multiple stakeholders customized views of the same underlying data source, whether it be a core banking system or an ERP system, increases exponentially with the number of channels through which that data must be provided. It also reinforces the need for data at the point of consumption to be decoupled and independent from the source data in the system of record, becoming variously more coarse-grained or fine-grained as the use case requires.

This problem lends itself to a service oriented approach in which application logic is broken down into individual services, and then re-used across multiple channels. Yet, the heavyweight, top-down implementation approaches previously noted are not a fit for the agility that today's digital transformation initiatives demand.

To meet today's needs we propose a new construct, API-led connectivity, that builds on the central tenets of SOA, yet re-imagines its implementation for today's unique challenges. API-led connectivity is an approach that defines methods for connecting and exposing your assets. The approach shifts the way IT operates and promotes decentralised access to data and capabilities while not compromising on governance. This is a journey that changes the IT operating model and which enables the realization of the 'composable enterprise', an enterprise in which its assets and services can be leveraged independent of geographic or technical boundaries.

Microservices

Microservices are a hot topic amongst enterprise architecture leaders. In our view, we believe that microservices not only validate a service oriented approach but are in fact one interpretation of how that approach should be implemented, by taking the need for well-defined services and re-usability to an extreme. In doing so, it highlights the need for governance, and that successful implementation must also consider non-technology factors such as development processes and methodologies. In this way, the principles and approach behind API-led connectivity are entirely consistent with a Microservices approach and vice versa.

API-led connectivity calls for a distinct 'connectivity building block' that encapsulates three distinct components:

1. **Interface:** Exposing data in a governed and secured form via an API

2. **Orchestration:** Application of logic to that data, such as transformation and enrichment

3. **Connectivity:** Access to source data, whether from physical systems, or from external services

Figure 1: Anatomy of API-led connectivity

Designing with the consumption of data top of mind, APIs are the instruments that provide both a consumable and controlled means of accessing connectivity. They serve as a contract between the consumer of data and the provider of that data that acts as both a point of demarcation and a point of abstraction, thus decoupling the two parties and allowing both to work independently of one another (as long as they continue to be bound by the API contract). Finally, APIs also play an important governance role in securing and managing access to that connectivity.

However, the integration application must be more than just an API; the API can only serve as a presentation layer on top of a set of orchestration and connectivity flows. This orchestration and connectivity is critical: without it, API to API connectivity is simply another means of building out point-to-point integration.

APIs vs API-led connectivity

Stripe, as an "API as a company" dis-intermediating the payments space, is an archetype of the API economy. Yet at MuleSoft's 2014 CONNECT conference, Stripe's CEO John Collison was quoted saying "you don't slather an API on a product like butter on toast". Thought of in isolation, the API is only a shim that while hiding the complexities of back-end orchestration and connectivity does nothing to address those issues. Connectivity is a multi-faceted problem across data access, orchestration and presentation, and the right solution must consider this problem holistically rather than in a piecemeal fashion. To only consider APIs is to only solve only one part of the connectivity challenge.

"Three-layered" API-led connectivity architecture

Large enterprises have complex, interwoven connectivity needs that require multiple API-led connectivity building blocks. In this context, putting in a framework for ordering and structuring these building blocks is crucial. Agility and flexibility can only come from a multi-tier architecture containing three distinct layers:

Each API-led connectivity layer provides context regarding function and ownership

Layer	Ownership	Frequency of Changes
System Layer	Central IT	6-12 months
Process Layer	Central IT and Line of Business IT	3-6 months
Experience Layer	Line of Business IT and Application Developers	4-8 weeks; more frequently for more mature companies

• **System Layer:** Underlying all IT architectures are core systems of record (e.g. one's ERP, key customer and billing systems, proprietary databases etc). Often these systems are not easily accessible due to connectivity concerns and APIs provide a means of hiding that complexity from the user. System APIs provide a means of accessing underlying systems of record and exposing that data, often in a canonical format, while providing downstream insulation from any interface changes or rationalization of those systems. These APIs will also change more infrequently and will be governed by Central IT given the importance of the underlying systems.

• **Process Layer:** The underlying processes that interact and shape this data should be strictly encapsulated independent of the source systems from which that data originates, as well as the target channels through which that data is to be delivered. For example, in a purchase order process, there is some logic that is common across products, geographies and channels that can and should be distilled into a single service that can then be called by product-, geography- or channel-specific parent services. These APIs perform specific functions and provide access to non-central data and may be built by either Central IT or project teams.

• **Experience Layer:** Data is now consumed across a broad set of channels, each of which want access to the same data but in a variety of different forms. Experience APIs are the means by which data can be reconfigured so that it is most easily consumed by its intended audience, all from a common data source, rather than setting up separate point-to-point integrations for each channel.

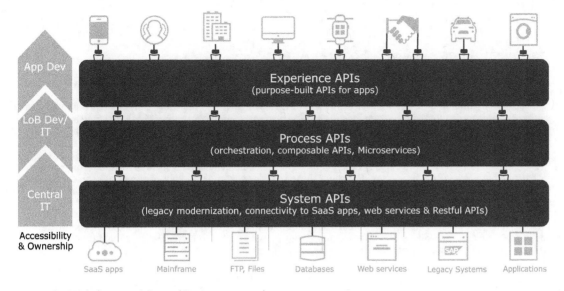

Figure 2: API-led connectivity architecture approach

Benefits of API-led connectivity

The benefits of thinking about connectivity in this way include:

Mission

- IT as a platform for the agency: By exposing data assets as a services to a broader audience, IT can start to become a platform that allows mission teams to self-serve.
- Increase developer productivity through re-use: Realizing an API-led connectivity approach is consistent with a service oriented approach whereby logic is distilled to its constituent parts and re-used across different applications. This prevents duplication of effort and allows developers to build on each other's efforts.
- More predictable change: By ensuring a modularization of integration logic, and by ensuring a logical separation between modules, IT leaders are able to better estimate and ensure delivery against changes to code. This architecture negates the nightmare scenario of a small database field change having significant downstream impact, and requiring extensive regression testing.

Technical

- Distributed and tailored approach: An API-led connectivity approach recognizes that there is not a one-size-fits-all architecture. This allows connectivity to be addressed in small pieces and for that capability to be exposed through the API or Microservice.
- Greater agility through loose coupling of systems: Within an organization's IT architecture, there are different levels of governance that are appropriate. The so-called bi-modal integration or two-speed IT approach makes this dichotomy explicit: the need to carefully manage and gate changes to core systems of record (e.g. annual schema changes to core ERP systems) whilst retaining the flexibility to iterate quickly for user facing edge systems such as web and mobile applications where continuous innovation and rapid time to market are critical. Separate API tiers allow a different level of governance and control to exist at each layer, making possible simultaneous loose-tight coupling.
- Deeper operational visibility: Approaching connectivity holistically in this way allows greater operational insight, that goes beyond whether an API or a particular interface is working or not, but provides end-to-end insight from receipt of the initial request call to fulfillment of that request based on an underlying database query. At each step, fine grains analysis is possible, that can not be easily realized when considering connectivity in a piecemeal fashion.

Driving Legacy Modernization at a Civilian Federal Agency

This government agency needed to overcome the challenge of serving an expanding user base while reducing service turnaround time - all while dealing with departmental budget cuts. Compounding the problem, requests were growing in complexity; customers were demanding increasingly sophisticated integration-dependent services, including voice support, and real-time self-service. The inflexibility and slow speed of their existing systems forced the agency to modernize legacy systems in order to support these new demands. MuleSoft was selected to support the agency's legacy modernization initiatives, and was able to significantly improve developer productivity by while lowering costs - thereby enabling the agency to meet customer needs.

To meet increased demands within a limited budget, this agency embraced the API-led connectivity approach. "The platform approach enables us to automate our existing data integration processes. Enriching these new flows with data exposed through Web services and APIs helps us meet the demand for reduced costs and shorter delivery times by," said the IT Director. "Using other types of integration tools, this would be unrealistic."

In the coming years, the agency plans to leverage MuleSoft for all of their integration needs - both within the agency, and with external agencies. "We rely on Anypoint Platform for modernizing our legacy systems and to help meet our SOA initiatives," said the IT Director "As we continue to scale, we see MuleSoft as a significant contributor to our ongoing priority projects."

Customer journey to API-led connectivity

Realizing an API-led connectivity vision must be much more than a technology decision. It requires a gradual but fundamental shift in IT organizations' architectural vision, development approach and the way developers approach their roles. The challenge is one as much about process change as it is about technology implementation.

However, realizing the API-led connectivity vision is not a discrete goal, but rather a continuous journey. Moreover, it is a goal that can be only be realized in incremental steps. Through partnering with dozens of Fortune 500 companies and government agencies on their API-led connectivity digital transformation journeys, we have distilled best practice into the following steps:

- Start-up mode: In order for the API-led connectivity vision to be successful, it must be realized across an organization. However, in large enterprises it is simply not possible to wipe the slate clean and start from scratch. Consequently, the API-led connectivity customer journey must start with a vertical slice of the organization, for a specific use case or for a specific mission objective. By bounding the problem, the scope of change is reduced and the probability of success increased. Training and coaching to drive role modeling of new behaviours is critical at this stage.

- Scale the platform: Once initial proof points have been established, these use cases will naturally become lightning rods within the organization that will build mindshare and become a platform to leverage greater adoption. In addition, the service oriented approach results in the natural creation of reusable assets which exponentially increases the value of the framework as the number of assets increases.

- Build Center of Enablement (C4E): Once scale has been established, it's critical to quickly codify best practices and provide a platform for discovery and dissemination through the organization. The result of such a process is mass adoption across the enterprise. The core of this C4E may also be built during the start-up mode and scaled as required.

Top-5 Global Bank

Digital transformation is often considered as external to the firm. However, whether in terms of enabling transformation outside the company, or in and of itself, digital transformation is a powerful phenomenon *inside* organizational boundaries also.

This multinational financial services company wanted to drive a firm wide architecture driving application development consistent with one of six best practice messaging patterns

This approach has initially seeded into one line of business. This success prompted subsequent rollout across 13 lines of business globally, connecting more than 1,000 applications in production.

In the initial startup mode, the enterprise seeded adoption via a central group which was better able to seed adoption and prove out the approach. As the company continues to scale across the business however, it is looking towards API-led connectivity as the means to decentralize elements of the architecture to drive scale, yet maintain control.

Central to the ability to realize this vision was a center of excellence which helped to codify knowledge and disseminate best practice. MuleSoft helped to build out this C4E through delivering on its proven customer journey approach.

MuleSoft: The API-led connectivity platform

MuleSoft's Anypoint Platform™ is the only solution that allows enterprises to truly deliver on their digital transformation through realizing API-led connectivity. In particular, Anypoint Platform is the only solution that enables end-to-end connectivity across API, service orchestration and application integration needs through a single unified platform. This allows developers to rapidly connect, orchestrate and enable any internal or external endpoint. The result is a 2x to 5x faster time to launch new initiatives, connect systems, and unlock data across the enterprise and a 30% reduction in integration costs.

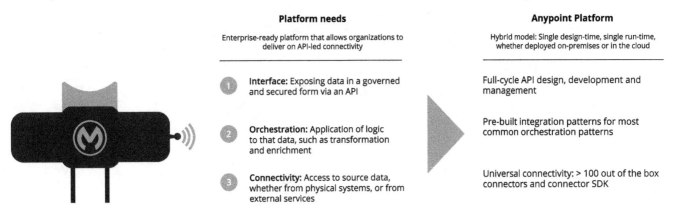

Platform needs

Enterprise-ready platform that allows organizations to deliver on API-led connectivity

1. **Interface:** Exposing data in a governed and secured form via an API

2. **Orchestration:** Application of logic to that data, such as transformation and enrichment

3. **Connectivity:** Access to source data, whether from physical systems, or from external services

Anypoint Platform

Hybrid model: Single design-time, single run-time, whether deployed on-premises or in the cloud

Full-cycle API design, development and management

Pre-built integration patterns for most common orchestration patterns

Universal connectivity: > 100 out of the box connectors and connector SDK

Figure 3: Anypoint Platform differentiators for API-led Connectivity

Since MuleSoft's solutions are easy to use and understand, any developer can quickly become productive without lengthy training in vendor-specific technology resulting in 10% higher employee productivity and 70% higher productivity for app development teams.

Finally, MuleSoft's experience in partnering with our customers to drive digital transformation initiatives allows our customer success teams to bring expertise in change management, organizational design and IT development best practices to complement our technology offerings and truly partner to drive success. Anypoint Platform is the world's leading integration solution and is trusted by 35% of the Fortune 500 and over 10 US federal civilian and defense agencies. MuleSoft is the only integration provider to be named a Leader across all three of Gartner's connectivity focused Magic Quadrant reports: the Gartner Magic Quadrant for On-Premises Application Integration Suites, the Gartner Magic Quadrant for Enterprise Integration Platform as a Service (iPaas) and the Gartner Magic Quadrant for Application Services Governance.

API-led Connectivity
The Next Step in the Evolution of SOA

Executive Summary

Key Challenges

- Companies must embrace digital transformation in order to stay relevant to their customers, else risk ceding market share to competitors who are able to adapt more quickly.

- At its core, digital transformation is driving companies to reframe their relationships with their customers, suppliers and employees through leveraging new technologies to engage in ways that were not possible before.

- These new technologies - SaaS, mobile, and the Internet of Things (IoT) - demand a new level of connectivity that cannot be achieved with yesterday's integration approaches.

Recommendations

- Adopt an API-led connectivity approach that packages underlying connectivity and orchestration services as easily discoverable and reusable building blocks, exposed by APIs.

- Structure these building blocks across distinct systems, process and experience layers, to achieve both greater organizational agility and greater control.

- Drive technology change holistically across people, processes and systems in an incremental fashion.

The Digital Transformation Imperative

We are in the midst of an unprecedented phase of digital transformation. Hospitals are extending care beyond the hospital ward; non-bank players are driving innovation in the payments space; media companies are distributing the content across multiple channels and partners. These changes are irreversibly reshaping industry boundaries and business models, and in the process, changing the winners and losers across verticals.

Technology is *the* critical enabler of digital transformation. Mobile and cloud, for years viewed as trends on the horizon, are now proven drivers for IT-enabled business disruption, both inside and outside the enterprise. The API, once seen as a tool for programmers, is providing both a new route to market as well as enabling disintermediation of the value chain that supports that route to market. For example, via its Product Advertising API, Amazon sells its goods through third-parties, thus extending its distribution reach. At the same time, the IT infrastructure on which these APIs run has in turn been made available for other uses through the Amazon Web Services API.

Business and IT leaders must act now in order to ensure their businesses stay relevant and competitive. Customers have the means to quickly identify and switch to companies that can better meet their needs, and businesses who do not act now will be left behind

However, digital transformation is not easily realized. It is certainly not the result of implementing a single application or a single technology. Rather, digital transformation can only be achieved when organizations are able to bring multiple technologies together to create truly distinctive

and differentiated offerings. In order to do so, they must bring data from disparate sources to multiple audiences, such as to customers, suppliers and employees. It is in this context that connectivity must be viewed as an executive concern and why Deloitte points to the CIO as being more appropriately described as the "Chief Integration Officer"[11]. Ultimately, connectivity is not only a critical enabler of digital transformation, it is arguably the biggest differentiator of success.

Despite its importance, far too many organizations are not approaching connectivity with this strategic mindset. Either, it's not a consideration at all — think lines of business heads driving credit card purchases of SaaS applications, without reflecting on how they will connect those applications to underlying ERP systems — or too often it is only considered with a short-termist approach, which values the success of an individual project to the detriment of the enterprise as a whole.

Traditional methods for integration applications do not work for digital transformation. These approaches, designed at a time with fewer endpoints and slower delivery expectations, often cannot move at the pace today's business requires. Just as digital transformation requires companies to embrace a new set of technologies, so they must embrace a new level of connectivity. This whitepaper proposes a new approach to integration - API-led connectivity - that extends traditional service oriented approaches to reflect today's connectivity needs. We'll outline the core of this approach and implementation challenges and discuss how IT leaders can realize this vision in their own organizations.

Why existing connectivity approaches will fail

The technologies underlying digital transformation have enabled companies to engage with their stakeholders in new and innovative ways. These technologies, notably SaaS, mobile and IoT, have dramatically increased the number of endpoints to connect to. Where once an organization may only have had to consider its internal systems, it must now consider an exponentially larger set of endpoints both inside and outside the enterprise. For example, financial payment transactions previously carried out by checks, are now transacted by an expanded set of channels — including telephone, online and mobile banking.

Moreover, the frequency with which these new systems change has also increased. For example, whereas the database schema of a core banking system may change only on an annual basis, the requirements of the online and mobile banking applications connecting to those systems may change weekly, daily or even hourly. It is this speed of innovation that is a defining characteristic of digital transformation and IT must strive to enable rather than hinder such change.

---

[1] Deloitte Tech Trends 2015, CIO as Chief Integration Officer, http://www2.deloitte.com/us/en/pages/technology/articles/tech-trends-2015-cio-as-chief-integration-officer-report.html

IT leaders then must meet two seemingly contradictory goals: they must ensure stability and control over core systems of record, while enabling innovation and rapid iteration of the applications that access those systems of record. This is the challenge now variously referred to as bi-modal or two-speed IT.

Existing connectivity approaches are not fit for these new challenges. Point-to-point application integration is brittle and expensive to maintain. Service-oriented Architecture (SOA) approaches provide some instruction in theory, but have been poorly implemented in practice. The principles of SOA are sound: well-defined services that are easily discoverable and easily re-usable. In practice, however, these goals were rarely achieved. The desire for well-defined interfaces resulted in top-down, big bang initiatives that were mired in process. Too little thought, if any, was given to discovery and consumption of services. And using SOAP-based WebServices technology to implement SOA proved to be a heavyweight approach that was ill suited then and even more ill suited now for today's mobile use cases.

A new approach is required, one that leverages existing investments, and enables IT to seize the moment to drive transformational change; one that enables agility, yet also allows IT to maintain visibility and control. This change is a journey that requires shifting IT's mindset away from project delivery, to delivering assets as services and enabling Line of Business IT to self-serve and build their own connections, processes and applications, while Central IT governs access, SLAs and data quality. In short, IT has to become a platform for the business.

API-led connectivity: The evolution of SOA

While connectivity demands have changed, the central tenets of SOA have not, that is, the distillation of software into services that are well-defined, re-usable and discoverable.

This vision is perhaps even more important given the proliferation of endpoints. The complexity of providing multiple stakeholders customized views of the same underlying data source, whether it be a core banking system or an ERP system, increases exponentially with the number of channels through which that data must be provided. It also reinforces the need for data at the point of consumption to be decoupled and independent from the source data in the system of record, becoming variously more coarse-grained or fine-grained as the use case requires.

This problem lends itself to a service oriented approach in which application logic is broken down into individual services, and then re-used across multiple channels. Yet, the heavyweight, top-down implementation approaches previously noted are not a fit for the agility that today's digital transformation initiatives demand.

Microservices

Microservices are a hot topic amongst enterprise architecture leaders. In our view, we believe that microservices not only validate a service oriented approach but are in fact one interpretation of how that approach should be implemented, by taking the need for well-defined services and re-usability to an extreme. In doing so, it highlights the need for governance, and that successful implementation must also consider non-technology factors such as development processes and methodologies. In this way, the principles and approach behind API-led connectivity are entirely consistent with a Microservices approach and vice versa.

To meet today's needs we propose a new construct, API-led connectivity, that builds on the central tenets of SOA, yet re-imagines its implementation for today's unique challenges. API-led connectivity is an approach that defines methods for connecting and exposing your assets. The approach shifts the way IT operates and promotes decentralised access to data and capabilities while not compromising on governance. This is a journey that changes the IT operating model and which enables the realization of the 'composable enterprise', an enterprise in which its assets and services can be leveraged independent of geographic or technical boundaries.

API-led connectivity calls for a distinct 'connectivity building block' that encapsulates three distinct components:

- Interface: Presentation of data in a governed and secured form via an API

- Orchestration: Application of logic to that data, such as transformation and enrichment

- Connectivity: Access to source data, whether from physical systems, or from external services

Figure 1: Anatomy of API-led connectivity

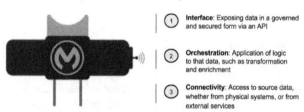

① **Interface:** Exposing data in a governed and secured form via an API

② **Orchestration:** Application of logic to that data, such as transformation and enrichment

③ **Connectivity:** Access to source data, whether from physical systems, or from external services

Designing with the consumption of data top of mind, APIs are the instruments that provide both a consumable and controlled means of accessing connectivity. They serve as a contract between the consumer of data and the provider of that data that acts as both a point of demarcation and a point of abstraction, thus decoupling the two parties and allowing both to work independently of one another (as long as they continue to be bound by the API contract). Finally, APIs also play an important governance role in securing and managing access to that connectivity.

However, the integration application must be more than just an API; the API can only serve as a presentation layer on top of a set of orchestration and connectivity flows. This orchestration and connectivity is critical: without it, API to API connectivity is simply another means of building out point-to-point integration.

APIs vs API-led connectivity

Stripe, as an "API as a company" dis-intermediating the payments space, is an archetype of the API economy. Yet at MuleSoft's 2014 CONNECT conference, Stripe's CEO John Collison was quoted saying "you don't slather an API on a product like butter on toast". Thought of in isolation, the API is only a shim that while hiding the complexities of back-end orchestration and connectivity does nothing to address those issues. Connectivity is a multi-faceted problem across data access, orchestration and presentation, and the right solution must consider this problem holistically rather than in a piecemeal fashion. To only consider APIs is to only solve only one part of the connectivity challenge.

"Three-layered" API-led connectivity architecture

Large enterprises have complex, interwoven connectivity needs that require multiple API-led connectivity building blocks. In this context, putting in a framework for ordering and structuring these building blocks is crucial. Agility and flexibility can only come from a multi-tier architecture containing three distinct layers:

* System Layer: Underlying all IT architectures are core systems of record (e.g. one's ERP, key customer and billing systems, proprietary databases etc). Often these systems are not easily accessible due to connectivity concerns and APIs provide a means of hiding that complexity from the user. System APIs provide a means of accessing underlying systems of record and exposing that data, often in a canonical format, while providing downstream insulation from any interface changes or rationalization of those systems. These APIs will also change more infrequently and will be governed by Central IT given the importance of the underlying systems.

* Process Layer: The underlying business processes that interact and shape this data should be strictly encapsulated independent of the source systems from which that data originates, as well as the target channels through which that data is to be delivered. For example, in a purchase order process, there is some logic that is common across products, geographies and retail channels that can and should be distilled into a single service that can then be called by product-,

geography- or channel-specific parent services. These APIs perform specific functions and provide access to non-central data and may be built by either Central IT or Line of Business IT.

* Experience Layer: Data is now consumed across a broad set of channels, each of which want access to the same data but in a variety of different forms. For example, a retail branch POS system, e-commerce site and mobile shopping application may all want to access the same customer information fields, but each will require that information in very different formats. Experience APIs are the means by which data can be reconfigured so that it is most easily consumed by its intended audience, all from a common data source, rather than setting up separate point-to-point integrations for each channel.

Each API-led connectivity layer provides context regarding function and ownership

Layer	Ownership	Frequency of Changes
System Layer	Central IT	6-12 months
Process Layer	Central IT and Line of Business IT	3-6 months
Experience Layer	Line of Business IT and Application Developers	4-8 weeks; more frequently for more mature companies

Figure 2: API-led connectivity architecture approach

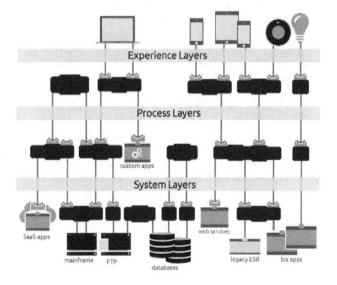

Benefits of API-led connectivity

The benefits of thinking about connectivity in this way include:

Business

- IT as a platform for the business: By exposing data assets as a services to a broader audience, IT can start to become a platform that allows lines of business to self-serve.

- Increase developer productivity through re-use: Realizing an API-led connectivity approach is consistent with a service oriented approach whereby logic is distilled to its constituent parts and re-used across different applications. This prevents duplication of effort and allows developers to build on each other's efforts.

- More predictable change: By ensuring a modularization of integration logic, and by ensuring a logical separation between modules, IT leaders are able to better estimate and ensure delivery against changes to code. This architecture negates the nightmare scenario of a small database field change having significant downstream impact, and requiring extensive regression testing.

Technical

- Distributed and tailored approach: An API-led connectivity approach recognizes that there is not a one-size-fits-all architecture. This allows connectivity to be addressed in small pieces and for that capability to be exposed through the API or Microservice.

- Greater agility through loose coupling of systems: Within an organization's IT architecture, there are different levels of governance that are appropriate. The so-called bi-modal integration or two-speed IT approach makes this dichotomy explicit: the need to carefully manage and gate changes to core systems of record (e.g. annual schema changes to core ERP systems) whilst retaining the flexibility to iterate quickly for user facing edge systems such as web and mobile applications where continuous innovation and rapid time to market are critical. Separate API tiers allow a different level of governance and control to exist at each layer, making possible simultaneous loose-tight coupling.

- Deeper operational visibility: Approaching connectivity holistically in this way allows greater operational insight, that goes beyond whether an API or a particular interface is working or not, but provides end-to-end insight from receipt of the initial API request call to fulfilment of that request based on an underlying database query. At each step, fine grained analysis is possible, that can not be easily realized when considering connectivity in a piecemeal fashion.

Customer journey to API-led connectivity

Realizing an API-led connectivity vision must be much more than a technology decision. It requires a gradual but fundamental shift in IT organizations' architectural vision, development approach and the way developers approach their roles. The challenge is one as much about process change as it is about technology implementation.

However, realizing the API-led connectivity vision is not a discrete goal, but rather a continuous journey. Moreover, it is a goal that can be only be realized in incremental steps. Through partnering with dozens of Fortune 500 companies on their API-led connectivity digital transformation journeys, we have distilled best practice into the following steps:

- **Start-up mode:** In order for the API-led connectivity vision to be successful, it must be realized across an organization. However, in large enterprises it is simply not possible to wipe the slate clean and start from scratch. Consequently, the API-led connectivity customer journey must start with a vertical slice of the business, for a specific use case or for a specific line of business. By bounding the problem, the scope of change is reduced and the probability of success increased. Training and coaching to drive role modeling of new behaviours is critical at this stage.

- **Scale the platform:** Once initial proof points have been established, these use cases will naturally become lightning rods within the organization that will build mindshare and become a platform to leverage greater adoption. In addition, the service oriented approach results in the natural creation of reusable assets which exponentially increases the value of the framework as the number of assets increases.

- **Build Center of Enablement (COE):** Once scale has been established, it's critical to quickly codify best practice and provide a platform for discovery and dissemination through the organization. The result of such a process is mass adoption across the enterprise. The core of this COE may also be built during the start-up mode and scaled as required.

Case Study
Top 5 Global Bank

Digital transformation is often considered as external to the firm. However, whether in terms of enabling transformation outside the company, or in and of itself, digital transformation is a powerful phenomenon *inside* organizational boundaries also.

This multinational financial services company wanted to drive a firm wide architecture driving application development consistent with one of six best practice messaging patterns

This approach has initially seeded into one line of business. This success prompted subsequent rollout across 13 lines of business globally, connecting more than 1,000 applications in production.

In the initial startup mode, the enterprise seeded adoption via a central group which was better able to seed adoption and prove out the approach. As the company continues to scale across the business however, it is looking towards API-led connectivity as the means to decentralize elements of the architecture to drive scale, yet maintain control.

Central to the ability to realize this vision was a center of excellence which helped to codify knowledge and disseminate best practice. MuleSoft helped to build out this COE through delivering on its proven customer journey approach.

MuleSoft: The API-led connectivity platform

MuleSoft's Anypoint Platform™ is the only solution that allows enterprises to truly deliver on their digital transformation through realizing API-led connectivity. In particular, Anypoint Platform is the only solution that enables end-to-end connectivity across API, service orchestration and application integration needs through a single unified platform. This allows developers to rapidly connect, orchestrate and enable any internal or external endpoint. The result is a 2x to 5x faster time to launch new initiatives, connect systems, and unlock data across the enterprise and a 30% reduction in integration costs.

Furthermore, unlike alternatives, MuleSoft's Anypoint Platform can be rapidly deployed on-premises, or accessed as a cloud solution. Since MuleSoft's solutions are easy to use and understand, any developer can quickly become productive without lengthy training in vendor-specific technology resulting in 10% higher employee productivity and 70% higher productivity for app development teams.

Finally, MuleSoft's experience in partnering with our customers to drive digital transformation initiatives allows our customer success teams to bring expertise in change management, organizational design and IT development best practices to complement our technology offerings and truly partner to drive success.

Anypoint Platform is the world's leading integration solution and is trusted by 35% of the Fortune 500. MuleSoft is the only integration provider to be named a Leader across all three of Gartner's connectivity focused Magic Quadrant reports: the Gartner Magic Quadrant for On-Premises Application Integration Suites, the Gartner Magic Quadrant for Enterprise Integration Platform as a Service (iPaas) and the Gartner Magic Quadrant for Application Services Governance.

APIS AND DEVOPS:

GREAT ALONE, BETTER TOGETHER

EXECUTIVE SUMMARY

DevOps has become not only trendy, but an important rethink of the IT culture at many organizations. And with good reason — the benefits to adopting DevOps are well-documented. A recent study, conducted by Utah State University and sponsored by Puppet Labs, revealed that DevOps practices can boost IT performance and ultimately improve a business's bottom line. High IT performance correlates with DevOps practices like proactive monitoring and continuous delivery and integration. Interestingly, the report also showed that the longer an organization uses and improves upon DevOps practices, the better it performs, which can lead to improved performance for the entire company. "This is where DevOps is different. It isn't just IT, it's the practice of IT," says Nicole Forsgren Velasquez, an assistant professor at Utah State University and one of the researchers on the study.

But it isn't just DevOps practices that improve the bottom line for companies. Similarly, the ability to create and implement a successful API strategy has become a critical competency for modern IT teams. According to MuleSoft's 2017 Connectivity Benchmark Report, 94% of IT leaders confirm they can deliver products and services to market faster with APIs. And an API strategy is critical to extracting maximum business value out of what IT teams are creating.

DevOps makes it easy to create and release software deployments. But when it's easy to build software, silos within organizations will replicate work without thinking about maximizing efficiency or about how to expose those assets to others for key business functions. What's needed is not only an emphasis on production but an emphasis on consumption that focuses on reusability and the exposing of existing assets to create new capabilities.

In this whitepaper, we'll talk about how organizations can shift from artifact production (the focus of DevOps), to consider a how these produced artifacts are consumed. One way this shift happens is through an API strategy called API-led connectivity. We'll take a look at how this change can be accommodated by the capabilities of MuleSoft's Anypoint Platform.

INTRODUCTION

Organizations today tend to take one of two paths when it comes to creating innovative experiences for their customers, employees, and partners. One path prioritizes rapid iteration over 'getting it right the first time'. It is taken by companies like Amazon, who are seen as leaders in innovation not only in their own industry but across all organizations. As a rule, Amazon does 136,000 software deployments per day.

The second path prioritizes stability above all and is best exemplified by a global bank that MuleSoft now works with. Early on in our engagement, this customer shared that it once took them three months and around $1.8 million to deploy one database field name change simply because they didn't have visibility into the impact of that change. Obviously, that is a crippling state.

Adopting DevOps can seem unnatural to organizations that don't have a culture of automation and that aren't set up, either for security and compliance reasons or because of company culture, to deploy software thousands of times per day. Adopting DevOps, therefore, becomes an iterative process; it's necessary to adjust the practice to fit the needs of the company.

Not every company needs to — or can — deploy code to production every few seconds like Amazon. But there is a way for any company to take the first path, even for the most regulated company with the oldest of legacy systems. It all depends on approaching the problem in the right way and with the right tools.

The danger of following the Amazon path is that it becomes very tempting, particularly with the power that DevOps unleashes, to simply create piles upon piles of software assets without thinking about how they might provide value for the wider company. Not only are these artifacts replicated in business silos, killing business productivity, but they are locked away from other parts of the business, who might be able to make use or and extract further value out of them.

Successful DevOps adoption has to include both an accelerated and efficient production model and an efficient, balanced consumption model. Companies that successfully implement DevOps should be stewards of a new operating model with a virtuous cycle in which teams produce reusable assets in a manner visible to central IT, which then enables consumption of those assets by making them discoverable and available for self-service, all the while monitoring feedback and usage.

In this model, those developing applications and other assets must change their mindset to think about producing assets that will be consumed by others in the business. And, in turn, central IT needs to change its mindset to an enabler of reusable, self-service consumption. Any assets built need to be discoverable and developers need to be enabled to self-serve them in projects. The virtuous part of this production-consumption cycle is to get active feedback from the consumption model along with usage metrics to inform the production model.

DevOps - a profound cultural as well as technological shift

DevOps has emerged as a practice that focuses on minimal disruption and maximum reliability; faster time to market is also an artifact of automated release processes that DevOps enables. There are thousands of articles and even industry conferences on the topic of DevOps itself, but at MuleSoft, we see one consistent theme that any organization thinking about adopting DevOps needs to consider: DevOps is a profound shift in IT culture, a shift the demands a rethink on IT processes, technology, and the way people work. The consumption model described above is an equally comprehensive shift.

Many start the journey to DevOps by selecting technology that helps development teams remove waste and inefficiency from their software development lifecycle. A common first step is to establish continuous integration processes, taking advantage of tools like Maven and GitHub to automate repeatable aspects of the SDLC where human intervention is typically error-prone. The next step is to produce and deploy software artifacts efficiently, creating a complete pipeline that takes code from concept to production in a repeatable and secure fashion and allows deployments to occur during business hours. Building this pipeline, a blend of technology and quality assurance processes, is the goal of most DevOps practices.

That said, code produced via this pipeline will not necessarily provide maximum business value unless it is given full visibility to the rest of the organization. DevOps can only take the code production machine so far; in order to scale, and more importantly, scale in a sustainable and secure way, IT needs to shift its thinking both to a model predicated on consumption and reuse. This is facilitated through the use of well-designed and built, documented, and visible APIs. This further increases the innovation possibilities DevOps provides and furnishes reusable assets that can grow, and change with ease depending on who wants to use them and what for.

Finally, processes and technology are nothing if your teams do not adopt them and think about them in the right way. If your team is not embracing agile delivery and thinking about test-driven development, then trying to implement DevOps will not be successful. An example of this is with one of our customers who thought about DevOps the same way they thought about delivering large energy projects — e.g. in a very waterfall-like fashion. But to deliver technology changes at the speed the market demands, software deployments have to happen faster than a construction project, so the company culture had to shift pretty dramatically.

The bene its of adopting DevOps

There are myriad benefits to adopting DevOps. Many view DevOps as a way to increase speed to market, getting new products out the door quickly without sacrificing the quality of those products, because the testing, QA, security and operation of code is baked into the pipeline itself. By removing some of the inefficiencies and waste in the process, the goal is to reduce the cost of development of new products and services, iterate rapidly on new business priorities and develop innovations that customers actually want more quickly.

Organizations are looking to DevOps to serve as a competitive advantage for their companies, so they can adapt to new changes in the market, and leverage their expertise to address customer needs and deliver innovative solutions to market with great speed.

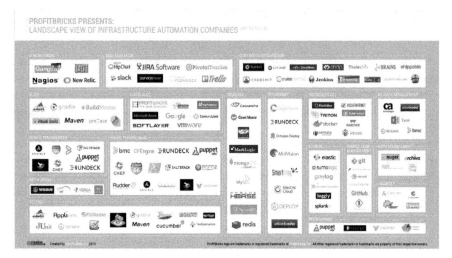

Figure 1. DevOps technologies on the market today

Figure 1 illustrates some of the technologies that we at MuleSoft have seen emerge within our customer base for customers pursuing DevOps practices. They fall into numerous buckets, from development and test, to deployment and monitoring, down to security and collaboration. Operations solutions like ServiceNow or Remedy for IT Service Management and JIRA for issue tracking are also common. Many of these technologies are open-source, or at least have open-source versions, so it's very easy for our customers to get started relatively quickly in building out the foundations of their DevOps practice.

How to use Anypoint Platform to set up DevOps in your organization

This whitepaper will help you conceptualize a generic rationale for DevOps adoption and how Anypoint Platform's capabilities can assist across a number of those categories.

First, we will consider the notion of build automation. As you are building your application, how do you create a recipe for the application to be reassembled correctly every time it needs to be taken apart for changes and updates? Applications built on Anypoint Platform (Mule apps) are often composite applications, containing multiple connectors, multiple file systems, artifacts like .jar files, databases, and even multiple tests. All of those connectors, databases, and tests have specific configurations. If you have to alter those configurations every time you make a change to the Mule application, that is going to slow you down, and that's also very error-prone. MuleSoft customers use built-in and supported build automation tools like Maven to address these concerns.

The next step is test automation. Most developers wait until their code is complete to author tests. How, instead, do you think through the emerging best-practice of test-driven development, where you're actually authoring tests before you write a single line of code? As MuleSoft started creating solutions for our customers, we learned that as you're building tests out to Salesforce or any other SaaS application, an active connection is required if you want to use real data. This is a pain point if a developer is doing this work on their laptop and can't maintain an active connection. We created MUnit, the MuleSoft integration testing framework, to help our developers and our customers create tests with mock data; and, in fact, both MUnit, and JUnit, a common Java testing framework, are used quite often within our customer base to deliver test automation successfully.

Version control is something that most developers today are very comfortable with. Developers know how to commit code across a disparate set of teams so they can drive parallel development and get instant visibility into changes that are not compatible with what others have been doing.

MuleSoft enables version control best practice via extensibility to GitHub, SVN, Team Foundation, and many others version control systems commonly used within enterprises.

Then, finally, there is deployment automation. As with creating a recipe for how an application is built, a recipe for how applications are deployed should also be created. Which environments should they be deployed to? How do you promote applications across environments: dev, QA, performance, security, stage, and production? How do the configurations change by environment? How do you create rules to block software from being deployed if it fails critical tests? Jenkins is a common solution that our customers use to deliver on this aspect of the pipeline.

Great DevOps practices focus on one additional element: reuse. As an asset is moving through the pipeline, how can you ensure others are aware of it, can access it securely, and know how to use it effectively? The API-led connectivity model is very informative here, as most developers are comfortable using Developer Portals and requesting API client keys and secrets. Industry trends suggest organizations are building an automation pipeline across the entire lifecycle of their APIs; there are a number of technologies across that lifecycle that have emerged as best practice, many of which MuleSoft supports and our customers are already leveraging today.

DevOps and API Lifecycle Capabilities on Anypoint Platform

Anypoint Platform provides a unified suite of design, management and runtime capabilities to make it easy for organizations to address the full API lifecycle. The components of Anypoint Platform guide developers from design to implementation to production and beyond - enabling discovery and self-service.

Lifecycle stage	Stage activities	Anypoint Platform components
Design	Create an API Spec Define data types Add security patterns	API Designer Anypoint Exchange
Simulate	Describe examples Author error messages	Mocking Service NOTE: With a mock service, front-end developers can begin crafting the user experience before the API is implemented, allowing parallel development and reducing time to market
Collect Feedback	Create on-ramp Publish portal	Developer Portal Anypoint Exchange
Validate	Create runnable tests Orchestrate API calls	Anypoint Studio Anypoint Exchange
Build	Import API spec Manage dependencies Compose with Connectors & Templates Static config analysis Link to Version Control system	Anypoint Studio Anypoint Exchange
Test	Author unit and functional tests Define pass/fail criteria	MUnit Anypoint Exchange
Deploy - Secure - Promote	Deploy artifacts Promote across environments Apply policies Control access	Anypoint CLI Anypoint Platform APIs Runtime Manager API Manager

Lifecycle stage	Stage activities	Anypoint Platform components
Operate - Secure - Monitor - Manage - Analyze	Measure SLAs Monitor utilization Adjust resources Track performance against KPIs	Runtime Manager Management Agent Anypoint Analytics

Each of the steps described above has certain aspects that can be automated. Most developers are familiar with the build stage; work done in Anypoint Studio can be easily plugged in to your continuous integration pipeline, leveraging some of the technologies that were mentioned earlier: GitHub for version control, Maven for dependencies management and build automation, JUnit and MUnit for test automation, and JIRA or ServiceNow for issue and service management. Customers with Microsoft investments building Mule apps often leverage Team Foundation and Visual Studio.

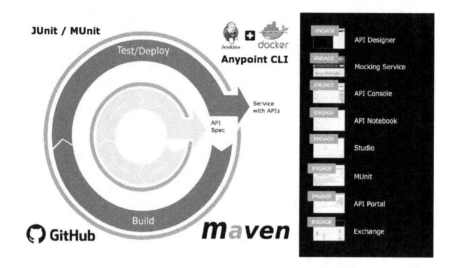

Figure 2. Design and Implementation Lifecycle

When the code is ready to be shipped, MuleSoft customers often leverage Jenkins, Puppet, Chef or HP ALM for both deployment automation and the orchestration of release processes across a number of different environments: dev, test, stage, and production. Puppet and Chef can also be used to automate the installation and configuration of Mule runtimes. Docker is rapidly gaining popularity to reduce the complexities of continuous deployment, and the Mule runtime can be shipped in a Docker container. And through the management agent, Anypoint Platform APIs and Anypoint Platform CLI, users can further automate processes using configuration automation and management tools such as Puppet, Chef, Ansible, and Salt instead of the Anypoint Platform user interface.

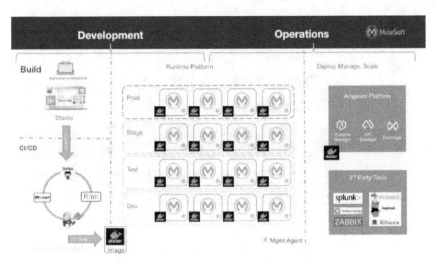

Figure 3. Operating Anypoint Platform

Finally, for monitoring and analytics, developers and Platform operators have the option to either use the out of the box capabilities provided by Anypoint Platform or plug into any existing third-party tools: monitoring and analytics tools such as Splunk, Nagios, AppDynamics, New Relic, or the open-source Elastic Stack: Elasticsearch, Logstash, and Kibana. All this is made possible through the extensibility of the Mule runtime engine.

Shifting from production to production + consumption

The more discoverable you make the assets that you create through your DevOps pipeline, the faster you will become at making them ready for reuse, enabling line-of-business IT, partner developers, and internal developers to securely self-serve on top of these assets. This will make your organization more innovative in creating new products and services because you're exposing capabilities to audiences that may or may not have otherwise known about them, or have had access to these pieces of data — these connectivity artifacts. Reusability enables speed, innovation, and agility.

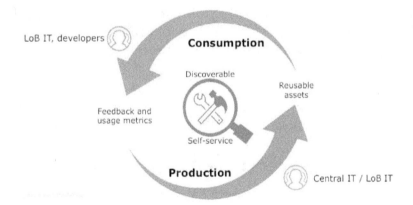

Figure 4. A new operating model: Focusing on production + consumption

DevOps increases reliability and minimizes disruption, with the pleasant side effect of increasing speed; what it doesn't do is provide control. An emerging construct for making sure that organizations aren't needlessly replicating effort, aren't creating applications and assets in business silos, and are effectively exposing the assets they create for maximum business value, is an approach to integration called "API-led connectivity." In our experience, this approach provides the answer to producing reusable assets and enabling their consumption to drive useful speed and innovation.

API-led connectivity provides an approach for connecting and exposing assets. With API-led connectivity, every asset becomes a managed API – a modern API, which makes it discoverable through self-service without losing control.

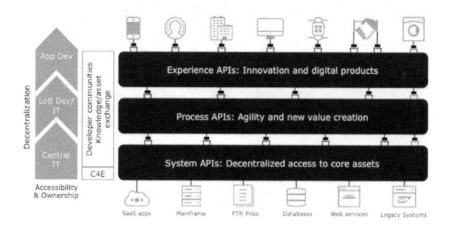

Figure 5. A new approach: API-led connectivity

- Systems APIs: These unlock data from your core systems by putting APIs in front of them. Then a "System API" layer is formed, which provides consistent, managed, and secure access to backend systems.

- Process APIs: It is possible to build on the system APIs by combining and streamlining applications with a certain amount of business logic, and then mapping them to create new capabilities. These "process APIs" take core assets and combine them with some business logic to create a higher level of value. Importantly, these higher-level objects are now useful assets that can be further reused, so they should also be APIs themselves.

- Experience APIs: Finally, an API is built that provides an end-user experience combining the capabilities exposed by the other two API layers. These are "experience APIs" that are designed specifically for consumption by a specific end-user app or device. These APIs allow app developers to quickly innovate on projects by consuming the underlying assets without having to know how the data got there. In fact, if anything changes to any of the systems or processes underneath, it shouldn't require any changes to the app itself.

- Center for Enablement (C4E) - A cross functional team across Central IT, LOB IT charged with being the stewards of assets created through the DevOps pipeline. This team is goaled to ensure assets are consumable, consumed broadly, and fully leveraged. Once established, this team ensures teams follow DevOps best practices, productizes and publishes assets, encourages collaboration and drives self-reliance.

Now, with API-led connectivity and a C4E, when you are tasked with building a new app or asset, there are reusable assets to build from, eliminating a great deal of the work needed to build them. Even better, it is now much easier to innovate, there is now greater visibility into what has been already created, and it easy to expose capabilities to partners, third parties, and other consumers; as we shall see below, this function is critical to even the most expert DevOps practitioners.

The benefits of the MuleSoft approach to DevOps

A customer that's really taken advantage of this API-led approach to connectivity is Spotify. Spotify already is a leader in DevOps; production and deployment was not a problem. It was so easy to deploy and produce assets, that there would be duplicates of applications created by multiple departments, and those applications were quite difficult to take advantage of outside their particular business silo.

What they needed was to expose the capabilities they were moving through that pipeline out to third parties, partners, and across internal channels so that they could more effectively drive new initiatives and create new opportunities for the business. Spotify is now leaning on MuleSoft to provide those reusable APIs and microservices that take advantage of their speedy time-to-market by pushing things through the existing DevOps pipeline. They are promoting self-service to enterprise data within teams, creating faster time to market for numerous business functions. With MuleSoft, Spotify can securely expose assets created through their existing DevOps practice out to systems such as data warehouses with company ERP infrastructure layers. This enhances functions like forecasting and reporting through improved information sharing across the enterprise.

But not every organization has the fortune to be in a position like Spotify who, from their founding had a DevOps practice and developer culture with automation at the core. Another example is a MuleSoft customer, Siemens, who, not that long ago had a software delivery model that will be familiar to many organizations. They had third party resources responsible for developing and testing code; that code was then handed off to the operations team to make sure it ran appropriately in various servers. On the side, a data management silo that slowly feed information to these development teams as it was requested.

Their first iteration of change was bringing in an ESB partner in MuleSoft and a BPM solution to help streamline some of the processes by which information was accessed. They started putting services on a bus and encouraging development teams to reuse those services and processes. Outside of Central IT, few of these services were utilized and the data management team often became a bottleneck to new services. As they started to establish their DevOps practice and followed an API-led approach, they quickly began seeing the value in having teams serve as champions for their own services and processes. Treating DevOps as a practice across people, processes, and technology, Siemens created a center for enablement.

This DevOps Center for Enablement plays a critical role in helping teams adopt best practices in developing and deploying code in highly reusable ways. With this approach, Siemens has removed data bottlenecks by securely exposing artifacts managed by the data management team via System APIs. Partners and internal teams can now self-serve and deliver innovative solutions.

Figure 6: Siemens DevOps Center for Enablement ROI

The results speak for themselves. Siemens' time to MVP — getting a first business-release of the capability out to the business on related projects — has decreased from 26 weeks to 13 weeks in just a quarter as a result of this capability enablement. They slashed that time in half in just over three months. Similarly, time to POC — demonstrating an idea to a business unit— has been slashed in half, from 13 weeks to six weeks. All the while, unplanned work has dropped below expectations, because teams are able to reuse some of the artifacts that they created with through an API-led connectivity approach. Siemens is not reinventing the wheel every time a new project comes up, improving productivity and speed. DevOps plays a key role in that, and an API-led connectivity approach and Center for Enablement promote reuse of the artifacts that come through the DevOps pipeline.

Conclusion

DevOps can help make companies increase reliability and minimize disruption, helping them move faster and adjust to change with greater ease. But it's an approach that needs to be undertaken with a holistic understanding of how technology, processes, and teams work together. MuleSoft has helped numerous organizations implement DevOps successfully and unlocked new capabilities with its API-led approach to connectivity.

 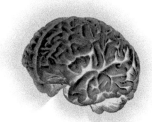

Architecting the Composable Enterprise
IT for the 21ˢᵗ century

Jason Bloomberg, President, Intellyx LLC

The Demise of Centralized IT

Enterprise IT was much simpler in the days before the cloud. Big companies owned their own technology and purchased enterprise licenses for many of the applications anybody in the organization might care to use. To connect everything together, IT executives would buy middleware – which naturally went in the middle of everything.

Furthermore, as Conway's Law would suggest, the organizational structures of the IT shop followed the centralized lines of the technology architecture. Simple hierarchical org charts would suffice, as different groups dealt with different tasks.

Outside this centralized oasis of technology? The vast unknown territory known to techies as *the business* – as though enterprises clove neatly into two parts, the tech cognoscenti here and everybody else over there.
Then along came the cloud. And social media. And mobile technologies. The world of IT has never been the same since. Not only are technologies distributed well beyond the perimeter of the enterprise as cloud computing has given birth to vast ecosystems of third-party technology providers, but the organizational principles have likewise transformed.

Technology has infiltrated every corner of the business – if we can even differentiate *the business* from IT anymore. Today's enterprises are software-driven organizations, shifting the roles and perspectives of everyone in the organization, whether they be "business" or "technology."

The opposite of centralized IT, therefore, isn't only decentralized IT – although distributing the technology effort in the enterprise is an important aspect of this trend. We're also decentralizing how the business accesses and uses technology resources as well.

The decentralized IT organization must build out the capabilities the business needs, while empowering business users to get their jobs done and thereby meet the needs of customers and the organization.

The end state of this combination of decentralization and empowerment is the *composable enterprise:* where people can support the changing demands of the organization by assembling and reassembling modular components – components made up of both technology and people.

Supporting this notion of the composable enterprise introduces profound business challenges for both business and technology leadership. If they don't take advantage of such cutting-edge approaches to addressing customer demands, they will fall behind or go out of business.
The organizational challenge at the heart of the composable enterprise centers on realigning every line of business and department along customer-driven lines. The technology challenge: how do you take crusty, monolithic legacy technology and unbundle it into components in order to assemble them in different ways, while retaining its value?

The Challenges of First Generation SOA

This notion of IT delivering composable capabilities to the business, as though application functionality and data were LEGO blocks for business people to assemble, is not a new idea. In fact, composability was an important benefit of Service-Oriented Architecture (SOA) – at least, the version of SOA IT shops struggled with during the 2000s.

SOA is an approach for abstracting enterprise software capabilities as reusable services in order to support more flexible business processes and ideally, more agile organizations. However, in retrospect, the original promise of SOA was largely unrealized.

Vendors used the approach to sell middleware, which led to expensive and difficult implementations. Deployments were centralized, leveraging hub-and-spoke technology that was ill-suited for the cloud. The SOA organization was centralized as well, with activities taking place internal to the organization, limiting the ability for teams at different organizations to share knowledge of lessons learned.

Eventually, the architectural focus on improving IT and organizational governance in order to achieve greater levels of business agility was largely subsumed into the technical minutiae of enterprise integration. The entire SOA exercise, therefore, became an exercise in tight coupling, connecting endpoints to endpoints.

The principles of SOA were solid, but most implementations were overengineered and too complicated. Web Services proved to be too challenging. And worst of all, enterprises failed to emphasize the *consumers* of the services – both in the sense of the software endpoints that interacted with services, as well as the people who would want to consume service capabilities and compose them to solve business problems.

The Rise of API-led Connectivity

The first generation of SOA centered on the role of the Enterprise Service Bus (ESB), and sported Web Services as the primary type of service. However, among the main roadblocks preventing greater success with SOA were the complexity and technical limitations of Web Services. Even though these XML-based standards promised loose coupling, most Web Services deployments were nevertheless excessively tightly coupled, limiting flexibility overall.

The rise of cloud computing also shifted the SOA discussion. What cloud computing brought to the SOA table were the principles of horizontal scalability and elasticity, automated recovery from failure, eventually consistent data (or more precisely, tunable data consistency), and a handful of other now-familiar architectural principles. The cloud also emphasized the importance of decentralized computing.

The appearance of the cloud coincided with the exploding popularity of Representational State Transfer (REST). REST arose largely out of

the ashes of Web Services, and helped organizations overcome many of the SOA roadblocks that had limited their success with the architecture.

As a result, second-generation SOA was REST-based and cloud-friendly, favoring lighter weight approaches to moving messages around than the heavyweight ESBs that gave SOA a bad rep. RESTful interfaces cleaned up a lot of the mess that Web Services left behind, as they were web-centric, lightweight, and far easier to use than Web Services.

The JavaScript Object Notation (JSON) also played an important role in the maturation of SOA, as it proved to be a simpler and more flexible data format than XML. The fact that JSON objects were themselves JavaScript also provided an ease of use that XML was ill-suited to deliver.

The combination of REST and JSON essentially moved the ball on application programming interfaces (APIs), leaving behind the challenges of Web Services. Today, APIs are more likely to be RESTful, HTTP-based interfaces than SOAP-based Web Services.

In fact, perhaps the most successful part of REST to date has been the simplification of the API. Enterprises no longer need a language-specific protocol that depends upon sophisticated network controls under the covers. Today they can take HTTP for granted, and a simple request to a URL suffices to establish any interaction they care to implement between any two pieces of software, regardless of language.

As a result, today's APIs are inherently Web-centric. They take advantage of Web-based, cloud-centric protocols and architectural principles, like horizontal scalability and automated recovery from failure. And most importantly, RESTful APIs' Web-centricity shifts the focus of enterprise integration to the consumer.

The Web, after all, is more about the human being interacting with a Web endpoint than it is about the Web servers, or any of the other infrastructure behind the scenes. It's no wonder, therefore, that today's digital transformations depend upon this Web-centricity to satisfy the needs and preferences of the customer.

APIs and the Composable Enterprise

The customer-centricity of digital efforts has led to the broader trend of the democratization of technology. No longer can enterprise apps afford to be immune to the pressures of consumer demands. Instead, everyone in the enterprise – or any other size organization, for that matter – expects the applications they use at work to be as convenient, flexible, and mobile-enabled as the apps they use anywhere else.

Enterprise IT, therefore, must respond to this rising tide of democratization, not only by supporting mobile interfaces to enterprise apps, but also by empowering an entire ecosystem of digital capabilities for both internal and external users. Such users expect to find apps in app stores – marketplaces of functionality, originating both inside and outside the organization.

(Photo credit: Joe Miserendino)

Furthermore, users are expecting to compose the functionality of APIs and the data they provide to meet shifting business needs. Sales data should connect to business intelligence should connect to analysis and visualization – the list of such composition opportunities is endless. This expectation of composability is at the heart of the composable enterprise.

From a technical perspective, the secret sauce that makes this app store-driven, user-centric composition vision come to life are the APIs that form the glue among the various application components and other services, including the small, modular components called microservices. And now that such APIs are web-centric, leveraging REST, JSON, and other easy-to-use protocols, there's no excuse for developers not to get them right.

Furthermore, there are so many available APIs that meet the needs

and business models of so many organizations that an *API economy* has grown up around them. In this API economy, developers and other people can assemble apps from a mix of components built in-house and available in the cloud.

Companies who may have never thought of themselves as offering software-based products or services to their customers are now able to leverage APIs to expand their offerings. As enterprises in multiple industries become software-driven organizations, APIs become the means for providing value to customers, for maintaining efficient relationships with suppliers, and for participating in the broader commerce communities to which they belong.

New Zealand Post is a great example of such an organization. This company developed a number APIs, empowering external users to integrate with its shipping, addressing, and postal systems. These APIs helped to build its parcel delivery business, which overtook mail delivery as the largest source of revenue in 2014. New Zealand Post is now using a commercial version of its addressing API to assist with identity verification on credit card applications.

Architectural Leadership for the Composable Enterprise

APIs support enterprise composability at two levels. Inside the organization, people leverage APIs at the team level, while external to the organization, customers and partners can mix and match APIs from different places, composing and recomposing capabilities and information at will.

In some cases, the business drives composability top-down. Executive-level concerns drive strategic initiatives that drive API-led composability. In other cases, composability is bottom-up, as developers put together capabilities to meet various project needs. However, in either case, the same APIs facilitate such composability – assuming, of course, they are architected properly to support such composability.

Architecture, in fact, is a critical enabler of the composable enterprise vision. APIs must be reusable and modular, and it goes without saying that nonfunctional requirements like compliance and security must be bulletproof. All of these requirements depend upon a lightweight, Web-centric architecture.

Where, then, should the IT organization go to get proper architectural leadership – or any other expertise necessary to execute on the composable enterprise? Perhaps a center of excellence will do.

Centers of excellence (CoEs) are teams and associated knowledge resources that provide leadership, best practices, research, and support for a focus area like architecture or APIs. On the surface, it sounds like such a center is just the ticket to help an organization transition to becoming a composable enterprise.

There's just one problem with this plan: CoEs are by definition *centralized*. They actually become roadblocks for IT, as well as for line of business people who want access to IT capabilities and data, because leveraging a center of excellence requires formal requests to a small, typically overworked team.

In contrast, the decentralized alternative to a C0E is a *center for enablement*. Centers for enablement focus on rolling out new capabilities and assets to a

skilled audience – often with the support of a self-service capability like a portal or app store.

Instead of acting as an ivory tower repository of expertise, a center for enablement distributes templates that various audiences can use as starting points. The goal is to teach people 'how to fish' as well as '*where* to fish' for the expertise and capabilities they require.

Templates, APIs, app stores, and marketplaces all facilitate self-service access to IT resources. However, moving to a self-service model requires changing behavior in the organization. Get this model right, however, and it frees IT to focus on more important tasks.

IT for the 21st Century: Supporting the Composable Enterprise

The vision of the composable enterprise is a vision of a world where IT is a partner to the business. IT is no longer a back office function, but rather an enabler of the business. To make this vision a reality, the approach can't only be top-down or bottom-up. It must be

customer-driven and end-to-end – the essence of digital transformation.

At one end, of course, are legacy systems, which will continue to present a challenge to the composable enterprise. However, rip and replace is rarely the best option. Instead, expose legacy assets as APIs, and modernize them how and when delivers the most value to the organization and its customers.

APIs make even inflexible legacy assets composable as part of the API economy. APIs are the lynchpin of a modern approach to integration that will create flexibility, agility, efficiency, and ultimately business success for years to come.

The business no longer has the time to wait for centralized IT. But that doesn't mean the IT organization goes away. Instead, there are the three roles that remain critically important for modern IT: security, governance, and maintaining access to systems of record – via APIs.

The role of architecture is shifting as well. The top priority for architecture is supporting the organization's business agility goals – helping the organization deal with the change at the heart of the composable enterprise.

In order to successfully become composable enterprises, organizations must decentralize the IT organization and support centers of enablement rather than centers of excellence. Implement lightweight, web-centric architectures and the design principles of API-led connectivity.

Such business and technological transformation is difficult, but the path to success is clear. Every organization has the power to become a composable enterprise.

Diversity
Limited

Software may be eating the world
but APIs are giving it teeth

Diversity
Limited

Table of Contents

Introduction

It's not an exaggeration to say that today we're in the middle of a series of epic changes in society, the economy and technology. Seen in isolation any one of these changes would be both challenging and disruptive. When regarded in totality however we're seeing an era-defining shift.

We believe that these macro changes mean that organizations will need to revisit how they fundamentally operate. Many predict that we will see the rise of a new type of organization that displays displays new structures, processes and strategies.

In this paper we detail the changes we see occurring in society and the economy that are driving this massive shift. We identify why the status quo will no longer be viable for organization in the future and will posit what the organization of the future might look like. Finally, we'll introduce some key technologies that will enable these new sorts of organizations to thrive.

Change Is The Only Constant

We contend that macro changes in society, economies and technology result in a completely new environment within which organizations operate. In order to understand the opportunities that exist, it is necessary to understand the underlying forces of change.

Generational shifts

While it is easy to overstate the very near term impacts of so called "digital natives," we believe that a workforce increasingly made up of individuals who have grown up used to flexible, accessible and intuitive technologies will change the expectations that workforces will have of enterprise technology. The rise of social networks such as Facebook and Twitter, the ubiquity of connectivity and smart devices, and the rise of distributed computing all result in individuals who are used to doing things differently from employees of previous generations.

The rise of the cloud

Over the past five to ten years we have seen a massive increase in the availability of cloud-based solutions. Whereas in the past individuals consumed music from local media, watched movies on physical (and local) storage, and generally stored their information locally, all of these functions have moved to the cloud. We now listen to music via Spotify, watch streaming movies on Netflix, and store our photos, files and memories on Facebook or Dropbox. As this trend moves from the consumer to the enterprise, there will be a fundamental shift in the way systems are designed and operated.

The internet of everything

Analysts predict that within a few short years there will be some 50 billion devices connected to the internet. Whereas today most connected devices are what we traditionally regard as "computers" – PCs, tablets, smartphones – in the future a host of less typical devices will be connected. From refrigerators to toothbrushes, from cars to thermostats, there will be a massive number of input devices that individuals and organizational systems need to interact with. This too will result in enterprise systems being forced to move from a siloed and ring-fenced paradigm, to one that is much more organic in nature.

Big data

One trend that not-surprisingly corresponds to the rise of the internet of things is the big data trend. With all of these connected devices, organizations are going to have to deal with a far greater volume of data than ever before. Already we're seeing examples of industrial companies inserting sensors into such varied devices as airplane engines and within concrete during construction. All of these sensors produce copious amounts of data that need to be transmitted, stored and analyzed and this will change the way systems are designed and run.

The demand for agility

The traditional paradigm where large organizations held a dominant position within a stable ecosystem have long gone. Increasingly, organizations are having to reinvent what they do on an almost daily basis. In the most basic example, this may mean having to roll out new pricing and packaging to react to changing marketplace conditions; in the most extreme case this might involve completely re-designing the products and processes an organization creates, and having to do so extremely quickly. Large organizations are increasingly having to emulate the speed and agility of startups and this is taxing their systems, culture and processes to the extreme.

Economic shifts

While the global financial collapse may have been a short term aberration, underlying it were some systemic changes which we believe are permanent. The pressure to do more with less remains. Organizations are facing seriously shortened product development cycles and lifespans and accordingly, the budgets they have are being similarly reduced. These tightened budgets and pressure for increasing productivity are driving organizations to find systems and processes that deliver better results with lower investments.

New sourcing and manufacturing approaches

Recent years have seen a marked increase in crowd-sourcing, a way for an organization to obtain outcomes from resources outside its boundaries. Crowd-sourcing is being utilized for research and design, funding, and intelligence gathering. While crowd-sourcing undoubtedly increases an organization's ability to be agile, it also creates challenges in terms of security, process and systems.

All of these changes, taken in totality, create a landscape of rapid and substantive change for organizations. Faced with such tectonic changes in the environment within which they operate, organizations are having to revisit the way they work.

With change come opportunities

While there are almost limitless examples of how these trends will enable new businesses, products, and services across industries, it's worthwhile to walk through a few examples of the ways that innovative companies will capitalize on these shifts to drive increased business value.

The efficient building site

Using a selection of these technologies, tradespeople on a building site can use mobile devices to get virtual reality overlays of building plans and specifications on top of pictures taken with the mobile device. A construction manager could hold a device up to a wall, press a button and see an overlay of the plumbing pipes, electrical wires and construction elements within the wall, effectively giving him a map of building infrastructure for more precise, efficient work.

Contextual marketing

Using location-based data and real time information feeds, a retail establishment can know when a particular customer enters their store. That customer can then be delivered personalized offers and information tailored to their buying history and personal demographics.

Health alerts

Patients can be connected to medical personnel in real time. Telemetry can deliver diagnostic data to physicians and alerts can be triggered when certain metrics (blood pressure for example) move beyond preset limits.

Optimized industrial equipment

By using sensors and big data analytics, big pieces of industrial equipment such as wind turbines and jet engines can deliver performance data to large-scale data analysis platforms. These platforms can in turn alter operational characteristics of the equipment in real time to ensure it performs at the highest levels of efficiency.

None of these examples are science fiction – they are all being used by innovative organizations today to deliver better outcomes for themselves and their customers. While these approach may today be outliers, they will move rapidly towards mainstream adoption and quickly become the modus operandi for most organizations.

The new organization

Faced with changes in the external environment, new expectations from their workforces and customers, and constraints on inputs into the operation, organizations will increasingly need to operate in a completely different manner. What will this new organization look like and how will it operate? This will vary by industry and individual company, but we believe that every new organization will exhibit a consistent set of core characteristics.

Distributed

An ever-increasing move towards globalization will mean that organizations will increasingly operate globally. Access to resources, skill shortages and the attractiveness of a global marketplace all encourage this trend to continue and increase. While this has been the norm for large organizations for decades, it will increasingly be the norm for even tiny operations. Organizations will make use of design, production and other functions that are distributed. An example might be a manufacturing organization that has a design team based in Europe, manufacturing in the Far East and distributed logistics hubs within the markets they work.

Hyper-local

Seemingly at odds with the previous trend, organizations will increasingly have to tailor their products, sales approaches and key messages to individual markets. While the previous business paradigm saw a global homogenization of business – McDonalds success was, in part, due to the fact that a Big Mac looks and tastes the same in Tokyo as it does in Timbuktu – this new paradigm will see organizations deliver something akin to the local greengrocer or butcher of old. Organizations will utilize technology to better understand individual customers and individual markets and deliver solutions that best fit with their wants. The days of the same product being sold in every market will soon be over.

Project based

Only a generation ago, employees signed on to an organization with the very real expectation that they would have a job for life. All the changes we detailed in the previous section mean that there is an unprecedented level of flux within the employee ranks. This trend will continue to accelerate and as a result, the future will be typified by "external employees," individuals that come to the organization to work on a distinct piece of work or project, and then move on to the next opportunity.

This level of change delivers great benefits to organizations in terms of agility and innovation, but it also introduces some real challenges to the way they operate.

Remote

The days of "going to the office" are a thing of the past for many people – technological advancement in terms of mobility and cloud computing mean that individuals can work anywhere there is an internet connection. This change has two benefits - it means employees can feel empowered to work in a setting that suits them - and it reduces the footprint that an organization needs – rather than investing in massive real estate spend, organizations can instead invest in the tools to allow their people to work wherever they want to.

Flat

The traditional model of an organization is hierarchical. Taking a militaristic approach, organizations have many levels of seniority, defined organizational charts and complex reporting lines. The organization of the future will be far flatter and systems will help to replace the complex structures and reporting lines that we know today. As the organization flattens, it allows for relatively junior employees to have a large impact on the organization. In the technology world it is often said that "developers are the new kingmakers" – this metaphor extends across the organization and in the future every employee will have the systems and ability to deliver substantive change to the organization.

All of these changes are positive for the organization, but introduce some real challenges to traditional IT structure, functions and tools. The iT department of the future will be a very different thing from what it is today.

The new technology stack

Underlying these new business models and innovations is a brand new technology stack. Traditionally, organizations have largely relied on monolithic stacks delivered by one or two massive technology vendors. These stacks were a technological embodiment of the hierarchical nature of the organization - they lent themselves to rigidity, structure, process, and lines of control.

As those attributes start to come to an end within organizations, we need to find a new metaphor for IT systems, one that ensures security, reliability and control, while offering the flexibility and agility for individual users to achieve their goals.

Whereas the past was typified by an organization using a single technology for each layer of the stack (software, infrastructure or other distinct functions) the future will be wildly heterogeneous. Different business units and individuals will use a diverse set of disparate systems that best deliver the outcomes they need. This will feel to traditional IT practitioners like a state of anarchy. If everyone is using something different, how will IT ensure security, compliance and control?

We believe that the IT organization of the future will be heterogeneous but knit together into a cohesive, high-performing whole by broad fabrics. A good example is infrastructure – while individual business units might use infrastructure from many different vendors (some public cloud from Amazon Web Services, a private OpenStack cloud and some traditional on-premises infrastructure) they will do so within the context of a broad management layer. This management layer is a fabric that spans the entire organization and allows the adoption of a plethora of different technologies while ensuring enterprise-wide consistency and visibility. This technology fabric will exist in multiple areas and levels of the technology stack but prominent examples include cloud management and control, application and infrastructure monitoring, enterprise social networking and the enterprise service bus.

This fabric approach will enable the organization of the future. With a broad integration layer, for example, organizations can more readily deliver highly specific mobile applications. Rather than a monolithic stack where mobile applications have a tendency to be "one size fits all," a broad enabling fabric means that virtually every employee can have their own application, tailored to their projects, preferences and the way they work.

The term "composable enterprise" has been coined to describe the way the new IT stack will look, but there is one critical element to enabling this composable enterprise to function, the Application Programming Interface or API.

APIs – The glue that binds it all together

The acronym API might not mean anything to most individuals, but APIs are a core enabler of new business models, product offerings and insights. An API is simply an interface to an IT application or data source that allows authorized applications or machines to easily access it. A well-defined API is the glue that ties data together the organization of the future. While traditionally used for the integration of discrete applications, APIs are now the key technology that enables all of the business and IT transformations we've discussed. Enabling software to interact with sensors, delivering contextual mobile applications, harnessing big data for analysis and insights - all are enabled by the humble API.

APIs have a myriad of value propositions within organizations.

Capitalizing on existing data

Traditional enterprise systems tend to silo data. A traditional system will have a storage layer, a processing layer and a presentation layer. Additionally, they have a number of systems that manage slices of data in discrete silos. For example, data about customers may live in the CRM system, but data about the order history of each customer lives is a discrete order management system.

New technologies are enabling the unlocking of this data, many times without the need to re-architect applications. In this way an existing organization, with its existing applications, can tap into the data locked within these systems to support new use cases. This might mean they deliver mobile applications to their employees using the data, it may mean they combine the data from these applications with other data or it might mean they monetize this data in new and creative ways.

Reaching new markets

APIs introduce the ability for organizations to reach entirely new markets and explore new partnerships. By taking core data and repurposing it in new ways, it is possible to create entirely new business models. By making data available to third parties, new business relationships can be explored. A possible example would be an e-commerce business exposing anonymized customer data via API and allowing market research companies to utilize that data. The primary organization can monetize what was previously wasted data, the third party organization can

get valuable source data, and consumers can be presented new and innovative products and services.

Enabling mobile opportunities

A plethora of opportunities exist when data is free from siloed stores and served up to mobile devices and applications. It is the role of the API to create the interface between core data and mobile devices/applications and hence the humble API can be seen as the enabler for an entirely new economy. The rise over the past few years of mobile app stores such as Apple's AppStore or the Google Play Store are directly attributable to the opportunities afforded by the API.

Key takeaways

Organizations are seeing unprecedented changes in the economy, the external environment and their internal operating situation. These changes are causing organizations to operate in vastly different ways from what they do today. As organizations increasingly move to the new operating model, they will in turn require a very different kind of IT organization to deliver upon their needs. The API is the glue and the enabler that allows organizations to leverage the opportunities inherent in these new approaches, react to constraints and externalities in their broader environment and deliver innovation, agility and ongoing business sustainability.

About Diversity Limited

Diversity is a broad spectrum consultancy specializing in SaaS, Cloud Computing and business strategy. Principal and founder Ben Kepes provides various services including:

- Commentary – Ben is a noted commentator about Cloud Computing and enterprise software – he has written for a broad selection of media outlets, and is often quoted as a subject matter expert and influencer.
- Consulting – Ben is in demand with large organizations who turn to him for advice on technology starting. He spends time with both customers and vendors advising on all aspects of their strategy.
- Advisory – Ben sits on a number of boards, both formal and informal. He enjoys helping startups get to market and grow to scale.
- Investment – Ben is an investor in a number of different companies. These investments revolve around Ben's focus of delivering technology that can make a difference in how organizations work.

About the author
Ben Kepes

Ben Kepes is a technology evangelist, an entrepreneur, a commentator and a business adviser. Ben covers the convergence of technology, mobile, ubiquity and agility, all enabled by the Cloud. His areas of interest extend to enterprise software, software integration, financial/accounting software, platforms and infrastructure as well as articulating technology simply for everyday users.

He is a globally recognized subject matter expert with an extensive following across multiple channels.

Ben currently writes for Forbes and his own blog. His commentary has been published on ReadWriteWeb, GigaOm, The Guardian and a wide variety of publications – both print and online. Often included in lists of the most influential technology thinkers globally, Ben is also an active member of the Clouderati, a global group of Cloud thought leaders and is in demand as a speaker at conferences and events all around the world.

As organizations react to the demands for more flexible working environments, the impacts of the economic downturn and the existence of multiple form-factor devices and ubiquitous connectivity, Cloud Computing stands alone as the technology paradigm that enables the convergence of those trends. Ben's insight into these factors has helped organizations large and small, buy-side and sell-side, to navigate a challenging path from the old paradigm to the new one.

Ben is passionate about technology as an enabler and enjoys exploring that theme in various settings.

Best Practices for Microservices
Implementing a foundation for continuous innovation

Executive Summary

Today's business environment is extraordinarily competitive. No company, no matter its size or what industry it is in is safe from disruption. It is easier than ever for new entrants to come into a market, turning entire industries upside down. Unless organizations can nimbly innovate at the speed of their competition, they will be left behind, and large organizations with calcified processes and structures will be hit the hardest.

It is possible for any organization to harness the opportunities that digital transformation provides; it simply requires a more agile enterprise. This type of business employs a framework of smaller, hyper-focused teams rapidly innovating on defined units of business value, working in concert to deliver something much larger. We call this becoming the composable enterprise. Making an organization composable requires changes to how IT supports the business. It means creating scale through reusable services and enabling self-service consumption of those services.

The ability of your business to change quickly, innovate easily, and meet competition wherever it arises is a strategic necessity today. This will allow you to thrive in a market which constantly changes, and create new customer experiences in new contexts using new technologies. Your business can shape innovative customer experiences only if your IT team provides digital assets in the form of core business capabilities that bring real value to your business in multiple contexts. This is how IT can be an enabler of the strategic goals of your business.

> Organizations that have successfully laid a foundation for continuous innovation and agility have adopted microservice architectures to respond rapidly to the demands of the business.

Organizations that have successfully laid a foundation for continuous innovation and agility have adopted microservice architectures to respond rapidly to the never-ending demands of the business.

Why Microservices?

Microservices are the evolution of best-practice architectural principles that shape the delivery of solutions to the business in the form of services. All businesses, no matter what industry they are in, must strive to deliver the ideal customer experience, as customers are more demanding than ever and will abandon a business that is too slow to respond. IT must deliver solutions that can be adapted to deliver a holistic and uniform experience to the customer across all the business channels. To achieve this the architecture should identify and define digital assets which align to core business capabilities. They offer the potential to break down the coupling between business channels and the backend systems of record that cater to them. A microservice that encapsulates a core business capability and adheres to the design principles and goals outlined below should be considered a true digital asset. It can bring value to the business because it can be adapted for use in multiple contexts. The contexts for use of the service are the business processes and transactions, and the channels through which your customer, employee, or partner interacts with your business.

Benefits to the Business

A microservice architecture **aligns with the business** in such a way that changes to your business can be dealt with in an agile fashion. Business processes and transactions are automated with the composition of microservices. When processes are changed or when new ones are introduced, IT can respond by re-wiring services into new compositions.

The ease and speed with which your company can change will determine your ability to react to trends in your industry and maintain competitive advantage. With solution logic in the form of composable services, IT can run at the pace of the business and match business changes with an **agile response** in the delivery of solution logic. Innovation is the face of this agility. It may take the form of new channels of business (like Google creating new revenue streams by productizing their APIs), new digital engagements with customers (like Spotify engaging with their customers through Uber), entirely new products and services which may demand entirely new business processes, or the simple modification of existing business processes. All of this speaks of change. Companies need to be able to alter direction based on market forces. IT must be able to facilitate change by composing existing digital assets into new business capabilities.

Your enterprise can deliver solution logic in a decentralized manner with the standardization of microservice contracts in the form of APIs. Multiple teams from different domains can implement services with their own choice of technology but yet remain aligned with the business in their purpose. This represents the evolution of IT's role from provider to partner resulting in the **enablement of teams** from the lines of business to adapt the core capabilities built by the central team to their own particular needs.

> The ease and speed with which your company can change will determine your ability to react to trends in your industry and maintain competitive advantage.

Microservices are natively able to communicate with each other because of industry-wide adoption of standards like HTTP and JSON. In other words, they are **intrinsically interoperable**. They facilitate an exchange of information independent of how they have been implemented because their interface is defined according to standards which already exist at the level of the industry and which are also defined by the teams in your organization.

Your business can **pick and choose best-of-breed vendor products** and platforms because of the interoperability that standardized interfaces bring. For the same reason, your teams can also choose the best technologies to implement the microservices with a polyglot approach to development.

What are microservices?

Traditionally, enterprises have delivered software applications in siloes. These arose from the isolated demands of individual departments. Software was developed or purchased in attention to these limited scopes. Customer facing business processes on the other hand typically span multiple departments. The lack of alignment between these two realities led to duplicate efforts and missing or inaccurate information in each solution. The latter was a major force behind enterprise integration.

The service concept evolved from attempts to respect the business process as focal point of solution requirements. The need to modify existing processes or invent entirely new ones should be met with an agile response from IT to adapt to the change. Rather than build or purchase "applications" in the traditional sense, a service approach stipulates the creation of services as the building block of solution logic which are composable to address the automation requirements of business processes.

Consumption Modes

Microservices are most often directly invoked by HTTP REST API calls. Standards like RAML (Restful API Modelling Language) allow for the formal definition of REST APIs. RAML can define every resource and operation exposed by the microservice. It's an industry standard which has gained popularity as a lightweight approach to microservice interface definition and publication.

In those cases where microservices collaborate for the realization of a complex business transaction or process, an event-driven approach is also adopted. The idea is for the microservice to subscribe to business domain events which are published to a message broker. Standards like JMS and AMQP are dominant in major broker technologies in the industry. The involvement of a message broker in the microservice invocation adds reliability to the consumption model. Even if the microservice subscribed to a particular queue, topic or exchange were down when the event was published, the messaging paradigm guarantees that the microservice will receive the message once it comes back online again.

The composition of microservices is realized with a mix of direct calls through HTTP and indirect calls through a message broker.

API-led Connectivity

With the conviction that building an adaptable business capability is much better than building a tactical point to point integration, IT should strive to deliver these assets which are accessible through API invocation and domain event subscription and which can deliver value to the business in multiple contexts.

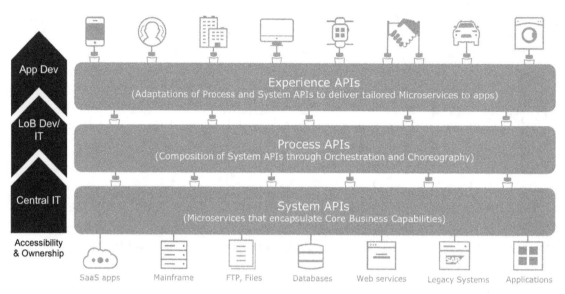

Figure 1. Microservices classification

The asset is primarily an encapsulation of a business entity capability, like Customer, Order, or Invoice. These system APIs or system-level microservices are in line with the concept of an autonomous service which has been designed with enough abstraction to hide the underlying systems of record. None of these system details are leaked through the API. The responsibility of the API is discrete and agnostic to any particular business process.

System APIs are composable with other APIs to form aggregate process APIs. The composition of system APIs can take the form of explicit API orchestration (direct calls) or through the more reliable API choreography by which they are driven by business events relevant to the context of the composition (order fulfillment, for example).

The API Gateway

Both process and system APIs should be tailored and exposed to suit the needs of each business channel and digital touchpoint. The adaptation is shaped by the desired digital experience and is what we call the experience API. Sometimes the adaptation of the API is technically motivated: a particular security mechanism might be needed on one channel; the types of channel may differ greatly as do mobile, web and devices; a composition of multiple APIs might be needed according to the backend for frontend pattern. In other contexts business differences must be catered to with adaptations that consider the special requirements of groups of users like employees, customers, and partners.

In all these cases the API Gateway pattern is a good approach because it is where API compositions and proxies are deployed. API Management facilitates the administrative application of recurring logic, like security, rate limiting, auditing and data filtering to the experience APIs on the gateway. The use of API management to apply policies that encapsulate the tailored logic makes the adaptation of system and process APIs relatively quick and easy.

The "Micro" of Microservices

Scope of Responsibility

The most obvious candidate microservice is the business entity easily identifiable with a glance at a business process or transaction. A *customer* is an example of such an entity. It is a business entity that may be relevant in a number of contexts both at the process layer and the experience layer. The responsibility is not limited to mere data carrying. A microservice should not be reduced to a simple CRUD service. Each entity encapsulates within itself all responsibilities relevant to the business domain for which it was designed. All of this goes hand in hand with a deliberate limitation of the scope of responsibility. "Discrete" is the best common sense interpretation of "micro" with respect to scope of responsibility. This helps in guaranteeing that the system level microservice doesn't take on any responsibility that more appropriately pertains to a business process level microservice. The system level microservices are agnostic to any particular business process and hence can be used in more than one composition.

The scope of a business process must also be considered. Some sub-domains have their own local business processes (*shipping*, for example). A system level microservice can be adapted for use in multiple processes within the *shipping* domain. Whenever its capability is needed outside the domain, it can be adapted for this with an experience level microservice. There are of course business processes, typically customer facing, which traverse multiple domains. The rule here is to compose multiple microservices adapted for this use in experience APIs.

Team Organization and Responsibilities

Teams should be small enough to work locally together and focus entirely on a single sub-domain of the business, and include domain experts so that the language of that sub-domain is modelled in the solution.

The ownership of the microservice includes everything from design to deployment and management. The API is considered a business product, an asset to be delivered to the business. There is no handoff to other teams to manage the running instance. The whole lifecycle belongs to the team who develop it.

Scope of Effort

Microservices that address the needs pertaining to a specific sub-domain will recognize that certain business concepts are perceived in a way that is particular to the sub-domain. No attempt is made to model a universal solution unless the entity is naturally shared across the entire organization.

Ease of deployment

The cost of delivery to production is greatly reduced by the combination of small teams with complete ownership, the discrete responsibility of the microservice, and the infrastructure which facilitates continuous delivery.

Fundamental Principles of Microservice Design

Microservice capabilities are expressed formally with *business-oriented* APIs. They encapsulate a core business capability and as such are assets to the business. The implementation of the service, which may involve integrations with systems of record, is completely hidden as the interface is defined purely in business terms.

The positioning of services as valuable assets to the business implicitly promotes them as *adaptable* for use in multiple contexts. The same service can deliver its capabilities to more than one business process or over different business channels or digital touchpoints.

Dependencies between services and their consumers are minimized with the application of the principle of *loose coupling*. By standardizing on contracts as expressed through business oriented APIs, consumers are not impacted by changes in the implementation of the service. This allows the service owners to change the implementation and switch out or modify the systems of record or even service compositions which may lie behind the interface and replace them without any downstream impact.

Identification of Candidate Microservices Identifying the microservices that you need to build and the scope of their responsibility can be helped by considering the types of information that are exchanged in the transactions they cater to. In a healthcare setting, *patient*, *encounter* and *claim* are examples. In an e-commerce setting there are: *order*, *item*, *discount*, or *customer*. In a banking solution, you might have *transfer*, *account*, *payee*. The responsibility ought to be lean and focused. The system level microservices are not an abstraction over an entire back-end system, but only that part of the system or systems responsible for the storage of the business entity. Business transactions and processes are often the focus of IT efforts because it is the business process that effectively defines the business. This may be *order fulfillment* in the e-commerce sector. A visit that a patient makes to a hospital could be driven by the *visit administration* microservice. This microservice is implemented with the composition of microservices in the system layer.

Autonomy is a measure of control that the implementation of the service has over its runtime environment and database schema. This enhances the performance and reliability of the service and gives

consumers more guarantees about the quality of service they can expect from it. Coupled with statelessness, autonomy also contributes to the overall availability and scalability of the service.
Each service is necessarily **fault tolerant** so that failures on the side of its collaborating services will have minimal impact on its own SLA. Services, by virtue of being independent of each other, have the opportunity to cut off communication to a failed service. This technique, called a "circuit breaker" and inspired by the electrical component of the same name, stops individual service failures from propagating through the larger, distributed system.

All of these design principles contribute to the principle of **composability** which allows the service to deliver value to the business in different contexts. Its composition together with other services to form a new service aggregate is effectively the new form of application development.

The aim of **discoverability** is to communicate to all interested parties a clear understanding of the business purpose and technical interface of the microservice. Thus, the service must be published in a way that ensures that developers of client software have everything they need to easily consume it.

Reuse
Reuse continues to be a principle of microservice design. However, the scope of reuse has been reduced to specific domains within the business. The effort of designing for this reuse, which in the early days of SOA included wasted efforts in designing enterprise-wide canonical models, was fruitless because it was too ambitious. However, it must be noted that the canonical model in its restricted scope can be of benefit. In line with the reuse it facilitates, its scope has been reduced. With the 'merit based reuse' approach, an emerging model is preferred over a predetermined one. Teams can agree on communication models for deciding how microservices must be adapted for use outside the contexts in which they were designed. A collaboration hub like Anypoint Exchange encourages Merit based reuse with reviews, ratings, etc. If an existing microservice API does not suit your domain or 'business group', you might be better off building another microservice that does it.

Business Domain orientation of Microservice Architecture

It is important to approach service design for a particular domain and NOT insist on doing so for every aspect of the business. The failure of enterprise-wide canonical modeling exercises of the last decade are evidence of this. The reality of the business is that business entities can be perceived in deeply different ways across the business units or sub-domains.

No attempt should be made to design enterprise-wide services if each domain has a very different perception of the same concept. An example business entity with very different perceptions is the *Customer* in the Customer Care, Orders, Invoicing and Shipping domains. In figure 2 you can see how each domain has its own microservices which encapsulate core business capabilities for that particular domain. This can result in apparent duplication of microservices as is the case for the Customer API.

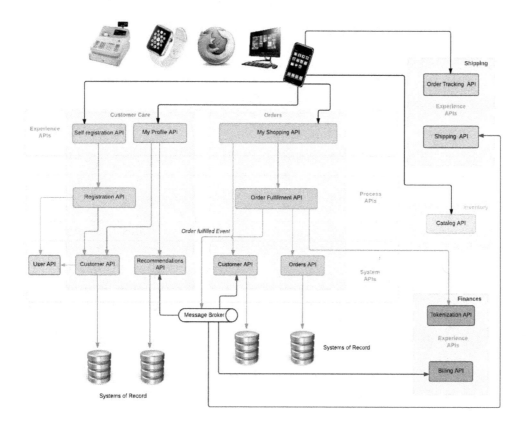

Figure 2. Microservices designed for particular Business Domains

As microservices communicate with each other, especially those designed for different domains, there may be a need to negotiate a contract that suits the needs of the consuming software. This particular adaptation will be manifest as an experience API tailored specifically to that client. It could also take the form of a domain event published to a queue.

Microservices and The Monolith

Microservices are a fundamental shift in how IT approaches software development. Traditional software development processes (waterfall, agile, etc) usually result in relatively large teams working on a single, monolithic deployment artifact. Project managers, developers and operational staff can reach varying degrees of success with these models, releasing application candidates that can be verified by the business, particularly as they gain experience using a particular software and deployment stack. There are, however, some lurking issues with the traditional approaches:

- Monolithic applications can evolve into a "big ball of mud"; a situation where no single developer (or group of developers) understands the entirety of the application. This problem is exacerbated as senior developers roll off a project and are replaced by junior or offshore resources for maintenance.
- Limited re-use is realized across monolithic applications. Monolithic applications, by definition, hide their internals. While some re-usability might be realized by API's at the "edge" of the monolith, chances for re-use of internal components is limited. When reuse is achieved it's usually through shared libraries which foster tight coupling and are limited to the development platform used to implement the monolith.
- Scaling monolithic applications can be challenging. Identifying and tuning specific aspects of application functionality for performance in isolation of other aspects is usually impossible since all functionality is bundled in a single deployment artifact. Scaling monolithic applications is usually not in "real time."
- Operational agility is rarely achieved in the repeated deployment of monolithic application artifacts. While operational automation can alleviate most of the manual pain in deploying these applications, for instance by automating the provisioning of VM's or automatically configuring network devices, there's still a point where developers are blocked by operations staff waiting for these activities to occur. In the worst cases, where automation is not in place, developers and operators are under great stress every time a deployment fails or a production issue is hit.
- By definition monolithic applications are implemented using a single development stack (ie, JEE or .NET.) In addition to limiting reuse for application not implemented on the stack it also robs the opportunity to use "the right tool for the job." For instance, implementing a small part of a JEE application with Golang would be difficult in a monolithic application.

A microservice architecture, in concert with cloud deployment technologies, API management, and integration technologies, provide an alternate approach to software development which avoids the delivery of monolithic applications. The monolith is instead "broken up" into a set of independent services that are developed, deployed and maintained separately. This has the following advantages:

- Services are encouraged to be small, ideally built by a handful of developers that can be fed by "2 pizza boxes." This means that a small group, or perhaps a single developer, can understand the entirety of a single microservice.
- If microservices expose their interfaces with a standard protocol, such as a REST-ful API or an AMQP exchange, they can be consumed and re-used by other services and applications without direct coupling through language bindings or shared libraries. Service registries can facilitate the discovery of these services by other groups.
- Services exist as independent deployment artifacts and can be scaled independently of other services.
- Developing services discretely allows developers to use the appropriate development framework for the task at hand. Services that compose other services into a composite API, for example, might be quicker to implement with MuleSoft than .NET or JEE.

The tradeoff of this flexibility is complexity. Managing a multitude of distributed services at scale is difficult:

- Project teams need to easily discover services as potential reuse candidates. These services should provide documentation, test consoles, etc so re-using is significantly easier than building from scratch.
- Interdependencies between services need to be closely monitored. Downtime of services, service outages, service upgrades, etc can all have cascading downstream effects and such impact should be proactively analyzed.

The SDLC lifecycle of services should be highly automated. This requires technology, such as deployment automation technologies and CI frameworks, but more importantly discipline from developer and operations teams.

Microservice Implementation Patterns

Command Query Responsibility Segregation

The classification of microservices into system, process, and experience types can be further subdivided into consideration of scalability requirements. Most requests to microservices are to retrieve information for presentation purposes. A lesser number of requests are to realize a state changing business function, like a customer modifying their personal profile, or submitting an order. We distinguish these types of requests as queries for the retrieval of information and commands for the state changing business function.
Some high traffic requirements may require a deliberate separation of the deployment so that the one business capability is split into two microservices: one for commands and the other for queries in line with the emerging pattern Command Query Responsibility Segregation (CQRS).

Event Sourcing

The autonomy principle of microservice design stipulates each microservice having its own data store. Database sharing is avoided. This creates a problem when we consider our approach to the automation of a business transaction. We recommended business process type microservices whose responsibility it is to compose system type microservices through orchestration and choreography. Naturally, the information exchange for any business transaction is related, but each system microservice executes its part in the collaboration independent from the rest. The end-state of the whole composition must leave all data in a consistent state.

The industry is moving away from distributed transactions to solve this problem. Hence, one can see that each microservice having its own data store to represent what ultimately is the same information at a higher level can result in an inconsistency between them at any moment in time. This reality is especially prevalent with a domain event driven approach in which the microservices collaborating in a choreography work asynchronously driven by domain events published to a message broker. Eventual consistency is the key here. When every microservice has completed its work, then the whole system is in a consistent state.

This leads to an emerging pattern in which changes to state are stored as journaled business events. The current state is known not by retrieving data from a store but by navigating the history of business events and calculating it on the fly.

Continuous Delivery of Composed Applications

Getting teams to continuously release software aligns with agile development principles. Continuous delivery of software lets business stakeholders verify, in real time, that an application is meeting the ultimate business objective. Continuous delivery also means, in terms of composed microservice applications, continuous integration. In applications that are composed of many services it is critical to ensure that the composition actually works when the software is built.
Having short release cycles, fast feedback on build failures and automated deployment facilities are critical in implementing continuous delivery.

Self-service Consumption of Microservices

Every corner of an enterprise needs technology to build new applications for their specific function or customer. IT needs to transform from its traditional function as the sole technology provider to become an adaptive, responsive and nimble organization that can keep up with the pace of the digital era as well as embrace the opportunities provided by a change driven environment. This transformation can occur only if IT transforms itself into an strategic business enabler rather than a centralized technology function.
Being an enabler means that IT has to decentralize and democratize application development and data access to the different Lines of Business (LoBs) and functional business partners. This way, IT can concentrate on a partnership with the business - i.e. providing a set of strategic and consistent assets and technology.

Service proliferation, however, is a trade off incurred by such an approach. Managing these services at scale raises a number of challenges:

- Service Discovery and Documentation
- Fault tolerance
- Quality of Service
- Security
- Request traceability
- Failure triage

It is imperative that you can easily manage your microservices in a way that facilitates self-service access to them across all the lines of business in your enterprise. API Management represents the evolution of service governance that allows you to do the following:

- Publish your APIs so that developers of consuming software have everything they need to self-serve their needs and understand clearly the purpose, scope and interface of your microservice.
- Adapt your APIs through injectable Policies of logic covering security, quality-of-service, auditing, dynamic data filtering, etc.
- Watch your APIs so that you can strategize scalability according to traffic levels and take a temperature gauge on the impact of your assets.
- Tailor your APIs to the specific needs of different lines of business so that API management becomes a decentralized or federated exercise in collaboration between LOBs and central IT.

Microservices on Anypoint Platform

Anypoint Platform solves the most challenging connectivity problems. It's a unified, highly productive, hybrid integration platform that creates a seamless application network of apps, data and devices with API-led connectivity.

Unlike alternatives, Anypoint Platform can be accessed as a cloud solution or deployed on-premises allowing developers to rapidly connect, orchestrate and enable any internal or external application. Anypoint Platform lifts the weight of custom code and delivers the speed and agility to unlock the potential of this connected era.

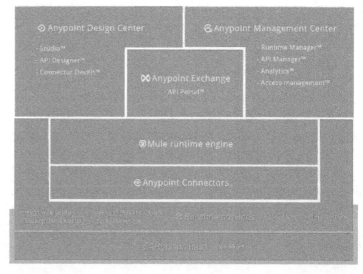

End-to-End Microservice Lifecycle

MuleSoft takes a holistic view of microservices. Unlike traditional apps, the ideal microservice development starts with a top-down API-first approach. Which means there are additional steps compared to traditional Software Development Lifecycles (SDLC).

For instance, the design aspect is usually an iterative process that includes:

1. Modelling your API using standard specs like RAML.
2. You typically want to simulate your spec with a mock API endpoint with which you can Solicit feedback from your API consumers.
3. You also want to validate with real code so you can touch and feel the API and provide feedback.
4. Once the API design is ratified, you would build it using your favorite language, with code that includes business logic and connectivity to appropriate back-end systems.
5. Then create test scripts if following the recommended Test Driven Design approach.
6. Once the microservice is deployed, you typically want to publish the documentation for your API using a portal that becomes your engagement tier with users of your microservice.
7. Finally, when operationalized, you want to manage the microservice runtime, as well as its APIs (for instance, apply security and throttling policies) and get usage analytics for your microservice. Analytics could be used for management/monitoring purposes or for metering and chargeback.

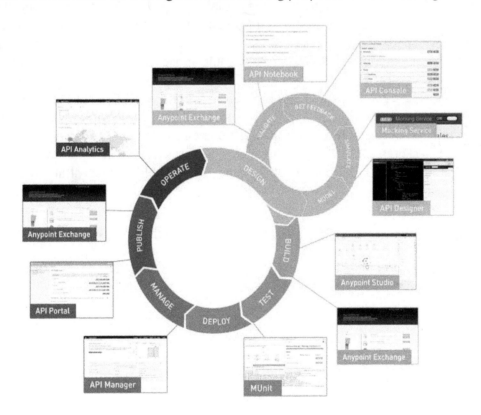

Figure 3. End to end lifecycle of microservices

Now let's go into each phase of the ideal microservice lifecycle in detail, and see how it can be accomplished with Anypoint Platform.

Design and Implementation with Anypoint Design Center

The design of a microservice should begin with its API definition. The API may be REST based or event-driven in line with the two modes of consumption (see Consumption Modes).

API Designer allows you to define a REST API using RAML. RAML is a standard which has achieved rapid adoption as the light-weight language of choice to define APIs. As you define the resources and operations for the API in RAML, API Designer auto-generates a console which centralizes documentation and testability. It also auto-generates a mocking service, deployed to CloudHub. This affords you the luxury of allowing the team responsible for the development of consuming software to write their code against the mocked implementation in parallel with the team who must implement the actual microservice. The team responsible for building the consuming software can showcase their work before the microservice is even developed.

If your team chooses to implement the microservice as a Mule application, then Anypoint Studio will allow them to do so rapidly with its scaffolding of RAML based APIs as a set of flows which implement all the operations. This is done with a graphical drag and drop of message processors. Anypoint Studio also allows the developer to build a true unit test of the application using MUnit, the unit testing framework for Anypoint Platform, with the same graphical approach. Anypoint Connectors encapsulate connectivity to many public APIs, like SalesForce and SAP. The suite of connectors is extensible with Anypoint DevKit, which allows you to turn a simple Java POJO into a reusable connector available for use within Anypoint Studio's palette.

Continuous Delivery with Anypoint Studio, Maven and Docker

A Mule application can be built in Anypoint Studio with Maven or Gradle and committed to an SCM like Github. From there a CI/CD framework like Jenkins can pull down the latest version, build it, execute all relevant tests and deploy it to the next environment in the build pipeline.

Differences in physical endpoints like databases that correspond to each environment are addressed by exploiting external properties files. Thus, the same Mule application progresses without change from dev through test and into production.

Traditional, monolithic applications are typically deployed using the operation convention for the given development platform. Monolithic Java applications, for instance, are usually deployed to multi-tenant application servers like JBoss AS or Tomcat.

IaaS frameworks, such as Chef and Puppet and virtualization technology such as VMWare or Zen can greatly accelerate the deployment of monolithic application stacks. Recent advances in container technology, particularly frameworks such as Docker and Rocket, provide the foundation for almost immediate deployment and undeployment of applications without necessarily provisioning new physical or virtual hardware. Numerous benefits arise from this deployment paradigm, including increased compute density within a single operating system, trivial horizontal and, in some cases vertical autoscaling as well as container packaging and distribution.

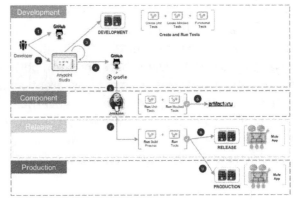

These advantages make containers the ideal choice for microservice distribution and deployment. Container technologies follow the microservice philosophy of encapsulating any single piece of functionality and doing it well. They also give microservices the ability to expand elastically to respond to dynamic request demand.

There is no such thing as a free lunch, however, and managing a container ecosystem comes with its own challenges. For instance, containers running on the same host will be bound to ephemeral ports to avoid conflicts, container failure must be addressed separately, containers need to integrate with front end networking infrastructure such as load-balancers, firewalls or perhaps software-defined networking stacks, etc. Platform-as-a-service technologies, such as Pivotal Cloud Foundry and Mesosphere DCOS, are emerging to address these needs.

Deployment as a Microservice Container

Anypoint Platform's runtime components support a variety of deployment mechanisms, ranging from traditional multi-tenant cluster based deployment to a Mule worker packaged and deployed as a container in CloudHub, MuleSoft's fully hosted and fully managed PaaS.

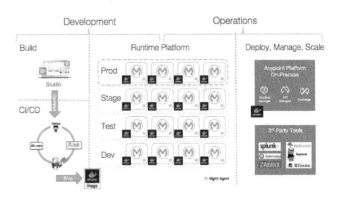

The Mule runtime can support a microservice architecture in an orthogonal manner using two complementary deployment approaches:

1. Mule as an API Gateway

When deployed in this manner the Mule runtime acts as an API Gateway to proxy HTTP traffic back and forth between microservices. This allows Mule to transparently apply cross-cutting policies, to enforce concerns like governance and security, to all API calls traversing a microservice architecture. It additionally allows Mule to asynchronously collect analytics about microservice traffic and consumption patterns, providing valuable insight back to the business.

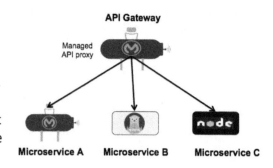

2. Mule as a Microservice Container

One of the benefits of microservice architecture is the freedom to "choose the right tool for the job" to implement a given service. For certain services, a development language like NodeJS or Java might be appropriate. Microservices that are focused on connectivity, orchestration or transformation however are usually easier to implement with an integration framework like Mule. Microservices implemented in Mule can present a managed API since it runs in the same runtime as the API management layer.

This provides a unified runtime for API management and integration unique to MuleSoft. The Anypoint Platform can be used for the composition and connectivity logic for your microservice, exposed as a managed API endpoint. It eliminates the need for a separate API gateway process by providing both capabilities on the same runtime. This simplifies the container creation scripts and the number of moving parts to maintain, which benefits large scale microservice deployments.

Both options can be configured on-premise or in MuleSoft's hosted CloudHub. Hosting your microservices on CloudHub simplifies the microservices DevOps complexity since MuleSoft automates most of the operations aspects and allows deployments in a self-serve, PaaS model.

However, if you choose to set up your own PaaS for microservices the Mule runtime has the following attributes that make it a perfect fit for on-premise containerization:

- The Mule runtime is distributed as a standalone zip file - a JVM is the only dependency
- It runs as a single low-resource process. For instance, it can even be embedded in a resource constrained device like a Raspberry Pi
- The Mule runtime doesn't require any external, persistent storage to share state. This means external resources like databases or messaging systems aren't required by default.

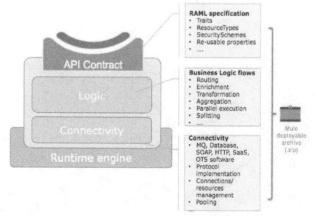

- The Mule application can be layered on top of a Mule runtime container (e.g. Docker) image

Deployment on CloudHub

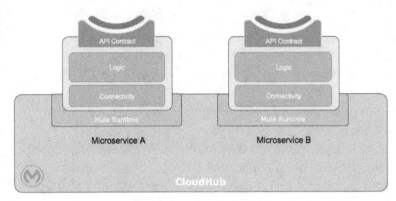

We saw how a containerized on-premise deployment can be achieved with MuleSoft. One disadvantage of this approach is that it puts the onus of maintaining the containerization and PaaS on the customer.

If you chose to host it on MuleSoft's PaaS (CloudHub) instead, the self serve aspect is handled by Anypoint Platform and the runtime is a fully hosted and managed service. Each microservice has it's own autonomous runtime. CloudHub is designed to be secure and fully scalable with built-in High Availability and Disaster Recovery. CloudHub also provides a single-click Global deployment of your microservice. Which guarantees your microservice runtime is compliant to local regulatory requirements, keeping traffic within geographical boundaries.

CloudHub drastically reduces barriers to adoption of a microservices architecture by avoiding the so called Microservices Premium required to set up and maintain your own containerization and PaaS framework. Which means, you can get started with microservices in minutes without having to worry about the infrastructure to support it.

Event-driven microservices with Anypoint MQ

Anypoint MQ is an enterprise-class cloud messaging service, fully integrated with Anypoint Platform and which can act as the means to invoke event-driven microservices. Process level microservices can publish domain events to queues. Those system level microservices which subscribe to the same queues will be invoked as soon as the event is published. In line with reliability requirements, even if they are down in the moment of publication, they will receive the message as soon as they come back up.

For scenarios where multiple microservices are interested in a particular business event, the process level microservice can publish the event to an exchange. Queues bound to the exchange will each receive a copy of the event and as described the microservices subscribed to them will be invoked.

Operational management with Anypoint Runtime Manager

Anypoint Runtime Manager provides a single operational plane to manage both microservice applications built with Anypoint Platform as well as the Mule runtimes that host them. Anypoint Runtime Manager can manage your Mule runtimes on-premises and/or hosted on CloudHub. Anypoint Runtime Manager allows you to start and stop these and cluster them. You can monitor memory and CPU usage and set alerts for when thresholds of their usage are exceeded.

Logs and business data can be viewed and analyzed from the console and can also be pushed out to Splunk, ELK or any DB (for analysis with tools like Tableau).

API management with Anypoint Platform's API solution

Anypoint Platform provides a number of features to manage microservices at scale in a large enterprise:

- API portals provide self-service documentation, test consoles, SDK client generation and programmable notebooks to allow developers to discover and learn how to consume the API for a microservice.
- Mule runtimes, deployed as API gateways, can proxy communication between microservices. This ensures policies, like security and throttling, are correctly applied across all microservices.
- For microservices built and deployed to CloudHub, you can leverage CloudHub Insight to get in-depth visibility into business transactions and events on your Mule applications deployed to CloudHub. Insight makes information searchable and helps you find and recover from any errors that occurred during processing and replay your transactions instantly if necessary.
  CloudHub Insight helps you answer questions about your integrated apps, such as:

  - What happened with a particular request or synchronization?
  - When did the request occur? How long did it take?
  - What was the result of a request?
  - If something went wrong during processing, at what point did the failure occur?

As the dependency graph between services grows, issues that were previously isolated, such as transient performance problems, can cascade across multiple services. API gateways can potentially act as a "circuit breaker" to quickly detect and isolate services from such failure.

Repeatedly implementing security and other cross-cutting concerns in microservices represents duplicated, potentially difficult, effort for developers. There is also the risk that developers will forget or incorrectly implement each concern. Consider the example of implementing security with OAuth 2.0. The API Management module of the Anypoint Platform includes an OAuth 2.0 Policy out-of-the-box. All you need to do is apply this policy to the microservice and you have OAuth 2.0 security. Leveraging shared policies ensures the correct security policy implementation is applied to all API's. If you have a cross-cutting policy (for instance, to selectively mask specified business data in a request), you can quickly and easily build a custom policy to reuse across other microservices, and non-microservices for that matter.

Publication and engagement with Anypoint Exchange

As digital assets with the potential to bring business capabilities to multiple contexts within or outside of your business domain, microservices ought to have their APIs published. This should be done in a way that minimizes the friction of informing and enabling developers of consuming software to understand everything they need to adapt and / or consume the microservice.

Anypoint Exchange allows you to publish and catalog RAML definitions as well as human-readable documentation for your microservice, which includes rich text, images, videos and attachments. Each API that is cataloged in Anypoint Exchange can have it's own private or public API Portal that is the landing page to learn everything about the microservice. The Anypoint API Portal contains all of the documentation as well as the access control mechanism to request/grant key-based access to the consuming app, this includes requesting tiered access via service level agreements (SLA).

Anypoint Exchange acts as a public / private library of API portals whose scope can embark any one or all of your business domains. An engagement model of this sort acts as the enabling mechanism to realize the ideal of having IT partner with LOBs in your business resulting in the democratization of application development and data access.

On the consuming side, Anypoint Exchange can be leveraged during multiple points in the Microservice lifecycle. It helps with discovery of existing assets that can include best practice templates, RAML snippets, API's (for instance, system API's from the same team/domain). The ability to provide user ratings, user forums and other collaboration tools encourage "Merit based reuse" in the context of microservices.

Contributing and cataloging all assets in one central repository takes the friction out of discovery, drives adoption and accelerates innovation. Note that Exchange can be a central microservice catalog used outside of the context of MuleSoft. Any IT developer, app developer, UI developer can login to Exchange with their corporate SSO, browse and discover microservices, play around with it in the sandbox, request access and start writing code against it in their language of choice. For instance, a Microsoft Visual Studio plugin is available for Anypoint Exchange that allows a .NET developer to browse microservice API's directly from Visual Studio IDE, pull it down and embed in .NET code.

Analysis with Anypoint Analytics

Real-time visibility of the consumption of your microservices is provided with Anypoint Analytics. You can see the frequency of calls, time to completion, policy violations, origin of calls across apps and geographies and much more. The data is visualized in customizable dashboards, available as reports for metering and chargeback as well as ingestible into external analytical tools like Splunk, ELK, tableau, Qlikview, and more.

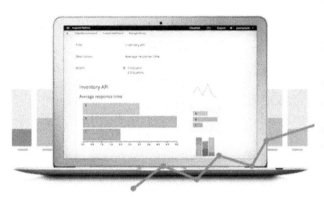

Decentralized Platform for Microservices

In traditional enterprises, the reality is that there will be a mixed mode for architecture. IT and lines of business could be operating in their own domains. There will be traditional global shared backend systems like ERP's, CRM's, FTP servers, mainframes, etc that are shared by multiple domains. And with microservices architecture on the other hand, certain lines of business may have their own isolated back-end systems with domain specific system/process/experience APIs. The key is for IT to enable the business that owns each domain, irrespective of which architecture they choose.

The Business Groups capability in Anypoint Platform allows IT to decentralize the platform and empower Lines of Businesses. Business Groups can be setup to map to Organization structure. Each Business Group can have its own administrator and RBAC with full autonomy (manage own microservice runtimes, MQ's, APIs).

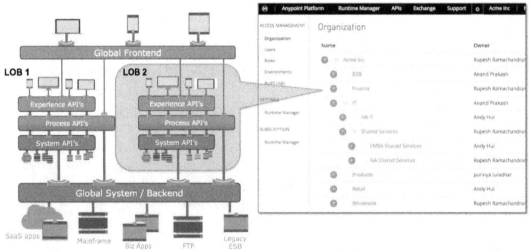

Figure 4: Business Groups feature in Anypoint Platform allows decentralization by domain

Business groups allow intra-domain collaboration and management of API's and MQ's within the domain. Whereas the top-level master group allows cross-domain collaboration and management. For instance, to leverage best practices with Mule, share RAML snippets, Mule application templates, custom connectors, custom API policies, etc. across the entire company, you could contribute these assets to the master group. Democratizing the platform so each business has autonomy for management, is crucial to enterprise wide microservices adoption. At the same time, IT can still take ownership of overarching capabilities like Single Sign On, shared services, overlay security policies configuration (e.g. OAuth server, IP blacklists, threat protection), etc.

In this model, IT truly becomes an enabler for the business's successful microservice rollout. Hence adopting a C4E or Center For Enablement model versus the legacy Center of Excellence model where IT traditionally became the bottleneck for delivery.

Unified Platform for Microservices

Anypoint Platform ties together the entire lifecycle of your microservices deployed across hybrid infrastructure with a single, unified platform. This includes the design, discover, deploy, run, document, manage, contribute and other aspects of the microservice. It also provides a '*single pane of glass*' management UI from which you can manage the microservice runtime, it's API's and its messaging endpoints.

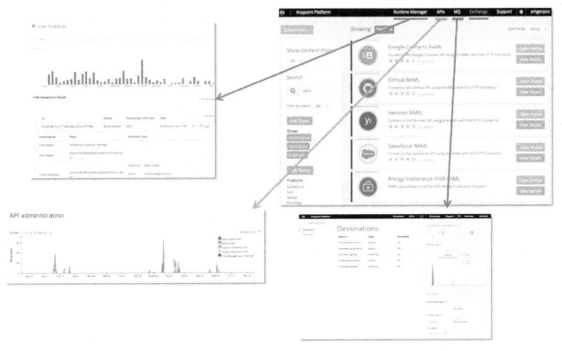

Figure 5: Unified platform with a single pane of glass

The benefits of having a unified platform for your microservice architecture include:

- End-to-end operational visibility. For instance, a slowdown in response times observed in the API dashboard can be correlated to individual transactions that may be erroring out, with the ability to drill down into corresponding logs for further troubleshooting. This reduces the Mean Time To Resolution by providing a single, unified console for operational visibility.
- Tooling leverage. The same skillsets, SDLC tools, single sign on, operation runbooks, engagement/collaboration portal, etc can be used for API management, on-prem microservice runtimes, cloud runtimes, MQ, etc.
- TCO optimization. Integrating the integration stack improves efficiency compared to swivel chair integration when working with disparate tools in your microservice ecosystem. With Anypoint Platform, not having to build your own additional layer to tie all your tools together drastically reduces the complexity, maintenance costs and overall Total Cost of Ownership.

Summary

Microservices is clearly an important and welcome trend in the software development industry, and has many advantages over previous architectural approaches. However, there are various concerns to be aware of when instituting a microservices architecture in your organization. Businesses need to implement microservices because of its ease of deployment and agile nature, but if not managed properly, this architecture can create disorganization and lack of governance. Products developed with a microservices architecture will also need to be integrated with legacy technology stacks, and if this is done poorly, it can create technical debt and more operational costs for the IT team. Therefore, instituting microservices in a way that will create competitive advantage and help your company innovate faster goes beyond a mere selection of products and software. You must also consider the people, process, and culture within the organization.

This is why we recommend a holistic, platform approach to microservices, centered around API-led connectivity. Not only does API-led connectivity create the integration component so crucial to the proper function of your technology stack, it will allow developers inside and outside the central IT team to create new solutions in a manageable, reusable, and governed way, eliminating concerns of too many applications that the business cannot control. In addition, MuleSoft's platform approach provides a unique operating model to allow both LoB and IT to build, innovate, and deliver new solutions wherever needed throughout the organization. Take a look at more resources on API-led connectivity and our vision for changing the organization's culture and process to enable IT to deliver faster at a lower cost.

In today's hyper-competitive business environment, it's important to stand out and provide a delightful experience for customers, employees, and partners. Microservices are a key way for a business to do that. Done in a holistic, manageable fashion, microservices will become a technological standard for the enterprise.

MuleSoft's mission is to help organizations change and innovate faster by making it easy to connect the world's applications, data and devices. With its API-led approach to connectivity, MuleSoft's market-leading Anypoint Platform™ is enabling over 1,000 organizations in more than 60 countries to build application networks that increase the clockspeed of business. For more information, visit https://www.mulesoft.com.

The Blueprint to Becoming a Customer Company

How to bring Salesforce's vision of a customer-centric company to life

At vero eos et accusamus et iusto odio dignissimos ducimus qui blanditiis praesentium voluptatum deleniti atque corrupti quos dolores et quas molestias excepturi sint

occaecati cupiditate non provident, similique sunt in culpa qui officia deserunt mollitia animi, id est laborum et dolorum fuga Et harum quidem rerum facilis est et expedita distinctio.

The Blueprint to Becoming a Customer Company:

How to bring Salesforce's vision of a customer-centric company to life

Enterprises are adopting more and more SaaS applications and customers are interacting with companies from an increasing number of channels. Many companies are not ready to provide the level of engagement, service and support their customers demand. New applications are added to the company's ecosystem, but not connected with the existing applications. Customer data is inconsistent and not synced across a customer's lifecycle.

This brief how-to-guide will give you insight into key technology trends, and show how integration allows you to connect with your customers, employees, partners and suppliers, putting you on the path to becoming a customer company.

About MuleSoft

MuleSoft provides the most widely used integration platform to connect any application, data service or API, across the cloud and on-premise continuum. Supporting billions of transactions per day, MuleSoft is used in production by global leaders in major industry verticals, including MasterCard, Nokia, Nestlé and Honeywell, and powers integrations with leading SaaS vendors such as salesforce.com, NetSuite, Workday, Intuit and Box.

Table of contents

Trend Spotlight:
The Fragmented Enterprise

The growth of SaaS applications and Big Data are leading to a fragmented enterprise

The world has changed and so has your corporate technology landscape. The growth of the SaaS market and Big Data are driving organizations away from a single provider for all IT needs. As companies acquire new applications or launch new business initiatives, they look to the cloud first. According to a Cap Gemini survey, 72% of companies are either working with or plan to work with more than one vendor, especially when looking to the cloud. Enterprises are looking to a variety of SaaS applications to meet their business goals, but are ending up with a highly fragmented ecosystem.

> **" Roughly half of companies rate themselves as only "fair to poor" in the collection & interpretation of customer data"**
>
> **The Economist, Intelligence Unit, 2013**

As companies purchase applications that meet the needs of a specific department or function, like sales or campaign management, ensuring data is consistent across these fragmented applications is increasingly challenging. If applications are not connected to each other, the business cannot move forward. Compounding the problem, the market is only getting larger as more mission critical applications move to the cloud, reaching an expected $140 billion by 2020 (IDC). In addition, these new SaaS applications need to connect back to the legacy applications, which largely remain on-premise.

SaaS applications also bring with them a wealth of data. There over 4.5 billion social users, having 150 million daily conversations about companies like yours using the 700 million plus smartphones sold each year. We are quickly reaching the point of over 450 billion business transactions per day (IDC). Customers are coming to you more often and from more channels, meaning information about who they are is fragmented across your business. To capture a larger percentage of those transactions and grow your business, you need to have one view of your customer data, across all applications, devices and touchpoints.

It's not just about IT infrastructure anymore; it's about using technology to revolutionize your fragmented business. It is no longer even just about connecting SaaS to SaaS or SaaS to on-premise. Customers, employees and partners are looking to interact with you through multiple channels and devices, and expect a seamless experience, regardless of where and how they interact. It's about connecting to your customers, partners, suppliers and employees.

Are you connected? Are your back end systems connected to your front office? Do you have all the information your employees, customers and partners need, connected in the cloud?

Cloud Technology is Now (only) 5% of Software Spending but Grows More Than 3 Time as Fast

Cloud Versus Enterprise Software Spending

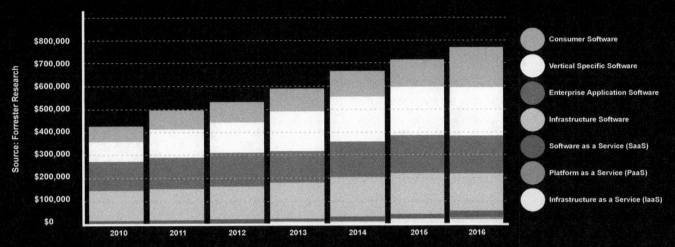

$17 billion of cloud versus $380 billion of enterprise software and vertical-specific software

Source: Forecast: Public Cloud Services, Worldwide, 2010-2016, 3Q12 Update

Integrating Data From A Variety Of Sources Is A Top Challenge

Which of the following challenges prevent your organization from making better use of customer analytics?

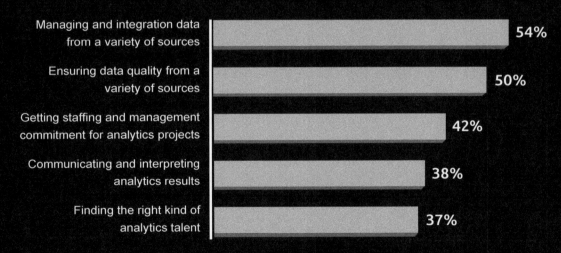

Base: 90 customer analytics professionals (multiple responses accepted)
Source: Q1 2012 Global Customer Analytics Online Survey

Contact us : ✉ Share : **f** 🐦 **in** **g+**

Step 1:

Identify all your customer touchpoints

Customers are highly opinionated. They expect a great product, delivered with superior service. They expect you to know who they are, no matter how they interact with your business. If they are unsatisfied, they have other choices and, with social media, an increasingly loud and far-reaching voice. You have to earn your customers' trust, and not just at the point of sale.

> " There is only one boss. The customer. And he can fire everybody in the company from the chairman on down, simply by spending his money somewhere else".
> - Sam Walton, 1977

Salesforce is promoting the idea of a "customer company", one that focuses on providing value to customers by listening to and engaging customers across multiple channels. Customer companies provide innovative products and services, streamline customer processes, and are available 24/7, everywhere. They are connected to not only their customers, but also employees, partners, suppliers and products. However, there's a dirty secret regarding the customer company vision. If you are missing this critical piece, you are doomed, and it's integration.

To become a customer company, you need to put your customer at the center of everything your business does; however, customers interact with your company across multiple touchpoints, each with its own application(s) to engage customers at each step in the buying process. No one application encompasses every direct and indirect customer touchpoint; it's all about how you connect your best-of-breed applications and legacy systems to deliver the right solution.

DID YOU KNOW?

Customers aren't just the CMO's problem. According to IBM, 4/5 of CIOs aim to digitize their front office within the next few years to sync with customers more effectively

As you begin your journey to becoming a customer company, you need to identify all applications that impact your customers across:

- Customer targeting: everything from development to communicating offers to your audience
- Acquisition: selling, configuring, quotes, contracting, order management
- Retention: installation, billing, support
- Collaboration: listening, working with customers
- Understanding: analyzing and reporting on customer information, maintaining customer data

These applications are not just across your front office: social media, marketing automation, call centers, CRM systems, support systems. They rely on the back office systems that produce, distribute, track, account and bill. These systems may not touch the customer directly, but they provide a view into a customer's history. You need to connect your SaaS applications to your on-premise systems, your new applications to your legacy systems to have a single view of your customers and your business.

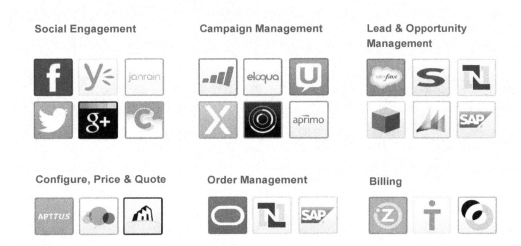

Once you've identified all applications that touch a customer through their lifecycle, it's time to think about how you integrate them to ensure consistent data, a consistent customer experience and superior customer service.

CUSTOMER IS KEY:

93% of CMOs, 96% of Customer Service leaders, 90% of Heads of Sales all say they are actively adopting new strategies for enhancing the customer experience.
(Source: The Economist Intelligence Unit, 2013)

Customer Company in Action

Leading UK Retailer

Goal: Drive in-store revenue and expand to new channels on the web

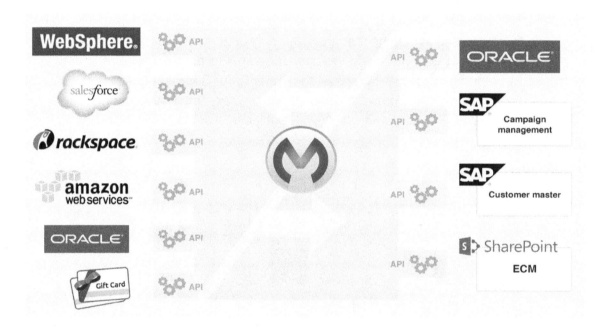

Business Initiatives	Connections	Benefits
• Grow in a fiercely competitive retail grocery market	• Salesforce & Force.com	• Single view of customer to support multichannel marketing
• Unlock data in silos across different brands and channels	• WebSphere Commerce	• Scalability to manage 5 million customers in Salesforce
	• Rackspace	
	• Amazon Web Services	
• Develop online presence to meet changing customer needs	• Oracle database	• No software or hardware to maintain
	• Loyalty card program	• Under 1 month from inception to go-live

Step 2:

Integration to deliver on you vision

To realize the vision of a customer company, you have to unlock your back office. It's not just about the data in your CRM system, but also the data in your marketing tools, your billing system, your support platform, etc. When you change a billing address in your CRM system, that change needs to be reflected across your order management and billing systems. When a customer logs a support ticket, it should be reflected in the CRM lead record.

> " There is massive buzz around SaaS, mobile and Big Data, but the secret nobody talks about is that enterprises can't make any of it work without connectivity".

- Ross Mason, MuleSoft, Founder

It is critical that data is consistent across the enterprise, regardless as to the application or system it touches. Siloed, fragmented data is the biggest barrier to becoming a customer company, with "poorly integrated business data often [leading] to poor business decisions, [reducing] customer satisfaction and competitive advantage, and [slowing] product innovation — ultimately limiting revenue." (Forrester, Information Fabric 3.0) To have one view of your data (and ultimately your customer) you need to integrate your cloud-based systems, where digital interactions happen, with the on-premise systems, which are the backbone of your organization.

Integration makes it possible to create a coherent whole across different starting points; it is the only way to ensure that data is always up to date and consistent across all applications, allowing you to improve customer experience and drive revenue. By integrating applications across the business, it becomes possible to orchestrate the execution of a sequence of business process activities, whether they are performed by software (apps or services), humans or devices. Essentially this means you can automate business processes across your ecosystem.

One view throughout the sales cycle

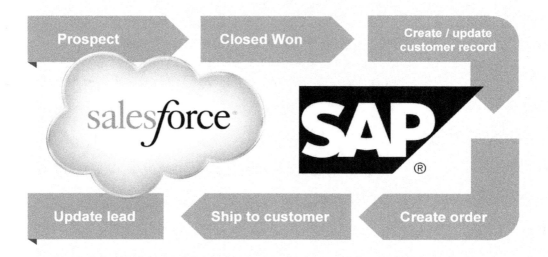

As the business gets more involved in IT buying decisions, there will only be more applications to connect. There are SaaS applications to meet (almost) every business need, with more and more hitting the market every day. The key now is figuring out how to connect those systems in a secure, repeatable and automated way so you can remain agile and react to customer needs.

PRO TIP

Not sure how to maximize your existing Salesforce investments? Sketch out what departments touch your Salesforce data, where that data comes from, and what other systems need to be in sync. With this picture, engage your IT department or an integration provider to connect the dots.

Step 3:

Beyond integration: Design for agility

Integration allows you to design your business for maximum agility; however, point-to-point or custom integration is not enough. If your IT team is custom-connecting your SaaS applications to each other and to your on-premise systems, as you add more and more touchpoints, your integrations become painful, restrictive and easily broken. The crucial point is to design for tomorrow's problems, not just today's endpoints. An integration platform can afford you that flexibility. Key considerations are where you want your business to be in 5, 10, 15 years and what you need to do to get there.

While the focus of your business design should be on a vision for future success, you cannot ignore what your already have. According to Cap Gemini, firms are increasingly taking a careful, step-by-step progression to Cloud maturity, rather than making an all or nothing decision. This means that there is always a new application to incorporate into your existing design. This drives the need for an open integration platform, one that can accommodate an ever-changing systems landscape.

In Step 1, we looked at all the possible customer touchpoints in your enterprise. Now, use the diagram on the next page to map out where you have applications today, and where you have gaps. You may not have any application in place, or you may have an application in place that does not meet all your needs. Then, think about how you will deliver on this design. How will you connect all your different applications? How will you plan for future technology purchases? How do you make sure customer data is the same across Salesforce, Marketo, SAP, etc.?

On this diagram, the lines connecting the different touchpoints make it seem very simple. In reality, ensuring consistency and connectivity across all applications can be very complex. In any given organization, sales and marketing alone use upwards of 10-15 applications to engage, onboard and maintain customer interactions. As business leaders take more control of cloud purchasing decisions, buying apps to fill gaps, it is up to IT to figure out how to make all of the pieces fit together. Integrating these with each other and your back office is crucial to running your business today and in the future.

Designing your business to have one view of your customer allow you to create demand and awareness, get details on your team's deals, create new and add-on business and provide customer service that is where your customers are. You'll be able to modernize cross-functional processes such as quote-to-cash and make it easy for employees to collaborate with customers, partners and suppliers across any device.

Where do you fall on the customer company continuum?

Questions to ask yourself:

What channels do your customers use to interact?

How can you improve these channels and experiences?

What functions have the largest impact on customer success?

How many SaaS applications are in use in your enterprise?

How many are connected to another application?

Use your answers to these questions to identify which applications you need to connect to become a customer company.

Do you have one view across marketing applications?

Are your sales, finance, support and services applications linked to each other?

Is your customer database up to date and complete?

Are you able to import, export and delete data in Salesforce via batch or real time?

Is your Salesforce instance linked to other systems in your enterprise?

Are your front office applications connected to your back office applications?

Do you have one view of your data from quote to cash? From ship to support? From entitlement to upsell?

Are you making business decisions based on your vision for the enterprise or your IT constraints?

Are you listening to your customers needs to improve your product?

Are you connected to your partners and suppliers?

If you answered no to more than one of these questions, integration challenges may be preventing you from becoming a customer company. Reach out to your IT department or an integration vendor today.

Customer Company in Action

Fortune 500 Pharmaceutical Company

Goal: **Create a 360 view of the customer, accessible from a mobile device**

Business Initiatives	Applications Used	Barrier to Success
• Create a 360 degree view of the customer to help increase revenues	• Customer Web Portal: Drupal	• Data silos, individual solutions & point-to-point integrations
• Make information accessible globally via multiple channels: eg. web, social, mobile devices	• CRM: Salesforce.com • Campaign Management: SAP, Marketo	• Existing application set did not connect to SaaS and mobile devices
• Lower costs & streamline processes	• Registration & Validation: Janrain, Ping Identity	

Step 4:

What's next?
Welcome to the New Enterprise

The New Enterprise has realized the vision of the customer company. In the era of the New Enterprise, companies can no longer compete with just the assets, technology and talent within their four walls. Companies must combine an explosion of applications, data, partners and customers into a single, high performing company. As the IT landscape becomes increasingly fragmented, the need for connection through integration becomes even more necessary.

A new enterprise:	Allows you to:
Has an **agile** IT department that delights line of business leaders, and exceeds their SLAs	**Unlock data** in legacy, custom and on-premise systems, facilitating automatic coordination between your front and back offices
Accelerates **time** to market from the inside out, by giving their HR, sales, marketing, services and finance departments a truly seamless way to collaborate and run their business	**Go to market faster**, by speeding up the development of mobile applications, offering data and services to employees, customers and partners at their fingertips
Has **no limits**, with a seamless path to the cloud, and way forward to manage their business in the future instead of through applications and services, but through APIs	**Connect Salesforce** - From the back office to a mobile device, giving one view of your customer

Conclusion:

Become a New Enterprise with MuleSoft

With Salesforce or your other CRM system as your hub for customer data, MuleSoft provides the necessary links to the rest of your business. With MuleSoft, you can seamlessly connect Salesforce to your other SaaS applications and on-premise software. Connect your 3rd party ERP and Finance applications in real-time, automate business processes across applications such as SAP, NetSuite, and Zuora, and incorporate your marketing tools to drive your business.

If you are ready to engage with a SaaS integration expert, MuleSoft is here to help. MuleSoft powers integrations for leading SaaS companies such as such as salesforce.com, NetSuite, Workday, Intuit, Box and many more.

About the Author

Sarah Burke

SaaS Integration Marketing, MuleSoft

Sarah is passionate about the SaaS market, understanding customer needs and technology trends. She brings over 4 years experience in enterprise software marketing to MuleSoft where she is the Senior Product Marketing Manager for SaaS Integration. Prior to joining MuleSoft, Sarah held various roles in enterprise software campaign planning, solution marketing, product marketing and analyst relations. Sarah is an expert in aligning marketing activities to the customer buying process.

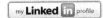

BUILDING A DIGITAL PLATFORM TO LEAD IN THE API ECONOMY

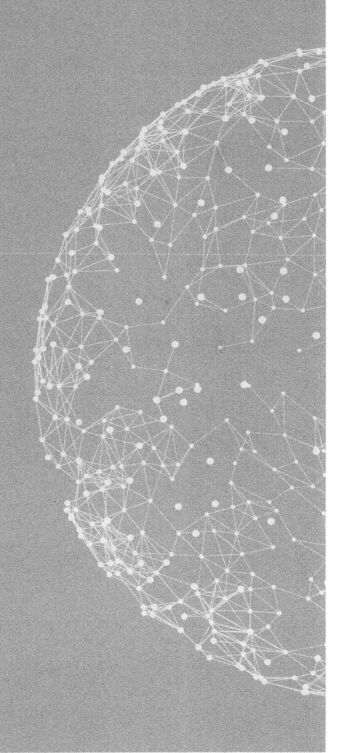

01 Introduction

Economic theory suggests that pursuing economies of scale and scope is a dominant competitive strategy: that organizations win by virtue of their scale driving down production costs, or by virtue of their scope driving efficiencies across business activities.
For example, Walmart, the world's largest retailer, is able to out-compete others on 'everyday, low prices' by virtue of the purchasing power that its size affords. And Johnson & Johnson, the world's largest pharmaceutical company, is able to leverage the same production, distribution and sales and marketing capabilities across its portfolio of brands, thus lowering the cost of bringing products to market.

Do these principles still hold true in today's digital age? As we enter the 'Fourth Industrial Revolution', SaaS platforms afford a startup founder access to the same infrastructure, at the same cost, as the largest multinational enterprise. Whereas previously, a small business may not have been able to afford the up-front capital investment that a Siebel CRM, or a SAP ERP system would require, the advent of SaaS platforms affords every company access to Salesforce.com CRM or Netsuite ERP at the same price.

Source: http://fortune.com/2017/01/04/amazon-marketplace-sales/

Not only that, Internet and Mobile provide that very same startup with access to a global audience. In this digital marketplace where the world's largest and smallest companies have access to the same resources, are traditional economic theories of scale and scope still relevant?

This article argues that not only are these competitive tenets as relevant as ever, but that today's market leaders are winning precisely because they are able to drive these economies at unprecedented scale. The companies that are winning are able to drive economies of scale and scope not just within their immediate organizational boundaries, but beyond them, by leveraging digital channels to build an ecosystem of buyers, partners and suppliers. In addition, it argues that the key to their success has been the ability to transform their business into a digital platform, and then leveraging that platform to build the surrounding ecosystem necessary to win.

02 Competing in a Digital Age:
From '1-sided' markets to 'N-sided' ecosystems

———

In today's competitive environment, winning companies have upended their respective industries by leveraging economies of scale and scope in unprecedented ways. The companies that are winning are those that are able to drive these economies not just within their immediate organizational boundaries, but beyond them, by leveraging digital channels to build a surrounding ecosystem of buyers, partners and suppliers.

For example, Amazon's success as a retailer does not come from simply selling goods online. Rather, it also comes from allowing other retailers to sell their goods through Amazon's platform and leverage the same marketing activities that drive visitors to Amazon's site (*Sell* on Amazon), and to leverage the same warehousing, distribution and logistics capabilities that Amazon uses for its own products (*Fulfillment* by Amazon).

Through exposing these capabilities, Amazon has built an ecosystem of retailers around it - that now account for some 50% of products sold through Amazon.com - that allow it to leverage *hyper*economies of scale and scope. Hypereconomies of scale in that Amazon is able to broaden its retail offerings and increase value to the customer, and hypereconomies of scope in that all of these sellers are using the same Amazon retail services, helping to

drive additional Amazon revenue streams and lower operating costs for all. By thinking of itself not as a retailer, but rather as a digital retail platform, Amazon has been able to effectively build a surrounding ecosystem that is driving its continued success.

This imperative for leaders to think of their organizations as platforms stems from an increasing complexity in competition (See Figure 1). The traditional market model that brings together consumers and suppliers in a 1-sided transaction i.e. a single party on either side of the transaction, has been superseded by ecosystem models in which organizations compete and collaborate across multiple fronts through monetizing digital platforms directly (Sell on Amazon), through partnering to leverage and embed those capabilities in third party offerings (Fulfillment by Amazon) or to expand into adjacent markets (Amazon Pay).

In this complex N-sided model with parties on either side of the transaction, organizations must compete across multiple dimensions, leveraging core capabilities across each dimension of competition. For example, an organization may be both a customer and a competitor to Amazon, leveraging Amazon's fulfillment capabilities to sell products that compete with those on Amazon.com. In either case, Amazon is able to capture value because it has delivered on a platform a vision that makes available these core capabilities to multiple stakeholders.

Figure 1:
From 1-sided markets to N-sided ecosystems

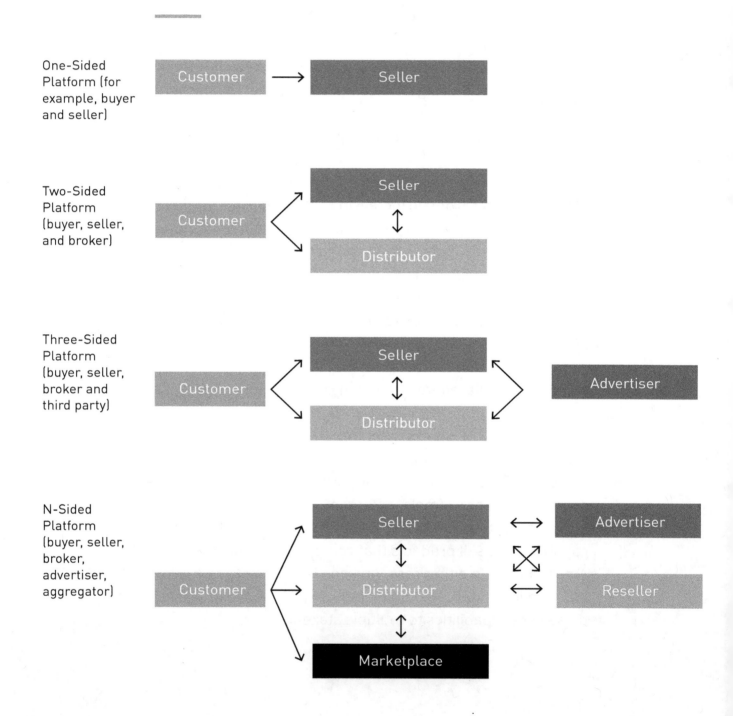

One-Sided Platform (for example, buyer and seller)

Customer → Seller

Two-Sided Platform (buyer, seller, and broker)

Customer → Seller ↕ Distributor

Three-Sided Platform (buyer, seller, broker and third party)

Customer → Seller ↕ Distributor → Advertiser

N-Sided Platform (buyer, seller, broker, advertiser, aggregator)

Customer → Seller ↔ Advertiser
Distributor ↔ Reseller
Marketplace

03 From Digital Business Models to Digital Platforms and Ecosystems

———

How then can organizations move towards building a digital platform? In our work serving digital leaders such as AirBnB, Netflix and Spotify, we see organizations closely follow the path below:

EXPLORE

As a first step, Business and IT leaders must come together and critically self-assess the core capabilities through which they wish to compete; they must objectively consider their unique advantages that will serve as the source of competitive differentiation.

Business and IT Leadership must also align around a common set of business outcomes that these core capabilities will support, to agree on the quantitative metrics that will define success, and to bring together the right organizational leaders.

See Table 1 below for examples of the types of thinking that MuleSoft's customers have engaged in to support their transformation to a digital platform.

Table 1: Examples of Digital Platforms

Company	Business Model From:	Business Model To:	Platform	Ecosystem
NZ Post	Monetize postal deliveries	Monetize end-to-end supply chain / logistics capabilities	Postal platform (Address lookup, Postal delivery rate finder, Parcel tracker etc.)	From postal branch only to any B2B or B2C company
Addison Lee	Monetize passenger trips via premium car service in UK	Monetize passenger allocation and dispatch capability in 20 countries globally	Taxi reservation platform	From UK only to EMEA-wide ecosystem
Wells Fargo	Monetize financial services through Wells Fargo channels	Monetize financial capabilities through non-Wells Fargo channels	Digital financial services platform	From direct Wells Fargo customers to consumers of financial services

PLAN

Once a company's core capabilities have been identified, they must then be 'packaged' so that they can easily be accessed, and monetized, by consumers. Consistent with the overarching construct of 'N-sided ecosystems', these capabilities may be leveraged by multiple parties and packaged and repackaged in different ways, and it is by bringing multiple capabilities together that a common platform emerges.

Increasingly, organizations are using Application Programming Interfaces (APIs) as digital interfaces that provide a common means to access these capabilities. As products and services are consumed through digital channels e.g. mobile, or digital means within a physical channel e.g. a tablet within a store, APIs have become instrumental as the channel for products and services to be consumed in a digital age. For example, Salesforce generates nearly 50 percent of its annual $3 billion in revenue through APIs; for Expedia that figure is closer to 90 percent and for eBay it's 60 percent.

It's worth noting that businesses who use APIs as part of their digital platforms see a strong improvement in business performance; according to MIT and Boston University economist Marshall van Alstyne, econometric evidence shows that organizations that adopt APIs "show a 2-10% gain in market capitalization". In addition, organizations that use APIs also report lower maintenance costs, more innovation, and greater customer satisfaction.

Van Alstyne, Marshall. The Platform Revolution. Presentation, CONNECT 2017

DELIVER

Once the plan is in place, leaders must then consider how to bring this vision to life. While the focus is typically on technology, and this is clearly important, successfully building a digital platform also requires changes in people and process, as well as technology. People in that how teams are structured and enabled may change to leverage the platform capabilities that have been created, and process in that how an IT organization thinks about software development may need to change, again to take advantage of the platform capabilities that have been built. For the platform to take hold, developers must look to leverage existing capabilities rather than duplicate efforts. Ideally, each existing capability that's a candidate for re-use should then be leveraged through a services-oriented approach like an API.

Typically, organizations may consider building out a central team that incubates the initial platform capabilities and then enables others, both inside and outside the organization, to consume these capabilities. Such a 'center for enablement' may also be charged with publishing self-serve materials and providing training and support.

One important point to highlight is that delivery of a digital platform should not be 'big bang' i.e. Business and IT leaders should not look to build a separate and distinct platform that the organization migrates to, but rather, take a blended approach in which delivery is in incremental phases.

In this way, organizations can move towards a long-term goal, yet still hit short-term business goals. The most pragmatic way of doing this is leveraging the joint business and IT dialogue to have an open conversation and find the balance between where platform capabilities would bring the greatest opportunity, and where the organizational investment would be greatest.

EVOLVE

Once the platform has been built, organizations must drive awareness, adoption and engagement with the platform to form the surrounding ecosystem. As the digital platform gains traction, what naturally evolves is an application network: a network of an organization's data assets that overlay and pull from an organization's IT systems. It is this application network that forms the digital platform that companies are looking to build.

Building a Digital Platform: Wells Fargo

Wells Fargo, one of the largest banks in the world, is driving a digital transformation journey to deliver an unified customer experience (CX). As part of this journey they built Wells Fargo Gateway, a Banking-as-a-Service (BaaS) platform that provides key services – such as account servicing, payments, and foreign exchange – through exposing APIs to Wells Fargo's partners and developers. This platform was foundational to One Wells Fargo, the bank's transformation program aimed at unifying customers' experience around any interactions with the bank - be it over phone, web or mobile. Through API-led connectivity, services from all partners and applications are seamlessly integrated into the Wells Fargo experience and consistently rendered on any channel.

"The FX API, which we are offering to our partners, has been a game changer ... they can seamlessly integrate their applications or their systems with our platform."

Sid Vyas
CTO, Capital Markets
and Investment Banking Technology
Wells Fargo

04 3 Keys to Successful Digital Platforms

In MuleSoft's work supporting organizations building digital platforms, we see a number of characteristics for those digital platforms that are successful and sustaining:

DRIVE REUSE

Platforms by their nature provide capabilities that can be accessed by multiple stakeholders. Digital platforms provide the ability to access the same capability in multiple ways. For example, Wells Fargo enables their corporate customers to access their foreign exchange capabilities through a banking relationship manager, online, or direct via an API.

SELF SERVE

For platforms to rapidly scale, organizations must enable rapid adoption of their platform capabilities. This means that consumers of those capabilities must be able to drive on-ramp with minimal manual intervention - from setup, through documentation, tooling to ease consumption i.e. software development kits and support. For example, New Zealand Post provides a developer portal that allows companies to learn about the platform capabilities that they are exposing, read documentation and experiment with the APIs in a training environment.

FEDERATE ACCESS

At the same time as providing access, organizations must also maintain a certain level of governance, in order to ensure security. For example, for existing corporate assets to which users must authenticate and access via Active Directory, extending that existing security and governance framework into the API layer (a capability that's built-in to some enterprise grade API management solutions like MuleSoft's Anypoint Platform).

Building a Digital Platform: NZ Post

APIs are seen as a key enabler to New Zealand Post's business strategy, allowing the organization to process digital impact on its traditional mail business while also keeping pace with the rapid growth in parcel delivery through e-commerce. Execution of its API strategy has effectively opened New Zealand Post's platform, providing a broader range of services and a fast and effective way of integrating with applications and other platforms. For example, e-commerce merchants can now provide integrated domestic and international delivery options, rate finding, tracking and delivery choices through New Zealand Post's new Shipping API.

"Every new proposition or service innovation requires connectivity of some sort, with everyone from global logistics partners to government authorities looking to create customer solutions by integrating our services with their web and mobile applications."

Brendan Shivnan
API product development manager,
New Zealand Post Digital

05 Building a Digital Platform
The Digital Platform as an Application Network

MuleSoft's mission is to help organizations change and innovate faster by making it easy to connect applications, data and devices. In our work helping organizations build digital platforms, we see the imperative to develop core capabilities as reusable building blocks that build on and complement one another. What emerges as a result of this approach is an application network whereby these capabilities can be recomposed and changed as necessary according to business needs. Underpinning the network is a set of reusable APIs that are the building blocks used to define how data is accessed, exposed and shared. This modular, easily pluggable infrastructure enables the digital platform by making it easy to create, change, and monetize new capabilities. These capabilities, built on owned infrastructure, creates and attracts value and resources outside the platform, providing greater customer stickiness and more opportunities for revenue. Contact us today to learn more about how to build an application network and make your digital platform vision, a reality.

Building a Digital Platform: Addison Lee

Addison Lee's iconic black cars transport more than 10 million passengers each year in London. Since it was founded in 1975, the company has harnessed technology innovations to stand apart from its competitors. To keep up with changing customer behavior and preferences shifting, Addison Lee had to react quickly with customer-centered innovations to stay competitive with new entrants. In fact, new revenue streams for Addison Lee have resulted from being able to seamlessly connect its mobile application users with its network of international fleets. A customer will be able to book a cab in 20 locations around the world using the Addison Lee app.

"API-led connectivity empowers us to be creative in how we connect our systems to deliver new digital products and offers."

Peter Ingram
CTO

06 About MuleSoft

—

MuleSoft makes it easy to connect the world's applications, data, and devices. With our market-leading Anypoint Platform™, companies are building application networks to fundamentally change the pace of innovation. MuleSoft's API-led approach to connectivity gives companies new ways to reach their customers, employees, and partners. Organizations in more than 60 countries, from emerging companies to Global 500 corporations, use MuleSoft to transform their businesses.

BUILDING A DIGITAL PLATFORM TO LEAD IN THE API ECONOMY

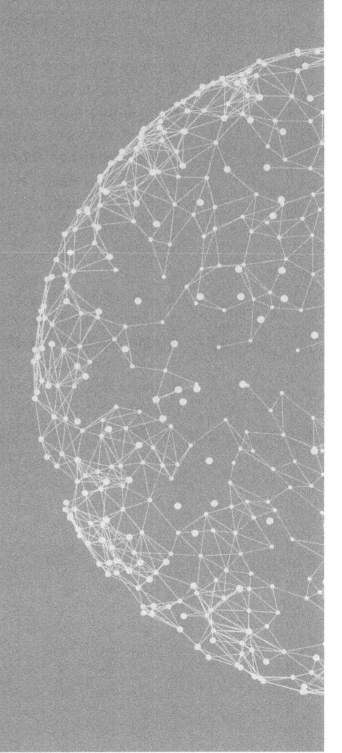

 MuleSoft

01 Introduction

Economic theory suggests that pursuing economies of scale and scope is a dominant competitive strategy: that organizations win by virtue of their scale driving down production costs, or by virtue of their scope driving efficiencies across business activities.
For example, Walmart, the world's largest retailer, is able to out-compete others on 'everyday, low prices' by virtue of the purchasing power that its size affords. And Johnson & Johnson, the world's largest pharmaceutical company, is able to leverage the same production, distribution and sales and marketing capabilities across its portfolio of brands, thus lowering the cost of bringing products to market.

Do these principles still hold true in today's digital age? As we enter the 'Fourth Industrial Revolution', SaaS platforms afford a startup founder access to the same infrastructure, at the same cost, as the largest multinational enterprise. Whereas previously, a small business may not have been able to afford the up-front capital investment that a Siebel CRM, or a SAP ERP system would require, the advent of SaaS platforms affords every company access to Salesforce.com CRM or Netsuite ERP at the same price.

Source: http://fortune.com/2017/01/04/amazon-marketplace-sales/

Not only that, Internet and Mobile provide that very same startup with access to a global audience. In this digital marketplace where the world's largest and smallest companies have access to the same resources, are traditional economic theories of scale and scope still relevant?

This article argues that not only are these competitive tenets as relevant as ever, but that today's market leaders are winning precisely because they are able to drive these economies at unprecedented scale. The companies that are winning are able to drive economies of scale and scope not just within their immediate organizational boundaries, but beyond them, by leveraging digital channels to build an ecosystem of buyers, partners and suppliers. In addition, it argues that the key to their success has been the ability to transform their business into a digital platform, and then leveraging that platform to build the surrounding ecosystem necessary to win.

02 Competing in a Digital Age:
From '1-sided' markets to 'N-sided' ecosystems

In today's competitive environment, winning companies have upended their respective industries by leveraging economies of scale and scope in unprecedented ways. The companies that are winning are those that are able to drive these economies not just within their immediate organizational boundaries, but beyond them, by leveraging digital channels to build a surrounding ecosystem of buyers, partners and suppliers.

For example, Amazon's success as a retailer does not come from simply selling goods online. Rather, it also comes from allowing other retailers to sell their goods through Amazon's platform and leverage the same marketing activities that drive visitors to Amazon's site (*Sell* on Amazon), and to leverage the same warehousing, distribution and logistics capabilities that Amazon uses for its own products (*Fulfillment* by Amazon).

Through exposing these capabilities, Amazon has built an ecosystem of retailers around it - that now account for some 50% of products sold through Amazon.com - that allow it to leverage *hyper*economies of scale and scope. Hypereconomies of scale in that Amazon is able to broaden its retail offerings and increase value to the customer, and hypereconomies of scope in that all of these sellers are using the same Amazon retail services, helping to

drive additional Amazon revenue streams and lower operating costs for all. By thinking of itself not as a retailer, but rather as a digital retail platform, Amazon has been able to effectively build a surrounding ecosystem that is driving its continued success.

This imperative for leaders to think of their organizations as platforms stems from an increasing complexity in competition (See Figure 1). The traditional market model that brings together consumers and suppliers in a 1-sided transaction i.e. a single party on either side of the transaction, has been superseded by ecosystem models in which organizations compete and collaborate across multiple fronts through monetizing digital platforms directly (Sell on Amazon), through partnering to leverage and embed those capabilities in third party offerings (Fulfillment by Amazon) or to expand into adjacent markets (Amazon Pay).

In this complex N-sided model with parties on either side of the transaction, organizations must compete across multiple dimensions, leveraging core capabilities across each dimension of competition. For example, an organization may be both a customer and a competitor to Amazon, leveraging Amazon's fulfillment capabilities to sell products that compete with those on Amazon.com. In either case, Amazon is able to capture value because it has delivered on a platform a vision that makes available these core capabilities to multiple stakeholders.

Figure 1:

From 1-sided markets to N-sided ecosystems

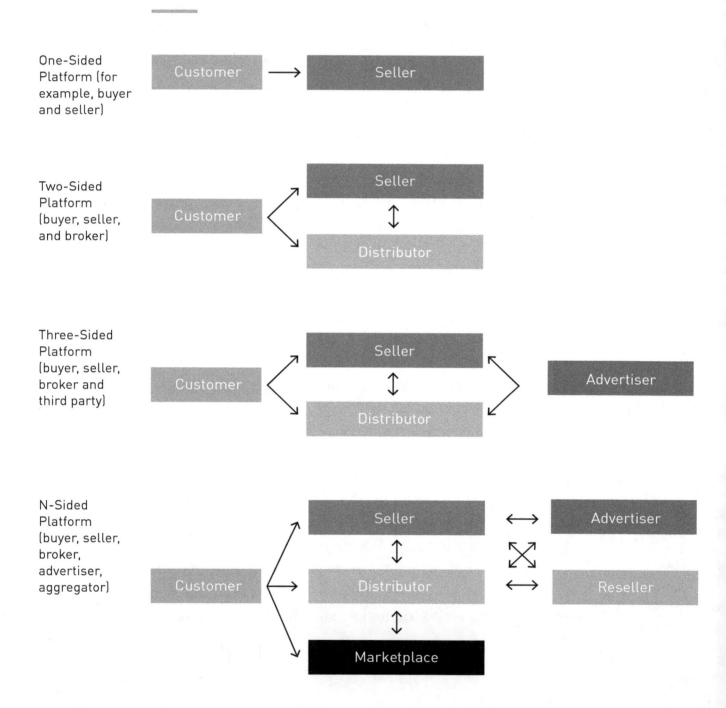

One-Sided Platform (for example, buyer and seller)

Two-Sided Platform (buyer, seller, and broker)

Three-Sided Platform (buyer, seller, broker and third party)

N-Sided Platform (buyer, seller, broker, advertiser, aggregator)

Customer

Seller

Distributor

Advertiser

Reseller

Marketplace

03 From Digital Business Models to Digital Platforms and Ecosystems

—

How then can organizations move towards building a digital platform? In our work serving digital leaders such as AirBnB, Netflix and Spotify, we see organizations closely follow the path below:

EXPLORE

As a first step, Business and IT leaders must come together and critically self-assess the core capabilities through which they wish to compete; they must objectively consider their unique advantages that will serve as the source of competitive differentiation.

Business and IT Leadership must also align around a common set of business outcomes that these core capabilities will support, to agree on the quantitative metrics that will define success, and to bring together the right organizational leaders.

See Table 1 below for examples of the types of thinking that MuleSoft's customers have engaged in to support their transformation to a digital platform.

Table 1: Examples of Digital Platforms

Company	Business Model From:	Business Model To:	Platform	Ecosystem
NZ Post	Monetize postal deliveries	Monetize end-to-end supply chain / logistics capabilities	Postal platform (Address lookup, Postal delivery rate finder, Parcel tracker etc.)	From postal branch only to any B2B or B2C company
Addison Lee	Monetize passenger trips via premium car service in UK	Monetize passenger allocation and dispatch capability in 20 countries globally	Taxi reservation platform	From UK only to EMEA-wide ecosystem
Wells Fargo	Monetize financial services through Wells Fargo channels	Monetize financial capabilities through non-Wells Fargo channels	Digital financial services platform	From direct Wells Fargo customers to consumers of financial services

PLAN

Once a company's core capabilities have been identified, they must then be 'packaged' so that they can easily be accessed, and monetized, by consumers. Consistent with the overarching construct of 'N-sided ecosystems', these capabilities may be leveraged by multiple parties and packaged and repackaged in different ways, and it is by bringing multiple capabilities together that a common platform emerges.

Increasingly, organizations are using Application Programming Interfaces (APIs) as digital interfaces that provide a common means to access these capabilities. As products and services are consumed through digital channels e.g. mobile, or digital means within a physical channel e.g. a tablet within a store, APIs have become instrumental as the channel for products and services to be consumed in a digital age. For example, Salesforce generates nearly 50 percent of its annual $3 billion in revenue through APIs; for Expedia that figure is closer to 90 percent and for eBay it's 60 percent.

It's worth noting that businesses who use APIs as part of their digital platforms see a strong improvement in business performance; according to MIT and Boston University economist Marshall van Alstyne, econometric evidence shows that organizations that adopt APIs "show a 2-10% gain in market capitalization". In addition, organizations that use APIs also report lower maintenance costs, more innovation, and greater customer satisfaction.

Van Alstyne, Marshall. The Platform Revolution. Presentation, CONNECT 2017

DELIVER

Once the plan is in place, leaders must then consider how to bring this vision to life. While the focus is typically on technology, and this is clearly important, successfully building a digital platform also requires changes in people and process, as well as technology. People in that how teams are structured and enabled may change to leverage the platform capabilities that have been created, and process in that how an IT organization thinks about software development may need to change, again to take advantage of the platform capabilities that have been built. For the platform to take hold, developers must look to leverage existing capabilities rather than duplicate efforts. Ideally, each existing capability that's a candidate for re-use should then be leveraged through a services-oriented approach like an API.

Typically, organizations may consider building out a central team that incubates the initial platform capabilities and then enables others, both inside and outside the organization, to consume these capabilities. Such a 'center for enablement' may also be charged with publishing self-serve materials and providing training and support.

One important point to highlight is that delivery of a digital platform should not be 'big bang' i.e. Business and IT leaders should not look to build a separate and distinct platform that the organization migrates to, but rather, take a blended approach in which delivery is in incremental phases.

In this way, organizations can move towards a long-term goal, yet still hit short-term business goals. The most pragmatic way of doing this is leveraging the joint business and IT dialogue to have an open conversation and find the balance between where platform capabilities would bring the greatest opportunity, and where the organizational investment would be greatest.

EVOLVE

Once the platform has been built, organizations must drive awareness, adoption and engagement with the platform to form the surrounding ecosystem. As the digital platform gains traction, what naturally evolves is an application network: a network of an organization's data assets that overlay and pull from an organization's IT systems. It is this application network that forms the digital platform that companies are looking to build.

Building a Digital Platform: Wells Fargo

Wells Fargo, one of the largest banks in the world, is driving a digital transformation journey to deliver an unified customer experience (CX). As part of this journey they built Wells Fargo Gateway, a Banking-as-a-Service (BaaS) platform that provides key services – such as account servicing, payments, and foreign exchange – through exposing APIs to Wells Fargo's partners and developers. This platform was foundational to One Wells Fargo, the bank's transformation program aimed at unifying customers' experience around any interactions with the bank - be it over phone, web or mobile. Through API-led connectivity, services from all partners and applications are seamlessly integrated into the Wells Fargo experience and consistently rendered on any channel.

"The FX API, which we are offering to our partners, has been a game changer … they can seamlessly integrate their applications or their systems with our platform."

Sid Vyas
CTO, Capital Markets
and Investment Banking Technology
Wells Fargo

04 3 Keys to Successful Digital Platforms

In MuleSoft's work supporting organizations building digital platforms, we see a number of characteristics for those digital platforms that are successful and sustaining:

DRIVE REUSE

Platforms by their nature provide capabilities that can be accessed by multiple stakeholders. Digital platforms provide the ability to access the same capability in multiple ways. For example, Wells Fargo enables their corporate customers to access their foreign exchange capabilities through a banking relationship manager, online, or direct via an API.

SELF SERVE

For platforms to rapidly scale, organizations must enable rapid adoption of their platform capabilities. This means that consumers of those capabilities must be able to drive on-ramp with minimal manual intervention - from setup, through documentation, tooling to ease consumption i.e. software development kits and support. For example, New Zealand Post provides a developer portal that allows companies to learn about the platform capabilities that they are exposing, read documentation and experiment with the APIs in a training environment.

FEDERATE ACCESS

At the same time as providing access, organizations must also maintain a certain level of governance, in order to ensure security. For example, for existing corporate assets to which users must authenticate and access via Active Directory, extending that existing security and governance framework into the API layer (a capability that's built-in to some enterprise grade API management solutions like MuleSoft's Anypoint Platform).

Building a Digital Platform: NZ Post

APIs are seen as a key enabler to New Zealand Post's business strategy, allowing the organization to process digital impact on its traditional mail business while also keeping pace with the rapid growth in parcel delivery through e-commerce. Execution of its API strategy has effectively opened New Zealand Post's platform, providing a broader range of services and a fast and effective way of integrating with applications and other platforms. For example, e-commerce merchants can now provide integrated domestic and international delivery options, rate finding, tracking and delivery choices through New Zealand Post's new Shipping API.

"Every new proposition or service innovation requires connectivity of some sort, with everyone from global logistics partners to government authorities looking to create customer solutions by integrating our services with their web and mobile applications."

Brendan Shivnan
API product development manager,
New Zealand Post Digital

05 Building a Digital Platform
The Digital Platform as an Application Network

MuleSoft's mission is to help organizations change and innovate faster by making it easy to connect applications, data and devices. In our work helping organizations build digital platforms, we see the imperative to develop core capabilities as reusable building blocks that build on and complement one another. What emerges as a result of this approach is an application network whereby these capabilities can be recomposed and changed as necessary according to business needs. Underpinning the network is a set of reusable APIs that are the building blocks used to define how data is accessed, exposed and shared. This modular, easily pluggable infrastructure enables the digital platform by making it easy to create, change, and monetize new capabilities. These capabilities, built on owned infrastructure, creates and attracts value and resources outside the platform, providing greater customer stickiness and more opportunities for revenue. Contact us today to learn more about how to build an application network and make your digital platform vision, a reality.

Building a Digital Platform: Addison Lee

Addison Lee's iconic black cars transport more than 10 million passengers each year in London. Since it was founded in 1975, the company has harnessed technology innovations to stand apart from its competitors. To keep up with changing customer behavior and preferences shifting, Addison Lee had to react quickly with customer-centered innovations to stay competitive with new entrants. In fact, new revenue streams for Addison Lee have resulted from being able to seamlessly connect its mobile application users with its network of international fleets. A customer will be able to book a cab in 20 locations around the world using the Addison Lee app.

"API-led connectivity empowers us to be creative in how we connect our systems to deliver new digital products and offers."

Peter Ingram
CTO

06 About MuleSoft

MuleSoft makes it easy to connect the world's applications, data, and devices. With our market-leading Anypoint Platform™, companies are building application networks to fundamentally change the pace of innovation. MuleSoft's API-led approach to connectivity gives companies new ways to reach their customers, employees, and partners. Organizations in more than 60 countries, from emerging companies to Global 500 corporations, use MuleSoft to transform their businesses.

BUILDING A DIGITAL PLATFORM TO LEAD IN THE API ECONOMY

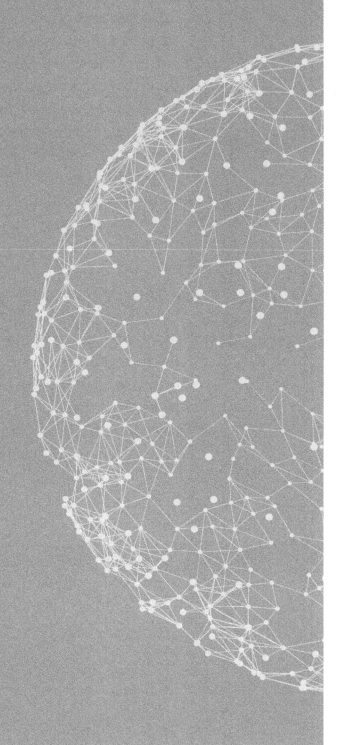

01 Introduction

___

Economic theory suggests that pursuing economies of scale and scope is a dominant competitive strategy: that organizations win by virtue of their scale driving down production costs, or by virtue of their scope driving efficiencies across business activities.
For example, Walmart, the world's largest retailer, is able to out-compete others on 'everyday, low prices' by virtue of the purchasing power that its size affords. And Johnson & Johnson, the world's largest pharmaceutical company, is able to leverage the same production, distribution and sales and marketing capabilities across its portfolio of brands, thus lowering the cost of bringing products to market.

Do these principles still hold true in today's digital age? As we enter the 'Fourth Industrial Revolution', SaaS platforms afford a startup founder access to the same infrastructure, at the same cost, as the largest multinational enterprise. Whereas previously, a small business may not have been able to afford the up-front capital investment that a Siebel CRM, or a SAP ERP system would require, the advent of SaaS platforms affords every company access to Salesforce.com CRM or Netsuite ERP at the same price.

___

Source: http://fortune.com/2017/01/04/amazon-marketplace-sales/

Not only that, Internet and Mobile provide that very same startup with access to a global audience. In this digital marketplace where the world's largest and smallest companies have access to the same resources, are traditional economic theories of scale and scope still relevant?

This article argues that not only are these competitive tenets as relevant as ever, but that today's market leaders are winning precisely because they are able to drive these economies at unprecedented scale. The companies that are winning are able to drive economies of scale and scope not just within their immediate organizational boundaries, but beyond them, by leveraging digital channels to build an ecosystem of buyers, partners and suppliers. In addition, it argues that the key to their success has been the ability to transform their business into a digital platform, and then leveraging that platform to build the surrounding ecosystem necessary to win.

02 Competing in a Digital Age:
From '1-sided' markets to 'N-sided' ecosystems

In today's competitive environment, winning companies have upended their respective industries by leveraging economies of scale and scope in unprecedented ways. The companies that are winning are those that are able to drive these economies not just within their immediate organizational boundaries, but beyond them, by leveraging digital channels to build a surrounding ecosystem of buyers, partners and suppliers.

For example, Amazon's success as a retailer does not come from simply selling goods online. Rather, it also comes from allowing other retailers to sell their goods through Amazon's platform and leverage the same marketing activities that drive visitors to Amazon's site (*Sell* on Amazon), and to leverage the same warehousing, distribution and logistics capabilities that Amazon uses for its own products (*Fulfillment* by Amazon).

Through exposing these capabilities, Amazon has built an ecosystem of retailers around it - that now account for some 50% of products sold through Amazon.com - that allow it to leverage *hyper*economies of scale and scope. Hypereconomies of scale in that Amazon is able to broaden its retail offerings and increase value to the customer, and hypereconomies of scope in that all of these sellers are using the same Amazon retail services, helping to

drive additional Amazon revenue streams and lower operating costs for all. By thinking of itself not as a retailer, but rather as a digital retail platform, Amazon has been able to effectively build a surrounding ecosystem that is driving its continued success.

This imperative for leaders to think of their organizations as platforms stems from an increasing complexity in competition (See Figure 1). The traditional market model that brings together consumers and suppliers in a 1-sided transaction i.e. a single party on either side of the transaction, has been superseded by ecosystem models in which organizations compete and collaborate across multiple fronts through monetizing digital platforms directly (Sell on Amazon), through partnering to leverage and embed those capabilities in third party offerings (Fulfillment by Amazon) or to expand into adjacent markets (Amazon Pay).

In this complex N-sided model with parties on either side of the transaction, organizations must compete across multiple dimensions, leveraging core capabilities across each dimension of competition. For example, an organization may be both a customer and a competitor to Amazon, leveraging Amazon's fulfillment capabilities to sell products that compete with those on Amazon.com. In either case, Amazon is able to capture value because it has delivered on a platform a vision that makes available these core capabilities to multiple stakeholders.

Figure 1:
From 1-sided markets to N-sided ecosystems

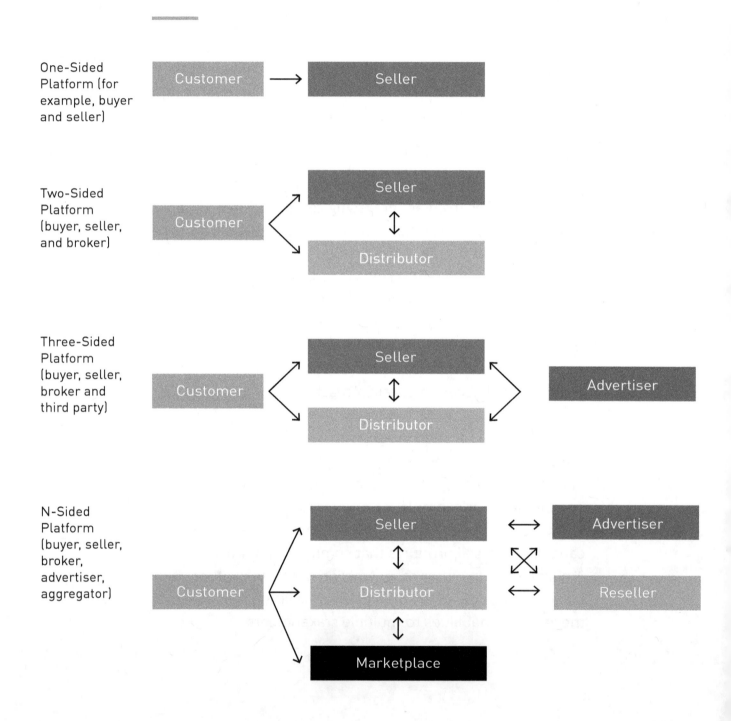

One-Sided Platform (for example, buyer and seller)

Customer → Seller

Two-Sided Platform (buyer, seller, and broker)

Customer → Seller ⇕ Distributor

Three-Sided Platform (buyer, seller, broker and third party)

Customer → Seller ⇕ Distributor → Advertiser

N-Sided Platform (buyer, seller, broker, advertiser, aggregator)

Customer → Seller ⇕ Distributor ⇕ Marketplace → Advertiser ↔ Reseller

03 From Digital Business Models to Digital Platforms and Ecosystems

—

How then can organizations move towards building a digital platform? In our work serving digital leaders such as AirBnB, Netflix and Spotify, we see organizations closely follow the path below:

EXPLORE

As a first step, Business and IT leaders must come together and critically self-assess the core capabilities through which they wish to compete; they must objectively consider their unique advantages that will serve as the source of competitive differentiation.

Business and IT Leadership must also align around a common set of business outcomes that these core capabilities will support, to agree on the quantitative metrics that will define success, and to bring together the right organizational leaders.

See Table 1 below for examples of the types of thinking that MuleSoft's customers have engaged in to support their transformation to a digital platform.

Table 1: Examples of Digital Platforms

Company	Business Model From:	Business Model To:	Platform	Ecosystem
NZ Post	Monetize postal deliveries	Monetize end-to-end supply chain / logistics capabilities	Postal platform (Address lookup, Postal delivery rate finder, Parcel tracker etc.)	From postal branch only to any B2B or B2C company
Addison Lee	Monetize passenger trips via premium car service in UK	Monetize passenger allocation and dispatch capability in 20 countries globally	Taxi reservation platform	From UK only to EMEA-wide ecosystem
Wells Fargo	Monetize financial services through Wells Fargo channels	Monetize financial capabilities through non-Wells Fargo channels	Digital financial services platform	From direct Wells Fargo customers to consumers of financial services

PLAN

Once a company's core capabilities have been identified, they must then be 'packaged' so that they can easily be accessed, and monetized, by consumers. Consistent with the overarching construct of 'N-sided ecosystems', these capabilities may be leveraged by multiple parties and packaged and repackaged in different ways, and it is by bringing multiple capabilities together that a common platform emerges.

Increasingly, organizations are using Application Programming Interfaces (APIs) as digital interfaces that provide a common means to access these capabilities. As products and services are consumed through digital channels e.g. mobile, or digital means within a physical channel e.g. a tablet within a store, APIs have become instrumental as the channel for products and services to be consumed in a digital age. For example, Salesforce generates nearly 50 percent of its annual $3 billion in revenue through APIs; for Expedia that figure is closer to 90 percent and for eBay it's 60 percent.

It's worth noting that businesses who use APIs as part of their digital platforms see a strong improvement in business performance; according to MIT and Boston University economist Marshall van Alstyne, econometric evidence shows that organizations that adopt APIs "show a 2-10% gain in market capitalization". In addition, organizations that use APIs also report lower maintenance costs, more innovation, and greater customer satisfaction.

Van Alstyne, Marshall. The Platform Revolution. Presentation, CONNECT 2017

DELIVER   Once the plan is in place, leaders must then consider how to bring this vision to life. While the focus is typically on technology, and this is clearly important, successfully building a digital platform also requires changes in people and process, as well as technology. People in that how teams are structured and enabled may change to leverage the platform capabilities that have been created, and process in that how an IT organization thinks about software development may need to change, again to take advantage of the platform capabilities that have been built. For the platform to take hold, developers must look to leverage existing capabilities rather than duplicate efforts. Ideally, each existing capability that's a candidate for re-use should then be leveraged through a services-oriented approach like an API.

Typically, organizations may consider building out a central team that incubates the initial platform capabilities and then enables others, both inside and outside the organization, to consume these capabilities. Such a 'center for enablement' may also be charged with publishing self-serve materials and providing training and support.

One important point to highlight is that delivery of a digital platform should not be 'big bang' i.e. Business and IT leaders should not look to build a separate and distinct platform that the organization migrates to, but rather, take a blended approach in which delivery is in incremental phases.

In this way, organizations can move towards a long-term goal, yet still hit short-term business goals. The most pragmatic way of doing this is leveraging the joint business and IT dialogue to have an open conversation and find the balance between where platform capabilities would bring the greatest opportunity, and where the organizational investment would be greatest.

EVOLVE   Once the platform has been built, organizations must drive awareness, adoption and engagement with the platform to form the surrounding ecosystem. As the digital platform gains traction, what naturally evolves is an application network: a network of an organization's data assets that overlay and pull from an organization's IT systems. It is this application network that forms the digital platform that companies are looking to build.

Building a Digital Platform: Wells Fargo

———

Wells Fargo, one of the largest banks in the world, is driving a digital transformation journey to deliver an unified customer experience (CX). As part of this journey they built Wells Fargo Gateway, a Banking-as-a-Service (BaaS) platform that provides key services – such as account servicing, payments, and foreign exchange – through exposing APIs to Wells Fargo's partners and developers. This platform was foundational to One Wells Fargo, the bank's transformation program aimed at unifying customers' experience around any interactions with the bank - be it over phone, web or mobile. Through API-led connectivity, services from all partners and applications are seamlessly integrated into the Wells Fargo experience and consistently rendered on any channel.

"The FX API, which we are offering to our partners, has been a game changer ... they can seamlessly integrate their applications or their systems with our platform."

Sid Vyas
CTO, Capital Markets
and Investment Banking Technology
Wells Fargo

04 3 Keys to Successful Digital Platforms

In MuleSoft's work supporting organizations building digital platforms, we see a number of characteristics for those digital platforms that are successful and sustaining:

DRIVE REUSE

Platforms by their nature provide capabilities that can be accessed by multiple stakeholders. Digital platforms provide the ability to access the same capability in multiple ways. For example, Wells Fargo enables their corporate customers to access their foreign exchange capabilities through a banking relationship manager, online, or direct via an API.

SELF SERVE

For platforms to rapidly scale, organizations must enable rapid adoption of their platform capabilities. This means that consumers of those capabilities must be able to drive on-ramp with minimal manual intervention - from setup, through documentation, tooling to ease consumption i.e. software development kits and support. For example, New Zealand Post provides a developer portal that allows companies to learn about the platform capabilities that they are exposing, read documentation and experiment with the APIs in a training environment.

FEDERATE ACCESS

At the same time as providing access, organizations must also maintain a certain level of governance, in order to ensure security. For example, for existing corporate assets to which users must authenticate and access via Active Directory, extending that existing security and governance framework into the API layer (a capability that's built-in to some enterprise grade API management solutions like MuleSoft's Anypoint Platform).

Building a Digital Platform: NZ Post

APIs are seen as a key enabler to New Zealand Post's business strategy, allowing the organization to process digital impact on its traditional mail business while also keeping pace with the rapid growth in parcel delivery through e-commerce. Execution of its API strategy has effectively opened New Zealand Post's platform, providing a broader range of services and a fast and effective way of integrating with applications and other platforms. For example, e-commerce merchants can now provide integrated domestic and international delivery options, rate finding, tracking and delivery choices through New Zealand Post's new Shipping API.

"Every new proposition or service innovation requires connectivity of some sort, with everyone from global logistics partners to government authorities looking to create customer solutions by integrating our services with their web and mobile applications."

Brendan Shivnan
API product development manager,
New Zealand Post Digital

05 Building a Digital Platform
The Digital Platform as an Application Network

MuleSoft's mission is to help organizations change and innovate faster by making it easy to connect applications, data and devices. In our work helping organizations build digital platforms, we see the imperative to develop core capabilities as reusable building blocks that build on and complement one another. What emerges as a result of this approach is an application network whereby these capabilities can be recomposed and changed as necessary according to business needs. Underpinning the network is a set of reusable APIs that are the building blocks used to define how data is accessed, exposed and shared. This modular, easily pluggable infrastructure enables the digital platform by making it easy to create, change, and monetize new capabilities. These capabilities, built on owned infrastructure, creates and attracts value and resources outside the platform, providing greater customer stickiness and more opportunities for revenue. Contact us today to learn more about how to build an application network and make your digital platform vision, a reality.

Building a Digital Platform: Addison Lee

Addison Lee's iconic black cars transport more than 10 million passengers each year in London. Since it was founded in 1975, the company has harnessed technology innovations to stand apart from its competitors. To keep up with changing customer behavior and preferences shifting, Addison Lee had to react quickly with customer-centered innovations to stay competitive with new entrants. In fact, new revenue streams for Addison Lee have resulted from being able to seamlessly connect its mobile application users with its network of international fleets. A customer will be able to book a cab in 20 locations around the world using the Addison Lee app.

"API-led connectivity empowers us to be creative in how we connect our systems to deliver new digital products and offers."

Peter Ingram
CTO

06 About MuleSoft

—

MuleSoft makes it easy to connect the world's applications, data, and devices. With our market-leading Anypoint Platform™, companies are building application networks to fundamentally change the pace of innovation. MuleSoft's API-led approach to connectivity gives companies new ways to reach their customers, employees, and partners. Organizations in more than 60 countries, from emerging companies to Global 500 corporations, use MuleSoft to transform their businesses.

 MuleSoft

www.mulesoft.com

FROM
TRANSACTIONS
TO
RELATIONSHIPS

Building the Connected Retail Experience

BUILDING THE CONNECTED RETAIL EXPERIENCE

Table of contents

Foreword

By Ross Mason, Founder of MuleSoft

It is easy to get drawn into the negative headlines about retail. One article, for example, suggests more retailers are headed into bankruptcy than at any time since the Great Recession. It often seems the retail industry is in crisis. However, the reality is that every industry, including retail, is going through massive change.

These changes, which include the rise of the smartphone, the internet of things and a globalized marketplace, alter how customers want to interact with retailers and how retailers get merchandise into customers' hands. Retailers used to follow a prescriptive formula of planning inventory, buying merchandise, moving it to retail outlets, and selling it to consumers on a particular schedule at a particular price. Now, however, retailers need to deliver seamless customer experiences across channels.

The practice and process of retail is evolving in large part due to Amazon. The convenient home access and deliveries were revolutionary, kickstarting a trend that forever changed the way we buy. Then more recently, Amazon decided to take its online world to the physical world by venturing into the realm of brick-and-mortar stores.

The terrifying thing for traditional retailers today is Amazon will operate stores much more efficiently and effectively because the company is driven by data and powered by software. Using data analytics, endless APIs and other intelligent tools, Amazon will monitor its online and physical stores to perfect its online-offline strategy.

For traditional retailers to survive in the age of Amazon, they need the agility to keep in step with the changing needs of consumers. In fact, 63 percent of consumers said they would switch retailers if they felt that they had a disconnected experience.[1] Additionally, 63 percent of British consumers recently claimed they would abandon a clothing purchase due to frustrations with the in-store experience.[2] Let's face it, modern day shoppers are fickle because they can be.

Today's shoppers expect more than a transactional relationship with retailers; they want a seamless and personalized journey that reflects the context of how they shop across devices and channels. The key to success lies in connecting in-store software with online systems so retailers can provide an uninterrupted experience wherever customers shop.

Our goal in this book is to provide retailers with a fresh strategy and roadmap around how to build and implement a retail application network to strengthen customer relationships and ultimately drive revenue. Let's get started.

[1] MuleSoft Connected Consumer Report 2017
[2] BarclayCard November 2016

"63 percent of consumers
would switch retailers if they felt that they
had a disconnected experience"

-MuleSoft Connected Consumer Report, 2017

INTRODUCTION

The retail industry is unique in that there are few other sectors which are so complex and varied. Retailers today are required to be multifaceted and adapt to dramatic socioeconomic changes. Not only has the retail industry gone through significant disruption because of technology, but the global economy, changes in working patterns, and new entrants have brought waves of change to the modern retailer.

Retail is a tremendously broad space, encompassing multiple segments such as quick service restaurants, car dealerships, drugstores, on-demand shopping, and subscription services — and that is just to name a few. And each segment has their unique demands and needs. For example, in the apparel sector, "Fast fashion" retail stores, such as Zara and H&M, have different needs and logistics than a midmarket department store like Nordstrom or a luxury retailer like Prada. Each type of retailer is unique and has its own strategy to engage with customers, the demands of which are increasing.

Just a few years ago customers were willing to accept tradeoffs. If you wanted that exact green sweater, you would maybe need to wait a week, or more, for delivery. If you wanted a new dress, you would shop at your local store. And if you went on Gap.com, there were just several options for a t-shirt. Today, this is all radically different - a retailer must match consumer expectations on all dimensions, across speed, convenience and choice.

Customer expectations today are leading retailers to rethink the goods and services that they offer, and are adding a multiplicity of new offerings to create convenience — and ultimately stickiness — for their customers. According to the Bureau of Labor Services, employed adult Americans have 20 minutes per day to purchase goods and services.[2] Consumers simply do not have the time to shop around for lots of different services, so numerous retailers have gambled on adding new services outside their core retailing functions to increase brand loyalty and customer engagement. For example, at one of our customers, the CIO of a major department store points out that "not only does the retailer sell everything from large furniture to fresh produce, it is also a bank, owns property, sells energy and owns data centers." What this means is that retail is now becoming a platform, which in turn means businesses need to create a broader value chain of capabilities and build that into the products and services they provide. Retail as a platform needs to be supported by an agile IT infrastructure for service delivery.

[2] Bureau of Labor Statistics June 2016

But no matter the size of the retail business, the sector, the customer expectations one must meet, or the kinds of services offered, there are four things all retailers have in common:

- There are selling channels, which can be digital, stores, franchisees, or wholesale;

- There is a supply chain, which can range from garment manufacturing and distribution (where products can be in transport for weeks) to fresh produce that have a shelf life of days;

- There is an important back office, running the operations through an ERP and other management systems

- There is data, resulting in analytics, information management, and insight

More and more, retailers today have adopted technology to augment each of these commonalities of the retail business in order to meet increased customer expectations. Retailers recognize the need to adopt technology and often have seen it implemented successfully in other businesses — perhaps even competitors who have done it. To adapt to these changes and outpace competition, this often results in more and more technology weaved throughout the retailers' ecosystem.

The increasing use of technology to digitize and improve these components, however, has created additional problems and questions. And across retailers, big or small, apparel or wholesale, there is a common theme: these digital initiatives have resulted in an increased project load for the IT team. Retail IT is struggling with issues like:

- How can legacy hosted, and digital systems, particularly cloud-based ones, exist in the same ecosystem?

- How do you integrate outdated (but still used) B2B communications standards like EDI, OAGIS, GS1, etc. into your modern systems?

- How do you implement the necessary integrations to make all the systems work in a standardized and sustainable way?

- And how do you do all of this at an acceptable cost?

What is becoming increasingly clear is that technology is not the silver bullet to solving retail's challenges; you cannot buy your way out of digital disruption. Rather, the secret to retail digital transformation lies in a new approach: an organizational shift in the IT culture and a well-thought out integration strategy to make sure the technology works together. At MuleSoft, we believe that IT can no longer be an order-taker for the business, but must rather be a strategic innovation partner to the entire enterprise. These two factors, correctly planned and implemented, will have dramatic improvements across the entire retail value chain:

- **Plan:** Across the value chain, there are more data and analytics to inform your planning cycle.

- **Buy:** There is improved decision-making and focus on buying the right inventory.

- **Move:** There is an emphasis on operational excellence, centered around an efficient and visible supply chain.

- **Sell:** There is increased customer engagement by meeting the customer wherever they are.

Overall, retail is changing due to societal and technology changes; customers today want a connected experience. As consumer expectations have changed, the entire retail value chain has changed. This book focuses on the commonalities among retailers and how IT can become your game changer.

Primary Business Functions

Feedback Loop

	Plan	Buy	Move	Sell
What is it?	Strategy & planning Product design Sales forecasting	Merchandising Purchase orders Pricing	Logistics & supply chain Inventory management Distribution	Store & channel operations Customer experience Customer support
What systems does it touch?	Demand planning, product information management (PIM), Design-centric apps	Purchase order management, ERP, financial systems	WMS, transportation management systems, RFID	CRM, POS, ERP, eCommerce, Returns, Digital marketing
Integration use cases	Legacy Modernization, Omnichannel, New products and channels	Legacy Modernization, Value Chain Innovation, New products and channels	Omnichannel, Legacy Modernization, New IT operating model	Field Sales Productivity, Omnichannel, Mobile

This book will provide a blueprint for the organizational structure necessary to implement this new IT operating model. We will also outline the integration strategy we suggest, called API-led connectivity, to link up all the systems across the retail value chain. In addition, we will also highlight retailers who have implemented this approach and resulted in strong business outcomes. Finally, we will then point you toward a number of best practices and implementation patterns to accelerate your journey toward achieving this new IT operating model, that will help you achieve your digital transformation goals.

With each change in consumer expectations or change in new technology, the entire value chain bears the impact. Our aim is to introduce you to a new way of thinking and a new approach to each part of the framework. The best retailers are the ones that embrace change and understand the ripple effect of change throughout the value chain. It is time to make this work for your company as well.

Chapter 1.1 New IT Operating Model & API-led connectivity

"Everything is changing and as a consequence you need a strategy that isolates elements of that change and enables you to move the parts around in a cost effective and risk effective manner. Our integration strategy and tools from MuleSoft is allowing us to do that."

–Julian Burnett, CIO of House of Fraser

The unique nature of digital transformation in retail

We are amid an unprecedented phase of digital transformation. Customers can videoconference with sales associates, experience a store through virtual reality, or custom-order jewelry that is 3-D printed. These changes are irreversibly reshaping retail boundaries and business models, and in the process, changing the winners and losers in retail.

As previously stated, implementing more technology is not the silver bullet to solving retail's challenges; you cannot buy your way out of digital disruption. Rather, the secret to retail digital transformation lies in a well-thought out integration strategy. At MuleSoft, we believe that IT is the strategic enabler for the business. A new IT operating model, correctly planned and implemented, will have dramatic improvements across the entire retail value chain.

When business and IT are not partners, the dissonance can block success. Perhaps this is a situation you are familiar with: your customers are growing ever more demanding, and unless you respond quickly to build relationships with them, they will take their business somewhere else. Line of business executives throw all kinds of digital initiatives at the IT team, all of which must be completed with the utmost urgency. Therefore, IT is responsible for an ever-growing laundry list of projects, all with ever-approaching deadlines, which is increasingly difficult to manage with the existing amount of resources. And this demand keeps pushing upward from sweeping trends such as omnichannel, the need for more flexible supply chains, complex customer analytics, and IoT. As the demand keeps growing, the ability to meet it actually diminishes.

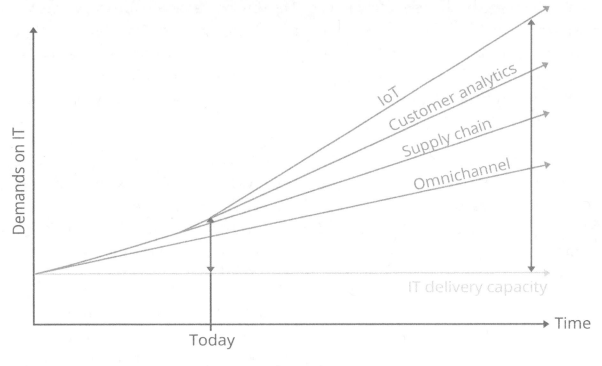

Increasing demands on IT

Based on conversations with our retail customers, to accomplish what has to be done to create those deep relationships with customers is difficult; it is not sufficient to implement more and more technology —an app here or a location beacon there. Rather what is needed is to increase both speed and scale; and to do that, a new operating model for IT and the business is required.

New IT Operating Model

The solution is that IT needs to change the way it thinks about meeting business demands. No longer can it simply view itself as a deliverer of projects; it needs to think about itself more as an enabler that allows LoB IT to self-serve. IT needs to enable self-service of assets and make them consumable and reusable by the rest of the organization, which in turn provides agility.

Imagine a franchise business like McDonald's. It has core assets such as recipes, retail layouts, and marketing offers, which it packages for reuse and self-service by their franchisees. Amazon has done something similar by creating core reusable services for its vendor partners on the platform—shipping, payments, inventory management, web presence, product search, returns, etc. These businesses encourage innovation at the edges by federating reusable assets and intellectual property for self-service and consumption at the edges. By leveraging the resources and capabilities outside of central IT, organizations can make a step change in delivery speed and capacity. It's only in this way, with a new IT operating model, that IT can deliver the agility necessary to meet the needs of the modern business.

An example of IT delivering business agility is implementing online purchasing. You need a website app and a mobile app, but what happens when you want to extend your eCommerce capability to in-store pickup or provide visibility into stock at local stores? You might also want to send personalized emails, but there are so many channels for engagement across messaging apps and social media. What happens when you want to extend offers in other channels?

The key is not to see these as separate problems but as a common base of small problems for which a repeatable set of solutions exists. This creates a much more agile way of responding to the various needs of the business. It changes how IT engages with the business in a way that is similar to how customers' relationships with brands are changing; things are moving from a transactional to a personal relationship.

In order to adapt to change, a new IT operating model is needed for retail. Customers today do not have to make trade-offs for speed, convenience and choice; and neither does a retailer's IT. With a new IT operating model, you can have:

- Speed

- Agility

- Visibility

- Security

- Scalability

This approach, and its benefits, will be a focus in the following chapters and across the retail value chain.

API-led connectivity: Reuse in Retail

As mentioned throughout this book, digital transformation is complex in the retail industry. It is certainly not the result of implementing a single application or technology. Rather, digital transformation can only be achieved when retailers are able to bring multiple technologies together to create truly distinctive and differentiated experiences. To do so, they must bring data from disparate sources to multiple audiences, such as customers, suppliers and employees.

In the retail industry, traditional methods for integrating applications do not work for digital transformation. These approaches, designed at a time with fewer endpoints, different objectives and slower delivery expectations, often cannot move at the pace today's retail business requires. Just as digital transformation requires companies to embrace a new set of technologies, so they must embrace a new level of connectivity. This book proposes a new approach to integration—API-led connectivity for retailers—that extends traditional service-oriented approaches to reflect today's connectivity needs. By adopting API-led connectivity retailers can build an application network to become more agile, change the clock speed of business, and respond to changes in the market. We will outline the core of an API-led connectivity approach and implementation challenges, and discuss how IT leaders can realize the vision of a retail application network.

Callout: Microservices

Microservices are a hot topic among enterprise architecture leaders. In our view, we believe microservices not only validate a service-oriented approach but are in fact one interpretation of how that approach should be implemented, by taking the need for well-defined services and reusability to an extreme. In doing so, it highlights the need for governance, and that successful implementation must also consider non-technology factors such as development processes and methodologies. In this way, the principles and approach behind API-led connectivity are entirely consistent with a Microservices approach and vice versa.

IT leaders must meet two seemingly contradictory goals: ensuring stability and control over core systems of record while enabling innovation and rapid iteration of the applications that access those systems of record.

Existing connectivity approaches are not fit for these new challenges. Point-to-point application integration is brittle and expensive to maintain. Service-oriented Architecture (SOA) approaches provide some instruction in theory, but they have been poorly implemented in practice. The principles of SOA are sound: well-defined services that are easily discoverable and easily re-usable. In practice, however, these goals were rarely achieved. The desire for well-defined interfaces resulted in top-down, big-bang initiatives that were mired in process. Too little thought, if any, was given to discovery and consumption of services by anyone outside of core IT. And using SOAP-based Web Services technology to implement SOA proved to be a heavyweight approach that was ill-suited then and even more ill-suited now for mobile use cases.

To meet today's retail needs, we propose a new construct—API-led connectivity—that builds on the central tenets of SOA yet reimagines its implementation for today's unique challenges. API-led connectivity is an approach that defines methods for connecting and exposing your assets. The approach shifts the way IT operates and promotes decentralized access to data and capabilities while not compromising on governance. This is a journey that changes the IT operating model and enables retailers with the realization of the "composable enterprise," an enterprise in which assets and services can be leveraged independent of geographic or technical boundaries.

API-led connectivity calls for a distinct "connectivity building block" that encapsulates three distinct components representing the modern API:

- **Full API lifecycle:** The modern API is a product, and it has its own software development lifecycle (SDLC) consisting of design, test, build, manage, and versioning.

- **Visible, secured, and governed by design:** The modern API has a stronger discipline for security and governance, and is monitored and managed for performance and scale.

- **Enterprise-grade connectivity:** Access to source data, whether from physical systems or external services.

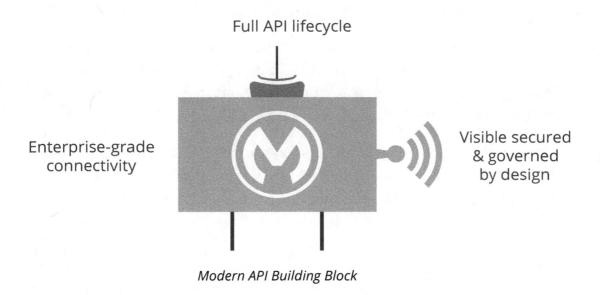

Full API lifecycle

Enterprise-grade
connectivity

Visible secured
& governed
by design

Modern API Building Block

Designing with the consumption of data top of mind, APIs are the instruments that provide both a consumable and controlled means of accessing connectivity. They serve as a contract between the consumer of data and the provider of that data that acts as both a point of demarcation and a point of abstraction, decoupling the two parties and allowing both to work independently (as long as they continue to be bound by the API contract). Finally, APIs also play an important governance role in securing and managing access to that connectivity.

However, the integration application must be more than just an API; the API can only serve as a presentation layer on top of a set of orchestration and connectivity flows. This orchestration and connectivity are critical: without them, API to API connectivity is simply another means of building out point-to-point integration.

"Three-layered" API-led connectivity architecture

Retailers have complex, interwoven connectivity needs that require multiple API-led connectivity building blocks. In this context, putting in a framework for ordering and structuring these building blocks is crucial. Agility and flexibility can only come from a multitier architecture containing three distinct layers:

- **System Layer:** Underlying all IT architectures are core systems of record (e.g., CRM, key customer and billing systems, proprietary databases, etc.). These systems often are not easily accessible due to connectivity concerns, and APIs provide a means of hiding that complexity from the user. System APIs provide a means of accessing underlying systems of record and exposing that data, often in a canonical format, while providing downstream insulation from any interface changes or rationalization of those systems. These APIs will also change more infrequently and will be governed by Central IT, given the importance of the underlying systems.

- **Process Layer:** The underlying business processes that interact and shape this data should be strictly encapsulated independent of the source systems from which that data originate, as well as the target channels through which that data are to be delivered. For example, in a purchase order process, there is some logic that is common across products, geographies and retail channels that can and should be distilled into a single service that can then be called by product-, geography- or channel-specific parent services. These APIs perform specific functions and provide access to non-central data and can be built by either Central IT or Line of Business IT.

- **Experience Layer:** Data is now consumed across a broad set of channels, each of which wants access to the same data but in a variety of forms. For example, a POS system, eCommerce site and mobile shopping application may all want to access the same customer information fields, but each will require that information in a different format. Experience APIs are the means by which data can be reconfigured so that they are most easily consumed by their intended audience, all from a common data source, rather than setting up separate point-to-point integrations for each channel.

Each API-led connectivity layer provides context regarding function and ownership

Layer	Ownership	Frequency of change
System Layer	Central IT	6-12 months
Process Layer	Central IT and Line of Business IT	3-6 months
Experience Layer	Line of Business IT and Application Developers	4-8 weeks; more frequently for more mature companies

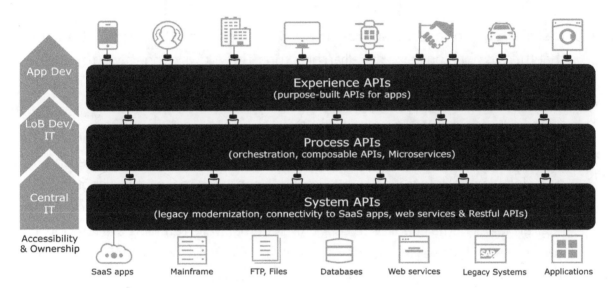

API-led connectivity architecture approach

Benefits of API-led connectivity

The benefits of thinking about connectivity in this way include:

Business

- **IT as an enabler:** By exposing data assets as a service to a broader audience, IT can enable lines of business to self-serve.

- **Increase developer productivity through reuse:** Realizing an API-led connectivity approach is consistent with a service-oriented approach whereby logic is distilled to its constituent parts and reused across applications. This prevents duplication of effort and allows developers to build on each other's efforts.

- **More predictable change:** By ensuring modularization of integration logic and logical separation of modules, IT leaders are better able to estimate and ensure delivery against changes to code. This architecture negates the nightmare scenario of a small database field change having significant downstream impact, requiring extensive regression testing.

Technical

- **Distributed and tailored approach:** An API-led connectivity approach recognizes that there is not a one-size-fits-all architecture. This allows connectivity to be addressed in small pieces, and for that capability to be exposed through the API or Microservice.

- **Greater agility through loose coupling of systems:** Within an organization's IT architecture, there are different levels of governance that are appropriate. The so-called bimodal integration or two-speed IT approach makes this dichotomy explicit: the need to carefully manage and gate changes to core systems of record (e.g., annual schema changes to core ERP systems) while retaining the flexibility to iterate quickly for user-facing edge systems such as web and mobile applications, where continuous innovation and rapid time to market are critical. Separate API tiers allow a different level of governance and control to exist at each layer, making possible simultaneous loose-tight coupling.

- **Deeper operational visibility:** Approaching connectivity holistically in this way allows greater operational insight that goes beyond whether an API or a particular interface is working by providing end-to-end insight, from receipt of the initial API request call to fulfilment of that request based on an underlying database query. At each step, fine-grained analysis is possible that cannot be easily realized when considering connectivity in a piecemeal fashion.

Bringing it together

Realizing an API-led connectivity vision must be much more than a technology decision. It requires a gradual but fundamental shift in IT organizations' architectural vision, development approach, and developers' approach to their roles.

22

With a new IT operating model, IT is able to drive transformational change yet maintain visibility and control. IT's mindset shifts from project delivery to delivering assets as services. Line of Business IT can self-serve and build its own connections, processes, and applications while Central IT governs access, SLAs, and data quality. In short, IT becomes an enabler. With API-led connectivity, retailers have an integration strategy that promotes agility, flexibility and reuse.

Chapter 1.2 Anypoint Platform

API-led connectivity provides a proven methodology for retailers to increase IT project delivery speed and close the IT delivery gap. This enables retail organizations to deliver on customer expectations, and drive massive competitive differentiation in doing so.

MuleSoft's Anypoint Platform™ was purpose-built to enable API-led connectivity. It delivers an unmatched combination of capabilities that allow retailers to realize this vision, including:

Support for the Full API Lifecycle: While many solutions in the market focus exclusively on API management, Anypoint Platform supports the full API lifecycle, enabling the modern API to be treated more like a product than just code. Anypoint Platform supports the entire SDLC, from design, collaboration, build, test, deploy, publish, version, to retire.

Security by Design: API-led connectivity embraces the importance of securing and governing APIs. With Anypoint platform, every connectivity asset can be governed using policies. In addition, every node, connection, and API is automatically registered within Anypoint Platform. This means that they are inherently secured. Anypoint Platform also provides unparalleled visibility into what applications access which systems. Last but not least, Anypoint Platform's dynamic policy enforcement enables security and governance requirements to be changed independently of the underlying code, increasing agility without compromising on security.

Ubiquitous Connectivity: Anypoint Platform can connect to any source of data, enabling rapid implementation of API building blocks. The platform allows users to connect any endpoint with pre-built generic protocol, transport and database, and application connectors.

A Unified Platform: Anypoint Platform provides enterprise grade connectivity and support for the full API lifecycle on a single platform, eliminating the need to manage multiple products, vendor relationships, and skillsets. Unifying the functionality required to realize API-led connectivity under a single platform and management plane streamlines development, and simplifies application maintenance.

 Flexible Deployment: On-Premise, or In the Cloud: On-Premise, or In the Cloud: Deployment environments are evolving with the emergence of public and private clouds. Anypoint Platform enables retailers to write once and deploy anywhere - on the cloud, on-premise, or within a hybrid environment. Retail organizations can manage their networks as a single fabric, regardless of where the API nodes are deployed.

All of these capabilities are required to successfully realize API-led connectivity and close the IT delivery gap. MuleSoft provides a unified solution that marries these capabilities on a single platform, which is purpose-built to enable retailers to innovate faster in the service of a better customer experience.

"Most retailers collect information on their customers, but only 11% of marketers report centralizing structured and unstructured data to make informed decisions. Few retail organizations have an integrated view of their customer."

-Forrester, The Operating Model For Customer Obsession

PLAN

Chapter 2.1 Plan - Business Case

Why is planning important?

There are few activities more important to a retailer's health and growth than planning. Planning is a systematic discipline, aimed at maximizing return on investment and minimizing waste and overages. Not only is careful planning key to maintaining the bottom line, it gives retailers a sense of direction of where customers are going and how the business will get ahead of their needs and desires. In a retail world characterized by massive amounts of societal and technological change, where buying cycles get ever shorter, planning is crucial to get right. We view planning as a key part of achieving business agility.

Accurate business planning has always been one part science and one part magic; getting it right could mean the difference between a good quarter and a bad one as planning touches so many different aspects of a retail business. At a time when retailers cannot afford to lose any of their thin margin of profit, one commentator outlined exactly what the benefits of accurate planning are:

An improvement in forecast accuracy can have a significant impact on the bottom line by reducing inventory buffers, obsolete products, expedited shipments, DC space required and other non-value added work. At the same time we see higher customer fill rates, improved customer satisfaction, and increased revenue and margins.[3]

Primary Business Functions

Feedback Loop

	Plan	Buy	Move	Sell
What is it?	Strategy & planning Product design Sales forecasting	Merchandising Purchase orders Pricing	Logistics & supply chain Inventory management Distribution	Store & channel operations Customer experience Customer support
What systems does it touch?	Demand planning, product information management (PIM), Design-centric apps	Purchase order management, ERP, financial systems	WMS, transportation management systems, RFID	CRM, POS, ERP, eCommerce, Returns, Digital marketing
Integration use cases	Legacy Modernization, Omnichannel, New products and channels	Legacy Modernization, Value Chain Innovation, New products and channels	Omnichannel, Legacy Modernization, New IT operating model	Field Sales Productivity, Omnichannel, Mobile

[3] Logility, "Simplify Supply Chain Forecasting"

How has planning changed?

Planning retail inventory used to be an intuitive, gut-feeling process. Tomoko Ogura, the senior fashion director of Barneys, the famed New York department store, said in 2012: "We're always trying to find new, cool things, or developing special projects, working with designers on exclusives." But now, with the availability of copious amounts of real-time customer data, generated by social media, customer interaction with digital channels, and actual purchases — just to name a few sources — planning is now a data-driven exercise and not a treasure hunt.

Ventures like branded credit cards and loyalty programs have offered retailers some insights into their customers' characteristics and buying habits. And the rapid growth of eCommerce has further expanded opportunities for retailers to get to know their customers. On top of that, customers are now actively sharing more information than ever about their tastes, needs, wants, and habits on social media. These and other sources of customer data from technologies like geolocation, NFC, and mobile payments are giving retailers access to an unprecedented amount of valuable new customer information.

Today, many possibilities are opened up by a data-based planning process. Morris Cohen, the Panasonic Professor of Manufacturing and Logistics at the University of Pennsylvania's Wharton School, notes: "Advanced machine learning and optimization algorithms can look for and exploit observed patterns, correlations, and relationships among data elements and supply chain decisions – e.g., when to order a widget, how many widgets to order, where to put them, and so on. Such algorithms can be trained and tested using past data. They then can be implemented and evaluated for performance robustness based on actual realizations of customer demands." [4]

The challenge, of course, is harnessing all the data available in its various silos, putting it in some sort of consumable format, and being able to analyze that data and extract insights from it. In order to plan effectively, businesses need to establish a single view of their customers and use all the data that each customer generates as the basis of their planning strategy.

[4] Harvard Business Review, June 2015

Which systems are involved?

There are more tools and data than ever to help retailers with the planning process, but is often hard to make use of them and integrate them with existing legacy systems. Retailers need to be able to adapt to changing patterns and trends sometimes within days. But how can this happen when it takes weeks to get the business analysis team to make sense of customer purchase data?

Our retail customers verify that integration is crucial to good planning. Planning today touches so many systems: demand planning, product information management (PIM), ERP, supply chain management, business intelligence, and more, that linking systems together and having them all in one place is critical to obtaining the necessary data.

Accurate planning is a matter of data integration

Simply having access to all that customer data is not enough. In fact, it can be — and often is — nearly useless, when retailers fail to synthesize the data and properly incorporate it into their business strategies. These various data streams are often unintentionally isolated in silos within a retailer's separate departments — like sales, marketing, customer service, IT, etc. — or systems, like an ERP system that manages inventory data and a separate CRM system that organizes customer information. For retailers to take full advantage of all this customer data, they need an effective way to aggregate the information and integrate it with their various systems and operations for inventory management, product development, advertising, customer relationship marketing, and sales.

Generally, backend systems like an ERP and front-end systems, often SaaS applications like Salesforce, tend to remain siloed as their contrasting architectures make it difficult to streamline integration. Legacy systems complicate matters, creating difficulties when it comes to sharing data, as they are outdated and inflexible. All these isolated pockets of data make it difficult for organizations to combine data sources for a unified customer view and use that data to optimize production. And as businesses employ SaaS and cloud based applications and systems, sharing data with on-premise systems becomes even more complicated. When organizations add new channels of engagement (e.g. mobile, computers, tablets, kiosks, sensors, etc.) it becomes increasingly difficult to manage all the information coming from numerous devices, databases, applications, and departments.

If the data integration problem is solved correctly, it enables a critical element of getting to the single view of the customer. However, many organizations do not see integration as a holistic strategy but rather a project-based means to an end. We see companies undergo data integration projects in a point-to-point way to enable one channel or update a particular system. And one of the pitfalls of this type of integration is that it keeps critical customer data in silos, not allowing it to be used to the benefit of the entire business. This project-based, point-to-point approach not only will hinder getting to the single view of the customer so crucial to accurate planning, it also has inherent weaknesses that will continue to self-reveal as more and more systems are integrated.

Custom point-to-point integrations are often seen as a quick and easy way to complete projects that require connecting systems together. For example, when planning time comes around a retailer may connect inventory data in an on-premises ERP with customer data in Salesforce with some hard code. But this method is fragile, expensive, and difficult to maintain; with point-to-point connections, a developer needs to manage connectivity and implement changes in an ad-hoc, unsustainable manner. Moreover, any changes to the connections impact the entire system, leaving room for errors and possible creating failed systems and downtime. These point-to-point integrations deliver a short-term solution, but become overly complicated as businesses grow and plan for the future.

Why API-led connectivity is a better approach for planning

Connectivity approaches, like point-to-point, do not work for the issues posed by a data-driven planning process. Point-to-point application integration is brittle and expensive to maintain. Service-oriented Architecture (SOA) approaches provide some instruction in theory, but they have been poorly implemented in practice. The principles of SOA are sound: well-defined services that are easily discoverable and easily re-usable. In practice, however, these goals were rarely achieved. The desire for well-defined interfaces resulted in top-down, big-bang initiatives that were mired in process. Too little thought, if any, was given to discovery and consumption of services by anyone outside of core IT. And using SOAP-based Web

Services technology to implement SOA proved to be a heavyweight approach that was ill-suited then and even more ill-suited now for mobile use cases.

A new approach is required, one that leverages existing investments and enables IT to seize the moment to drive transformational change; one that enables agility yet allows IT to maintain visibility and control. This change is a journey that requires shifting IT's mindset from project delivery to delivering assets as services and enabling Line of Business IT to self-serve and build its own connections, processes, and applications while Central IT governs access, SLAs, and data quality. In short, IT has to become an enabler.

While connectivity demands have changed, the central tenets of SOA have not: that is, the distillation of software into services that are well-defined, reusable, and discoverable.

Take a look at one company using MuleSoft's unified integration platform, Anypoint Platform, to bolster their inventory planning strategy.

Chapter 2.2 Plan - Customer Spotlight: Global CPG Company

"Rather than be reactive to what's happening in the marketplace, we'll have the ability to be proactive and determine what that next thing we need to do to reach our consumers."

–IT Director at Global CPG Company

A large food manufacturing and CPG company employs over 30,000 employees worldwide. The business manufactures in 18 different countries, sells its products in over 180 countries and has offices all over the world. Recently, this CPG company approached MuleSoft with the need to better plan their inventory at a global scale.

Due to changing customer preferences, the CPG company realized that their business depended on better customer experiences and modern, personalized customer engagement. For example, their data told them that their customers wanted more natural products, wanted to know where ingredients come from, how those are being produced and if products are environmentally friendly. Not only were consumption habits changing, but the company also saw global changes in shopping habits. "The age of everybody going to the store and purchasing their food is over," said their project manager for integration. "Customer preference is now shaped by social media, and how we keep our brand loyalty is changing."

To better prepare for and meet their customer demands, the CPG company wanted to leverage their valuable data for a more efficient planning process across their various brands and manufacturing. This required the IT team to deliver better analytics. These goals proved difficult, however, as most projects in the past were done with point-to-point integration using old-fashioned EDI data. The team needed a new approach as everything needed to be done quicker to meet the changing demands of consumers. For example, the business needed to respond swiftly to a Greek yogurt fad or branded snacks by a new movie release.

The integration team wanted to engage a new strategy to improve the planning process and have better visibility into the needs of consumers. The team began shifting resources into innovation and brand building positions to move the company forward, including a focus on analytics. With analytics, it would help the company plan, innovate and build brand positions therefore the team built a comprehensive analytics platform to allow the company to look at trends. The IT director said, "Rather than be reactive to what's happening in the marketplace, we'll have the ability to be proactive and determine what that next thing we need to do to reach our consumers." Gathering digital marketing, purchasing, and social media data will help plan the company's next strategic moves.

Analyzing data is indeed a very powerful tool in the retailer's planning arsenal, but it's not as easy to do as one might think. The CPG company quickly realized that without integrating systems together to consume the data, the company simply has a lot of unusable data sitting in various databases and systems. For example, when a customer buys their products in a supermarket, how does that information make it back to the company? There needed to be a way to unlock the data assets in the backend systems. As the IT director points out, " Because we have all of these disparate systems all over the place, we really needed to beef up our integration capabilities. We were not processing data in near real-time, we were doing batch oriented processing and maybe could get the data once per day. We had to find a holistic way to look at common data usages and to standardize them using APIs." Therefore, the CPG company turned to MuleSoft to figure out how to expose those data services so that they can be used and consumed by multiple end points in a consistent and reliable way. MuleSoft gave the company an opportunity to build that standardized, holistic data integration framework.

With an API-led connectivity approach to integration, the CPG company has been able to expose data assets to help all parts of the business better use data to achieve their objectives. It has given the CPG company the ability to open up common data usage, so that multiple stakeholders can consume the data according to their particular business needs. For example, the marketing team can receive data about customers that can be reused for sales forecasting, drastically improving the planning process.

This new approach to data integration has resulted in a number of positive business effects. Internally, MuleSoft is helping the company gain visibility into their disparate systems globally. There is now a single source of truth and the ability to provide data efficiently to consumers who need it on a global basis.

Another benefit of API-led connectivity for planning is its emphasis on reuse, rather than just building project after project after project. This allows the company to remain agile to new opportunities in the market. Rather than viewing each project as individual solutions that need to be delivered, the company can build each project for reuse, building for the next person. By having one source of truth, and being able to slice and dice the data in different ways, it means the CPG company can plan for the change that will occur.

This new real-time availability of data, consumable and reusable by anyone who needs it throughout the business, has made the integration team excited about their role in the strategic planning process." The CPG company is excited about the future. "This gives IT the ability to become a true partner for the business. Rather than just being an order taker as we have in the past, and having them come to us with the ideas, we can pursue innovative ideas ourselves, and use our existing technology to create transformative and efficient initiatives."

That's a definite shift in the way that the company used to plan. Rather than being reactive to the marketplace, the business is able to leverage data analytics to build connected relationships with their customers. This becomes increasingly important as the CPG company plans for the future.

"Only 45% of retailers feel they are able to understand online touchpoints and the interplay with in-store behavior. This makes it difficult for associates to understand past shopper behavior and view inventory across locations to make informed buying decisions. "

-Source: Real-Time Data Drives The Future Of Retail

BUY

Chapter 3.1 Buy - Business Case

Why is buying important?

The rise of consumerism has shifted a retailer's buying efforts from a subjective approach to an objective one as every retailer now has to measure the likes and dislikes of customers before a buying decision can be made. In the planning cycle of a retailer (Chapter 2), a retailer plans their inventory and delivery experience across channels. To make this informed buying decision, it becomes necessary to have a single view of the customer in order to have a holistic picture of a customer's likes and dislikes and have proper integration to access real-time data.

In the buying process, a retailer uses their plans and forecasts to buy materials and goods. The buying process today is broad and complex, consisting of vendor management, purchasing, replenishment and pricing. [There are many retailers that manufacture their own goods; however for the simplicity of this section, we we will assume that retailers are buying goods from manufacturers, wholesalers and importers.]

Primary Business Functions

Feedback Loop

	Plan	Buy	Move	Sell
What is it?	Strategy & planning Product design Sales forecasting	Merchandising Purchase orders Pricing	Logistics & supply chain Inventory management Distribution	Store & channel operations Customer experience Customer support
What systems does it touch?	Demand planning, product information management (PIM), Design-centric apps	Purchase order management, ERP, financial systems	WMS, transportation management systems, RFID	CRM, POS, ERP, eCommerce, Returns, Digital marketing
Integration use cases	Legacy Modernization, Omnichannel, New products and channels	Legacy Modernization, Value Chain Innovation, New products and channels	Omnichannel, Legacy Modernization, New IT operating model	Field Sales Productivity, Omnichannel, Mobile

What's changed?

For a retailer, the buying process is centered around relationships. Globalization has expanded these relationships as there is now an opportunity to purchase goods from around the world. With speedy delivery and international trade, gone are the days of retailers needing to purchase local goods. In this increasingly complex retail ecosystem, the buying process now expands across numerous global vendors and partners.

And ultimately, the retailer is trying to build a relationship with their customer. By providing the right product or sharing new trends with a customer, a retailer's assortment is a critical lever in developing brand loyalty. And with increased customer demands, a retailer also cannot risk being out of stock as they will easily turn to a competitor's inventory.

For some retailers, buying the right assortment for their "target" customer may be easy. For instance, they carry work professional clothing for the millennial woman. But with the rise of eCommerce and availability of channels for purchase, the "target" customer is often much more varied for a retailer making the buying process even more complicated.

Recently, there has been an upward trend in more subscription based retailing with personalized goods delivered to a customer. For example, Stitch Fix curates fashion collections for their customer, selected by style specialists. Stitch Fix needs to be able to carry more inventory, but less across a set of SKUs to satisfy more diverse customer demand. This requires a leaner inventory than ever before, from buying 100 shirts in one style, to 20 shirts in 5 targeted styles. Additionally, Stitch Fix needs to be more responsive than ever. Whereas we speak of H&M and Zara as "Fast Fashion", what a celebrity wears at the Grammys during the weekend must be reflected by Stitch Fix's buyers and sellers on the following Monday. This is "Fast Fashion" at speed, and at micro scale. Stitch Fix therefore needs to buy the right inventory of goods and brands that will resonate with a variety of customers.

Which systems are involved?

There are more tools and data than ever to help retailers with the buying process, but is often hard to make use of them and integrate them with existing legacy systems. Especially in the fast-paced retail industry, buying the right inventory at the right time becomes critical.

We have learned through our retail customers that integration is crucial to the buying process. Buying today touches so many systems: purchase order management, ERP, financial systems partner systems, and more, that linking systems together and having them all in one place is critical to obtaining the necessary data.

Many retailers often resort to inefficient methods in order to get various systems to work together is what is called "swivel chair" data entry. This method requires an individual to manually retrieve data from one system and enter it into another (e.g., one must re-enter information from System X to System Y). This approach will complete the purchase order in a timely process but such a procedure is error-prone and takes an extensive amount of time and human resources.

As a lack of integration creates inefficiencies in the organization, retailers need a robust integration solution in order to streamline their business processes. Sharing information and providing visibility into both frontend and backend systems increases productivity and simplifies business process. With all systems properly integrated, organizations can focus more on the buying process and less on the hassles of trying to make data available. So how does a retailer buy the right assortment? Integration between systems becomes key.

As retailers undergo digital transformation, there are three strategies in particular that will create the accurate buying apparatus that retailers desire that will benefit from a holistic integration strategy.

- **Legacy Modernization**

  It becomes critical to unlock data between partner and vendor systems. Often times, this inventory or supplier data is in proprietary databases or older legacy systems. Well-managed APIs become very important to providing governed access to this key business data.

- **Value Chain Innovation**

  Technology has disrupted the buying process. It is now possible to complete purchase orders electronically from any corner of the world; and to receive your order to your warehouse quickly

- **New products and channels**

  Customers expect a dizzying array of new products delivered at speed and retailers need to buy new products.

More accurate buying is possible through a strong integration strategy. Take a look at how MuleSoft partnered with Buffalo Wild Wings to improve their buying process.

Chapter 3.2 Buy - Customer Spotlight: Buffalo Wild Wings

"We can help our general managers make better decisions, faster. It used to take a day, or more, to get sales data but now we can see sales data hourly."

–Dave Lenzen, Director of Enterprise Applications

Buffalo Wild Wings is an international restaurant chain with 1,200 locations in the US, Mexico, and Canada. Their mission, in the words of Dave Lenzen, the Director of Enterprise Applications, is "beer, wings, and sports. Our big goal is serving our guests, who we call fans, and trying to give them a fan experience within our restaurant and also through our digital channels." And that fan experience is predicated around the products that are available in the restaurants for customers. But how does Buffalo Wild Wings know that what they purchase is the right product?

The restaurant chain's biggest competition, according to Lenzen, is the couch. "Today everyone has large screen TVs," Lenzen points out. "We have to improve the fan experience. How do we bring different aspects of your experience in a stadium into the restaurant?" Buffalo Wild Wings therefore looked to build relationships with their customers and deliver a more compelling experience.

To do this, managers wanted to add local beer assortments to the menu to personalize the restaurant experience and to create a "home town" sensibility. But doing this proved difficult because it was complex to manage the growing assortment of beers available in the market. And more importantly, how did Buffalo Wild Wings know they were buying the right inventory and enough of it?

To solve the problem, the restaurant chain implemented new technology to help ensure the company was not sacrificing profits in its effort to personalize the dining experience with new, local beer assortments. By installing IoT-enabled flow meters on their tap lines, the business was able to capture pour data of all their beer served. They then planned to use that data to inform beer buying decisions.

Gathering sales insights from the IoT devices and pour data proved to be difficult, however. Buffalo Wild Wings' sales data had historically resided in databases isolated from the retailers' multiple backend POS systems. The retailer needed a way to integrate that data for a real-time, comprehensive view of their inventory; so, Buffalo Wild Wings turned to MuleSoft as the right solution to solve this connectivity challenge.

"Using Anypoint Platform, we implemented a solution, a new application called Smart Bar where a General Manager can log-in and manage their inventory of tapped beers and request new ones," says Lenzen. "All of that is automated now with integrations to various systems for requesting and approving those requests as well as setting up the menu items so they show up on the POS terminals at the restaurant. So not only do restaurant managers have good data on what beer is selling and how much of it, we've made the process of ordering it and making it available to customers as easy as possible.

This implementation has allowed general managers to easily personalize the buying process for each individual restaurant. As Dave highlights, "a general manager now can see, very quickly, much more quickly and easier than in the past, what is selling based on the sales information that we've integrated into the beer application through MuleSoft." The general managers can request new purchases and changes through the application, now entirely automated. Once the new purchase order is approved, "it'll show up within a day or two, on their POS terminals, versus previously, it would take a couple weeks to get that information set up."

By integrating this pour data with point of sales (POS) data, Buffalo Wild Wings is able to improve efficiency by measuring the volume of beer poured against the sales transaction to ensure it matches the type and size of beer that was ordered. With access to POS data and pour data, Buffalo Wild Wings sends this data to the SmartBar platform and evaluates the data to ensure the business is making sound business decisions. Using MuleSoft, the results have exceeded expectations. The new beer management solution was introduced at eight pilot restaurants and resulted in double-digit reductions in the amount of beer shrinkage. It has also led to better informed buying decisions.

With a better understanding of the beer inventory usage, MuleSoft is helping

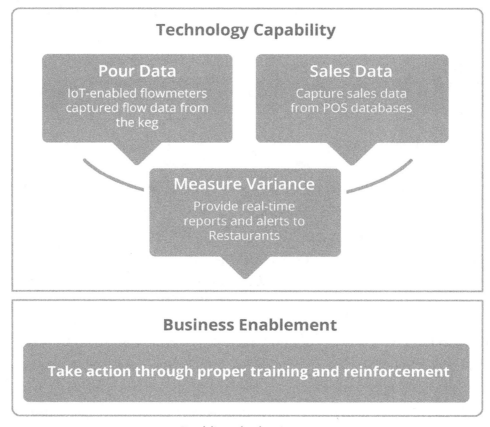

Enabling the business

Buffalo Wild Wings drive future purchasing decisions. For example, a general manager can specifically track preferences in a region such as a favorite beer in an area of New York.

As Buffalo Wild Wings thinks about the future, they believe that greater insight into beer inventory could perhaps even lead to an auto-replenishment solution to ensure that beers are always flowing and never in short-supply. It would be a radically different, and automated, buying process for inventory.

"Technology is pervasive in today's supply chains in every possible area, ranging from processing and tracking transactions to planning, scheduling and managing."

-Paul Anderson, the Professor of Practice in Supply Chain Management at Lehigh University

MOVE

Chapter 4.1 Move - Business Case

Why is moving important?

Once a retailer has made a purchasing plan and then bought inventory, it then becomes necessary to move that inventory from port to warehouse to the actual point of sale. The move process for a retailer involves both the movement and storage of raw materials, work-in-process inventory, and finished goods from point of origin to point of consumption.

Previously, supply chain management was often a back-office activity. Today, however, a company's ability to quickly move goods is crucial. Inventory management, logistics, and distribution are top-of-mind for retailers.

Primary Business Functions

Feedback Loop

	Plan	Buy	Move	Sell
What is it?	Strategy & planning Product design Sales forecasting	Merchandising Purchase orders Pricing	Logistics & supply chain Inventory management Distribution	Store & channel operations Customer experience Customer support
What systems does it touch?	Demand planning, product information management (PIM), Design-centric apps	Purchase order management, ERP, financial systems	WMS, transportation management systems, RFID	CRM, POS, ERP, eCommerce, Returns, Digital marketing
Integration use cases	Legacy Modernization, Omnichannel, New products and channels	Legacy Modernization, Value-Chain innovation, New products and channels	Omnichannel, Legacy Modernization, New IT operating model	Field Sales Productivity, Omnichannel, Mobile

What's changed?

Customers are becoming increasingly accustomed to being able to receive packages they order online almost immediately. According to one study, 69% of consumers say that one-day shipping would induce them to shop online more.[5] In the age of Amazon Prime, fast, free shipping is a competitive differentiator. To meet these increased expectations, companies need to make the business of delivering products smooth and invisible to the end consumer. Customers simply will not tolerate delays because of a supply chain issue as there are such low switching costs.

---

[5] Walker Sands Future of Retail report

The need for speedy delivery means that the distribution of goods is also drastically changing. Amazon is exploring autonomous trucking and robot vans to make delivery more efficient. New entrants into the market, such as Boxed, are using automated warehouse distribution centers to fill customer orders. Warehouses and delivery services are becoming the new shopping centers. Wal-Mart is tracking quantity and expiration dates on household items to better automate delivery by leveraging sensors at strategic points in the home, as well as attached to certain products.

In fact, the ability to track shipments in a more sophisticated way than ever before are transforming supply chain logistics. Paul Anderson, the Professor of Practice in Supply Chain Management at Lehigh University notes, "Technology is pervasive in today's supply chains in every possible area, ranging from processing and tracking transactions to planning, scheduling and managing." Technology trends like the ubiquity of mobile, improvements in human-machine interaction, and the rise of smart sensors are transforming how goods are delivered. The cost of a RFID tag has fallen from a dollar to a dime since 2003[6] and retailers such as Macy's plan to have every item tagged to help manage inventory across multiple channels. Anderson notes that companies need "a truly integrated, visible and efficient supply chain that benefits from collaboration."

This level of operational excellence required in the retail supply chain is the 'new normal.' To adjust to the necessity for efficient supply chain operations, most businesses depend on the central IT organization to deliver the technological infrastructure for supply chain logistics. Unfortunately, because most supply chain operations are dependent on outdated technology standards like EDI, IT teams often have to resort to custom solutions to bridge the gap. For example, customers now demand a real-time view of product availability yet legacy technologies were not built for this purpose; this requires IT teams to build out project after project. That backlog of projects is so great that IT is losing the capacity to deliver solutions to the business on time.

[6] "Forbes, "RFID Revolution"

Which systems are involved?

Supply chain logistics touches so many systems like warehouse management systems, transportation management systems, RFID and more. Linking systems together and having them all in one place is critical to obtaining the necessary data to ensure smooth, seamless product delivery.

As supply chain management becomes more international, complex and dynamic, there are more tools and data than ever to help retailers with the move process. The problem with a multiplicity of tools and data, however, is that they need to be made useful, which is a problem that falls squarely into IT's lap. There are three IT challenges that are proving particularly thorny for businesses looking to modernize their supply chain operation:

1. Decreasing partner on-boarding time (partner setup, message mapping, business logic). Normally when businesses start working with partners, B2B/EDI partner setup, trading profile management and message processing is core to the on-boarding process. That on-boarding can take a significant amount of time, often weeks to months, and in the case where such work is outsourced to a VAN provider, can be a black box. In a world where speed is a competitive differentiator, shaving time off the partner on-boarding process is extremely important.

2. Decreasing time needed to make changes to partner configurations. Change is constant. Business scenarios may change. Customer demands may change. The suppliers businesses rely on today may not be there tomorrow, but the customer still wants goods and services quickly. Changing partner configuration needs to be easy for IT to do.

3. Decreasing risk and/or cost by replacing a legacy or custom point-to-point B2B/EDI solution. EDI technology is 20-30 years old, so the EDI solutions that are in place already at most companies are 20-30 years old as well. They're either custom solutions that have had extensions built over layer by layer, or they are legacy systems with value that the original vendor is no longer supporting or certainly no longer actively investing in.

Why API-led connectivity is a better approach for moving

According to Hong-Kong based apparel manufacturer TAL, B2B transactions have traditionally been convoluted and long-winded. Logistics data, particularly at the speed customers now demand, needs to be interoperable, processed in real-time — nobody has time to wait for a daily data batch processing operation — and visible to analytics teams and other lines of business. As a lack of integration creates inefficiencies in the organization, retailers need a robust integration solution in order to streamline their supply chain processes. Sharing information and providing visibility into both frontend and backend systems increases productivity and simplifies business process, resulting in a visible supply chain. Data is delivered in a way that enables managers to have access to the right data and take the necessary action.

So how does a retailer improve their supply chain processes? Integration between systems becomes key. This is why we propose the holistic integration strategy, called API-led connectivity, to obtain operational excellence.

In the supply chain context, an API-led connectivity approach provides both the flexibility to work with different partners and make alterations easily, but retain control over core ERP systems:

- **Experience API layer:** Different experience APIs by channel, perhaps eCommerce, or SaaS application, or data interface

- **Orchestration API layer:** Different process APIs by business process e.g. executing a purchase order, checking inventory level

- **Data Access API layer:** Different data access APIs to wrap key key systems of record

As an example, here is a diagram of how API-led connectivity works to automate purchase orders:

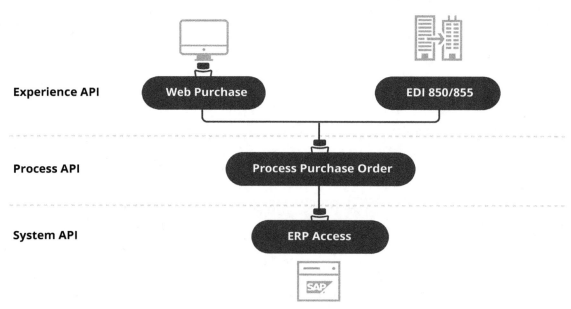

Purchase Order Automation Through API-Led Connectivity

The architectural benefits of the API-led connectivity approach include a decoupled architecture that abstracts away complexity and a more agile response to change. All of your channels are able to reuse the same process logic, so as you make changes to your supply chain partners and on-board new partners, you only need to manage the logic of receiving messages. The purchase order processing logic is already baked in, thus allowing you to move quicker.

This retailer in the above example could take this approach one step further. They could apply the API-led connectivity approach at the Experience API layer too. In this scenario, one can think of supply chain partners submitting Purchase Orders via a RESTful API with Anypoint Platform driving the downstream work to create the required EDI 850 message. In this way, they can onboard partners more quickly because they do not have to deal with the intricacies of messaging standards for franchisees that may not have a EDI gateway or for new retail channels like kiosks that do not 'speak' a standard language. The possibility of making frequent changes with few downstream consequences to your supply chain, responding quickly to the needs of your customers, suddenly become enormous.

To see how a robust, holistic integration strategy creates dramatic business outcomes, take a look at how TAL Apparel uses MuleSoft's unified integration platform, Anypoint Platform, to bolster their supply chain strategy.

Chapter 4.2 Move - Customer Spotlight: TAL Apparel

> *"The fashion world has been disrupted: 2 seasons has become 52 micro seasons and brick-and-mortar stores have been overcome with eCommerce. This requires world class supply chain and logistics services."*
>
> –Kai Yuen Kiang, VP, TAL Apparel

TAL Apparel, a Hong-Kong based apparel manufacturer TAL, is the world leader in producing technologically advanced garments. Founded in 1946, the company is one of the largest apparel suppliers globally. The company has been the pioneer in manufacturing garments by developing process and supply chain solutions, tailored to the exact needs of the customers. With 11 factories in Asia and 25,000 employees globally, TAL Apparel relies on its operational excellence. Serving over 50 global top brands such as Burberry and Brooks Brothers, the company produces 1 of every 6 dress shirts in the US.[7]

Supplying the customers of a global brand is a daunting challenge and requires the retailers to quickly adapt. As described by Kai Yuen Kiang, VP at TAL Apparel, "the fashion world has been disrupted: 2 seasons has become 52 micro seasons and brick-and-mortar stores have been overcome with eCommerce." These changes have dramatically impacted supply chain operations and prompted the need for a faster time-to-market. Traditionally, information would flow from retailers to distributors to manufacturers. With the modern supply chain, however, information flows from eCommerce sites directly to manufacturers.

These changes in the fashion world parallel changes in the IT landscape at TAL Apparel. Their simple IT landscape of web, ERP and BI has exploded to include

---

[7] Financial Times, "Shirt tales from TAL"

digital platforms, eCommerce, WMS, sensors, robots, SCM and more. On-premise IT systems have transitioned to cloud platforms and multi-year projects have been replaced with monthly releases. This disruption has paved what TAL Apparel calls "modern digital manufacturing."

Modern Digital Manufacturing...

- System Calling Manufacturer's API for Product Selection, Order, Checking Order Status

- Manufacturer's System Calling Courier's API for Shipment, Tracking, Proof of Delivery...

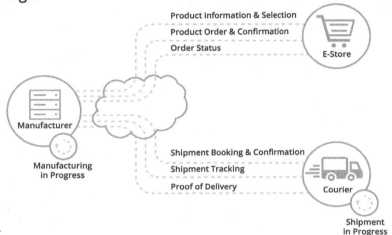

Modern Manufacturing

To become a modern manufacturer equipped to handle eCommerce, TAL Apparel required better data and analytics to optimize the movement of products throughout their supply chain. Additionally, it needed to be a quick solution to meet the new demand from high value prospects such as Michael Kors and Paul Fredrick, including the ability to offer real time order status and order cancellation.

Critical to meeting this demand was leveraging APIs as a new connectivity interface. This proved difficult, however, as their current MFT solution was inefficient. They needed to replace overdue Sunset IBM Websphere Partner Gateway which integrates over 15 partners with consolidated B2B trading process and transaction management. Even more complicated, these new technologies and implementation needed to be done on a massive scale, as TAL Apparel produces over millions of shirts yearly. And since the company has multiple partners worldwide, managing supply chain operations proved complex.

TAL Apparel and its partners looked to IT to build unified and connected capabilities to lower costs and increase speed to market. As described by Kai Yuen Kiang, they wanted to have "one technology platform to support rapid innovation."

TAL Apparel began to develop a more visible supply chain. The goal was to have greater visibility into product and inventory data for different lines of business for a more efficient supply chain. They had different systems for factories and partners and wanted to simplify and unify all these experiences into a single location in their headquarters. IT quickly realized that their current architecture was rooted in disjointed data and locked in legacy systems, causing project backlog to grow, pushing out these project deadlines.

To improve operations, the team decided to adopt a cloud first strategy, with the hope of introducing self-service and reusable assets to establish a more future-state architecture. They decided on MuleSoft to enable an API-led approach. This allowed them to decouple their data sources while standardizing on reusable templates that their partners could leverage and customize. They have since enabled lines of business to self serve and build good portions of projects on their own - thus eliminating bottlenecks by federating the work to where the expertise exists. For example, they could build reusable APIs such as Shipping API and Delivery API that could be leveraged across the supply chain. All of this is built on MuleSoft's unified runtime for Hybrid Integrations and APIs on one single platform.

TAL Apparel recognized that these challenges could be solved by an agile, adaptable approach to integration — API-led connectivity. They have a much more visible supply chain that is prepared for the future. Moving forward, TAL Apparel is experimenting with garment technology innovations such as 3D virtual fitting and 3D body scanning. By supporting fast deployments of new APIs to expand new business, TAL Apparel continues to outpace competition with its efficient supply chain.

"By 2020, customer experience will become the #1 factor for shoppers as the key brand differentiator, overtaking price and product."

-Walker Study

SELL

Chapter 5.1 Sell - Business Case

Why is selling important?

Digital transformation has drastically impacted the selling part of the value chain; its scope now expands to comprise of not only store operations but eCommerce initiatives, marketing, loyalty programs and returns.

Retailers are now responding to a digitally enabled customer. With more customers using app-enabled solutions in their own home, they expect the same level of technology in a connected store.

Primary Business Functions

Feedback Loop

	Plan	Buy	Move	Sell
What is it?	Strategy & planning Product design Sales forecasting	Merchandising Purchase orders Pricing	Logistics & supply chain Inventory management Distribution	Store & channel operations Customer experience Customer support
What systems does it touch?	Demand planning, product information management (PIM), Design-centric apps	Purchase order management, ERP, financial systems	WMS, transportation management systems, RFID	CRM, POS, ERP, eCommerce, Returns, Digital marketing
Integration use cases	Legacy Modernization, Omnichannel, New products and channels	Legacy Modernization, Value Chain Innovation, New products and channels	Omnichannel, Legacy Modernization, New IT operating model	Field Sales Productivity, Omnichannel, Mobile

What's changed?

In the retail industry, the selling process used to comprise of a customer visiting a store and making a purchase. With the explosion of store technologies and eCommerce, selling for any retailer now spans across a variety of channels.

The store itself has evolved into a connected store, often referred to as Brick-and-Mortar 2.0. These digital technologies are designed to foster personalization in the store. Visible to customers, digital signs and interactive product kiosks improve customer engagement. Behind-the-scenes, beacons are leveraged to monitor shopping behavior in a store and sales associates are alerted when a known customer walks into the store.

It is not just technology, however, that has changed the modern storefront; it is the experience within the store. Retailers are no longer relying on offering a product transaction to build relationships with customers, but rather focused on offering an experience. Retailers are now experimenting with new ways to entice customers to enter their store. For example, Harrod's recently added a 10,500 square-foot extension to offer customized services for skin and spa services. Tesco, a large grocery chain, now offers a "relaxed" checkout lane to offer an improved experience for older customers, who might need more time to complete a purchase. Retailers are focused on getting more customers in the store, and getting those customers to come back more.

Beyond the store, retailers have extended their offerings to web and mobile channels. Unlike a mobile-optimized site, a mobile app allows a retailer to directly connect with their users and build brand loyalty. This ability to directly have a relationship with customers digitally is a new phenomenon. And for retailers, such as Walgreens, they have found that their mobile customers are six times more valuable than their in-store only customers.

Additionally, eCommerce initiatives are top-of-mind for retailers. If retailers have not yet made the leap to online, they are no longer just late to the party -- the party has all but passed them by. A study from WalkerSands shows that one-third of consumers now shop online at least once a week.

By giving customers so many options, however, it has placed the burden of operational excellence on retailers. The increased number of goods ordered online and shipped directly to the customer has also radically increased the amount of returns. Yet for a retailer to compete, they must offer an easy return service; in fact a National Retail Federation study found that 59 percent of retailers currently offer free return shipping.

It is clear that the selling process has expanded beyond the 4 walls of a store; and will retailers are now able to reach a customer anywhere, especially in their home. And in the future as more customers embrace Smart Home technology, retailers have an opportunity to embrace new smart home channels. For example, Domino's has partnered with IFTTT to enable consumers to automate smart home devices to make pizza delivery tracking even easier. The brand's order tracking app can now sync with connected devices to turn off the garden sprinkler or turn on the outside lights when a delivery is expected. And while smartphone annual growth is expected to slow to 4% in 2018, smart home devices are expected to grow to 4 billion units by 2021. This is a new channel that presents a great deal of opportunity for retailers therefore posing the question, what's the next big change for the retail industry? For example, it is predicted that by 2020, most online retailers will develop virtual reality to improve the customer experience.

Which systems are involved?

As customer loyalty becomes more difficult to obtain, there are more tools and data than ever to help retailers with the selling process. It is often hard to make use of them and integrate them with existing legacy systems. Especially in the fast-paced retail industry, your selling process and customer experience is your critical success factor.

We have learned through our retail customers that integration is crucial to the selling process. Selling goods to customers touches so many systems: CRM, POS, ERP, eCommerce, returns management, digital marketing and more, that linking systems together and having them all in one place is critical to obtaining the necessary data.

With different systems unable to communicate with one another, it becomes nearly impossible to track all customer interactions and obtain information through one interface. For examples, sales representatives spend time jumping between applications to create a 360 degree view of their customers, slowing down sales processes.

Furthermore, integration of cloud services and applications is becoming ever more important as many retailers are now deploying cloud-based applications into their business processes and even moving large parts or even all of their retail operations to the cloud.

As a retailer looks to offer an omnichannel experience, it is not a matter of connecting system A to system B to create this new mobile app or that new channel online. Omnichannel is much more about becoming channel-agnostic. And if there is one thing the last decade has taught us, it is that new channels and new ways of interacting with consumers emerge rapidly. Omnichannel then becomes more about future-proofing your business — creating the capacity for change in your organization so that no matter which channel your customers, employees, and partners want to use across the business, it can be accommodated quickly and easily.

An API-led approach to connectivity will allow old and new systems to seamlessly coexist to deliver an omnichannel experience. By driving reuse of APIs, you can deliver consistency across channels and deliver at the speed that customers expect.

So how does a retailer improve their selling processes? Integration between systems becomes key.

As retailers undergo digital transformation, there are four strategies in particular that will create the efficient selling process that retailers desire that will benefit from a holistic integration strategy.

- Field Sales Productivity

   A retailer can now offer sales associates the necessary tools to build, deliver and manage digital customer journeys. A sales associate can walk a customer through purchasing options and comparing products, while making a recommendation based on a customers' individual needs. In the retail industry with such low margins, improving this efficiency becomes very beneficial.

- 360-degree customer view

   It is well known how crucial a single view of the customers, and it is now possible to have a holistic understanding of your customers' channel patterns for each scenario. Not only are retailers able to better target and drive business based on these insights, you can also minimize costs by avoiding ineffective marketing tactics. This insight provides retailers deeper visibility into their customers and their behaviors, allowing them to better market and sell products.

- Omnichannel

   Retailers that do omnichannel well have one key attribute in common: their operations architecture is built to be agile and flexible. In the absolute best case scenario, retailers would be able to spin up and spin down capabilities as needed.

- Mobile

  With more and more customers purchasing goods through smartphones, leveraging mobile channels becomes increasing important.

An integrated customer experience and seamless selling process is possible through a strong integration strategy. Learn how PetSmart is leveraging MuleSoft to build an omnichannel brand.

Chapter 5.2 Sell - Customer Spotlight: PetSmart

"We are unleashing the full power of having a clear view of customers through MuleSoft. MuleSoft has helped us to build those relationships with customers"

–Max Rodriguez, EIM Development Manager, Petsmart Inc

PetSmart is a leading retail chain in the U.S. specializing in pet supplies and services such as grooming, training, daycare, and boarding. The chain was founded in 1986 and is now a pet services leader with more than 1,500 stores across the country.

PetSmart is on a mission to be the trusted partners of pets and their parents throughout their lives. The company has adapted to the changing retail landscape and has developed more digital offerings, such as new website, to connect with customers. But to deliver these innovative pet offerings and build this deep relationship with pet owners, they needed to tie together their vast portfolio of products and services. They needed to become an omnichannel retailer to meet their customer needs.

But doing this was easier said than done. PetSmart offers 30,000 products, and a full array of services like, their store, PetsHotel (dog and cat boarding facilities), PetSmart Doggie Day Camp, as well as digital channels such as PetSmart.com, Pet Food Direct, Pet 360, and others. The vast portfolio of different services and purchasing channels, supported by a numerous and siloed back-end systems and data sources, made it difficult for PetSmart to offer a seamless experience for customers. For example, if you brought your dog Fluffy into the grooming salon and then into the PetsHotel, a customer would need to re-submit all the same profile information - the definition of a disconnected experience.

PetSmart therefore looked to MuleSoft to develop an omnichannel strategy.

By using Anypoint platform, PetSmart built reusable APIs, such as a customer profile API, that can be leveraged across the company. This customer API is used in multiple platforms such as PetSmart's mobile app, grooming services and pet hotel, enabling a single view of the customer. The aggregated customer data from a number of online applications, systems, and data sources provides a 360-degree view of their customer-base due to a robust customer data foundation. This means that the next time a customer updates their address on the PetSmart website, the address change will be reflected in the Pet Food Direct online store as well. By having this information connected, it gives PetSmarts a better view of their customer across channels and allows for more targeted marketing. Today, the Customer Profile API is leveraged across a number of web and mobile channels.

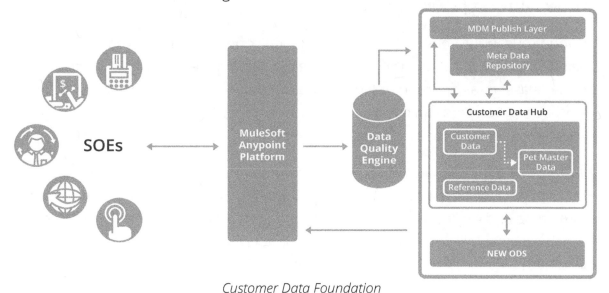

Customer Data Foundation

Now using MuleSoft's Anypoint Platform, PetSmart is able to execute an omnichannel strategy from their mobile and web systems such as Salesforce Commerce Cloud, to backend systems such as Manhattan Associates, their order management system. As Max Rodriguez, Sr. Manager of EIM, explains, "MuleSoft powers our omnichannel strategy." Each time Petsmart connects with its customers, that connection is made possible by MuleSoft.

As PetSmart builds an application network, they have accelerated their go-to-market strategy, launching omnichannel initiatives 2x faster. Furthermore, by reusing work across channels, they are able build APIs that can be leveraged across multiple channels. According to Max Rodriguez, EIM Development Manager, with MuleSoft's API-led connectivity approach, "the experience for the customer is the same. If they go to our salon for grooming, if they go to PetSmart's hotel, if they go to the store. We know who our customers are and who their pets are." This has increased PetSmart's ability to fully understand their customer behavior across channels, while allowing PetSmart to deliver a consistent experience to pet parents, regardless of which channel they choose to engage.

With MuleSoft, PetSmart is on their way of becoming an omnichannel retailer. MuleSoft's API-led connectivity approach allowed the company to create a foundational layer of reusable API building blocks, which, in turn, increased time-to-market by 2x and reduced development effort by nearly 50%. Their omnichannel initiatives have resulted in improved revenue for the business and deeper relationships with their customers.

Beyond reusability, PetSmart found that API-led connectivity improved maintainability and reduced costs because developers are now working with reusable assets, as opposed to large complex components. As a result of this new approach, developers can now build medium to complex API integrations in 2 week agile sprints, compared to the initial 4 weeks.

Moving forward, PetSmart aims to build more internal, reusable APIs. They are currently working on building a Pet Profile Data API, which will aggregate pet data-- from name and weight to address and dietary preferences. PetSmart also plans to launch external APIs for third-parties in order to create new revenue channels and build better, connected experiences for pet parents.

Today PetSmart is determined to be the first and continuous touchpoint for pet parents. With MuleSoft as their partner in their new service model, PetSmart is set-up for the future. As they adapt to the changing retail industry and expand to offer new services, such as home delivery, PetSmart will leverage MuleSoft to remain omnichannel.

RETAIL APPLICATION NETWORK

Chapter 6.0 Retail Application Network

The customer journey to API-led connectivity

Realizing an API-led connectivity vision must be much more than a technology decision. It requires a gradual but fundamental shift in IT organizations' architectural vision, development approach, and developers' approach to their roles. The challenge is as much about process change as it is about technology implementation.

However, realizing the API-led connectivity vision is not a discrete goal but a continuous journey. Moreover, it is a goal that can be be realized only in incremental steps. Through partnering with dozens of Fortune 500 companies and more than 150 retailers on their API-led connectivity digital transformation journeys, we have distilled best practice into the following steps:

- **Startup mode:** For the API-led connectivity vision to be successful, it must be realized across an organization. However, in large enterprises it is simply not possible to wipe the slate clean and start from scratch. Consequently, the API-led connectivity customer journey must start with a vertical slice of the business, for a specific use case or line of business. By bounding the problem, the scope of change is reduced and the probability of success increased. Training and coaching to drive role-modeling of new behaviors is critical at this stage.

- **Scale the platform:** Once initial proof points have been established, these use cases will naturally become lightning rods within the organization that will build mindshare and become a platform to leverage greater adoption. In addition, the service-oriented approach naturally creates reusable assets, which exponentially increases the value of the framework as the number of assets increases.

- **Build Center for Enablement (C4E):** To balance the creation of reusable assets and provide federated access to integration, a new organizational capability, C4E, is required. C4E is in charge of enabling business divisions to successfully fulfill specific connectivity needs. It is responsible for providing a framework and set of assets to allow both the business and IT to build, innovate, and deliver their objectives in an agile and governed way. The long-term aspiration is for C4E to enable LoBs, as well as IT, to consume and create these reusable assets.

Retail Application Network

As our retail customers follow API-led connectivity and embrace the C4E model, something powerful takes shape, which we call the application network. An application network seamlessly connects a retailer's applications, data and devices. It takes a different approach to the methods used to connect applications, data, and devices today. Instead of utilizing point-to-point connections or isolated architectures, the application network provides an infrastructure for information exchange by allowing applications to be "plugged" into the network. The network can be as simple as two nodes that enable two applications to share information, or it could span the enterprise and external ecosystems.

Every node added to the network will increase the network's value since the data and capabilities of that node are discoverable and consumable by others on the network. For example, a retailer can build an Order API that can be reused for the web and mobile apps, becoming part of the application network. In other words, it makes it easier for someone in the organization to create a useful application, use of data, or an API creating a particular experience, and then expose that value to the network. And when a new system, such as an order management system, is added, it seamlessly becomes another node in the application network.

With the massive number of applications, data, and devices that need connecting in the modern enterprise, and with the incredible amount of time and resources that retailers spend trying to tie everything together, an application network can provide the agility, flexibility, and speed retailers urgently need in today's environment. New applications can be plugged into the application network as easily as you plug in a printer. The application network can deliver unified vision and control and offer intelligent data about the relationships between applications. With an application network built with Anypoint Platform, retailers can transform themselves into composable enterprises.

Chapter 6.1 Catalyst Accelerator for Retail

Jumpstart API-led connectivity with Catalyst Accelerator for Retail

Alongside Anypoint Platform, MuleSoft offers Catalyst Accelerator for Retail, a publicly available set of API designs and implementations designed to accelerate the journey to API-led connectivity for retailers. These assets reflect best practices from leading retailers who have successfully implemented API-led connectivity. Catalyst Accelerator for Retail is intended to both support the transition to API-led connectivity, and to accelerate the development of common retail applications.

Its components include:

- **API-led reference architecture for retail.** Catalyst Accelerator for Retail provides a model for API-led connectivity, drawn from working with industry leaders, that promotes asset self-service and reuse.

- **Packaged API designs and implementations.** Leveraging our work with 2 of the top 5 global retailers, MuleSoft has built out a set of API definitions and packaged implementations. Each of the API building blocks in the above architecture is included as part of the Catalyst Accelerator.

- **Support for common retail applications.** The assets included in Catalyst Accelerator for Retail can be leveraged out-of-the-box to support accelerated development against common retail use-cases including omnichannel

Note that many APIs, such as the Product Availability API, are reused across these distinct use cases. Accordingly, the architecture and assets provide a strong reference model to guide retailers as they think about driving asset reuse across different retail projects across the enterprise.

Getting started with Catalyst Accelerator for Retail is easy. All of the assets discussed above can be downloaded for free on Anypoint Exchange. We encourage retailers to make full use of these assets to more quickly adopt API-led connectivity within their enterprise. Doing so allows IT teams to realize the benefits of reuse conferred by this model even faster than before.

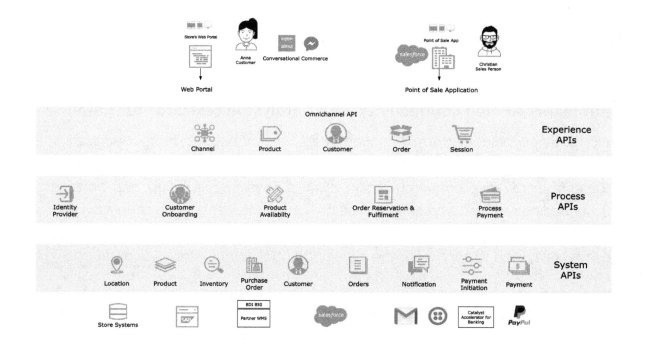

Catalyst Accelerator for Retail Architecture

For more information, please visit:

https://www.mulesoft.com/integration-solutions/api/retail/catalyst-accelerator

CONCLUSION

Chapter 7. Conclusion

Customer demands within the retail industry continue to grow, expecting a connected retail experience. With increasing competitive pressures from tech-driven startups disrupting the retail space, retailers are facing growing pressures to accelerate their go-to-market strategies in the face of shrinking margins.

With disruption knocking at the door, retailers are pressured to address the source of these disruptions: customer expectations. To do so, they must turn to IT to drive strategic initiatives that mitigate customer dissatisfaction – whether it is by building digital channels, developing a connected store or adopting technologies to enable a faster supply chain.

The difference between retail businesses that are thriving and those that are struggling is being able to provide these connected experiences for customers. Amazon is not in a leading position because it is an online retailer; Amazon dominates the eCommerce landscape because it provides connected experiences as well as speed and operational agility, and has the technological infrastructure to do so. The retailers that will win are those that are able to meet customers' needs both today and in the future. And in a world where those needs are as much about the customer experience as about the product, technology becomes the critical differentiator. It is not just how technology is used (which is table stakes), but how agile and flexible is the IT function.

API-led connectivity provides a means for retailers to transform IT from a bottleneck hindering innovation into a platform that enables the rapid delivery of innovation. Over time, this approach leads to the emergence of a Retail Application Network, which allows for any system, application, data, and device to be seamlessly "plugged" in and out in a lego-like manner. Equipped with an Application Network, retailers can not only respond to today's industry disruption, but put themselves in position to easily accommodate whatever business needs may emerge in the future.

Our goal in this book was to give you the strategy and the tools you need to implement the agile IT infrastructure so important to today's business. The critical capability that retailers need to enable is the capacity for change. Rather than focusing on individual connected experience as one-off projects, we provided you with a strategy and a roadmap to creating an efficient yet personal retailing experience for your customers throughout the retail value chain — plan, buy, move and sell. We provided practical advice to build the digital operations needed for a modern retailer, offered an integration strategy that will increase productivity and business agility, and revealed case studies from our retail customers that prove dramatic business outcomes.

We encourage retailers to join in driving this change by applying the principles and methodologies prescribed in this book to evolve from disrupted to disruptor, leveraging technology to not only improve the customer experience, but to establish market leadership in doing so. You now have the chance to seize the unique opportunities available to retailers and create a powerful, connected retail experience.

MuleSoft's Anypoint Platform is trusted by over 1000 enterprises worldwide including 2 of the top 5 global retailers. It is the only vendor to be named a Leader in both the Gartner Magic Quadrant for Full Lifecycle API Management and the Gartner Magic Quadrant for Enterprise Integration Platform as a Service (iPaaS).

Business Process Management
Best practices for integrating BPM with Anypoint Platform

Executive Summary

Business Process Management is an important part of continuous improvement and business transformation, but many organizations struggle with implementing it effectively. The question is often whether BPM is a technological problem or a cultural one. Are business processes dependent on the technologies they use or the people who use them?

The answer is both. Ultimately, the issue is not to think about BPM separately from how your services and processes work, but how to make them work together. In other words, in order to be successful with business processes first you need to have all your systems and apps exposed as services via APIs.

Business Process Management is the discipline used to coordinate and distribute tasks across people and systems within an organization, based on well-documented process and business rules, in order to ensure business consistency between teams and systems. It is commonly thought that there is only one way to execute process management, but there is in fact another, more effective way.

In this paper, we will show how Business Process Management can be realized using a strategy called API-led connectivity. It will also cover recommended best practices for BPM design with Anypoint Platform.

Introduction: The capabilities of BPM

What is BPM?

Business Process Management (BPM) can be a fundamental building block of many business functions. The primary function of a BPM solution is to assist business analysts in modeling and optimizing the processes of their organization, and its ultimate goal to improve the functioning of a human-centric business process.

The strength of a BPM solution lies in its ability to orchestrate between different systems, people and processes to improve the overall function of human-centric business activities.It is meant to provide a solution to a business audience, like a packaged application, with the following capabilities:

- A Business Process Modeling tool (for business), typically web-based, to model complex Business Processes involving human & system (commonly called task) business rules using BPMN annotation.
- A Business Rules engine, where complex routing conditions within the Business Process can be outsourced and parameterized separately
- A Business Process Simulator to measure process efficiency, in terms of average time to complete a process and the cost of a process (how many people will get involved, and how long they will spend to complete the task)
- A Business Process Development tool, for IT developers to "enrich" the provided business process, with specific IT artifacts
- A Business Process Runtime Engine, to execute the "enriched" Business Process using BPMN annotation. The runtime engine also provides a built-in persistence store to keep in-flight processes state to prevent failure

- A Task List, used for humans to retrieve the business process tasks assigned to him/her, or a business role that s/he belongs to
- A Business Process Reporting tool for business performance checking (for example the performance on a call center) and auditing purposes (for instance who made a litigious approval 3 months ago on a business case)

What BPM isn't

BPM is not, technically speaking, an integration tool, because it is mainly targeted at business audiences looking for a centralized tool to document, simulate, and optimize internal processes. And once the processes are fully executable, business people can track and audit the pending or completed processes.

The only technical aspect of BPM is the capability to "enrich" the Business Process Model with technical artifacts in order to make the process executable. This includes constructs such as variables/payload, a user interface to present human tasks in the BPM Tasklist, Web Service callouts, etc. This is possible since BPMN version 2.0, where OASIS decided to merge BPEL and BPMN into a unified specification for both Business Process Annotation and Execution languages together. The objective was to streamline the process design lifecycle between business and IT teams.

Given the BPMN 2.0 background and the BPM trend, some traditional vendors are positioning BPM as an integration layer because their solutions were built on top of an existing SOA stack. However, the overhead introduced by the native BPM requirements is too high, making it unsuitable for integration or API initiatives where connectivity and performance are key.

When to use BPM

BPM is ideal for long running business processes, which involves heavy human interactions across multiple lines-of-business. BPM is also suitable when business tracking is important - the capability to know who did what from a historical perspective. Here are some examples:
- Case Management
- New Hire Interview Process
- Expenses Approval

Common Challenges in BPM Implementations

The first challenge is that organizations adopting BPM must have good Business Role Management, either via Role Management tools, or just some simple internal practices (like Excel), that BPM can leverage to distribute tasks. A lot of implementation failures stem from this, because BPM is not able to distribute the task to the worker in a consistent way. And this requirement is too often underestimated and all the business benefits vanish.

The second major challenge is the Business Process "enrichment" itself. While on paper it sounds promising to have a single modeling language suitable for both Business and IT in order to streamline the process delivery lifecycle, in practice the story is different. The person designing Business Processes does not typically know the technical assets of the IT infrastructure, so tends to abstract system tasks into one single box (like 'create order') which after all is fully understandable.

However when the IT developer inherits this process and he/she is responsible for enriching it, this create order 'box' might end up being replaced with ESB-like mediation logic embedded inline with the Business Process. Hence muddling the business perspective.

At this stage the process can actually be executed. However because of the verbose enrichment, the process owner can no longer understand the process, making it difficult to iterate and optimize. This is the 'one-off agility' phenomenon that we see too often in BPM projects.

The solution to these challenges - API-led connectivity through Anypoint Platform

Taking an API-first approach provides a natural abstraction for System Tasks like 'create order,' which can and should be implemented outside of the BPM.

Traditional SOA stack vendors that also provided BPM products, relied on a Web Services (SOAP, WSDL, XML) interface for System Tasks, and these services were typically hosted on their SOA product. However, enterprises have long learnt that Web Services API's are too heavyweight for enterprise-wide consumption. For instance, a Web Service created for BPM (createOrder) cannot be used by a mobile developer working on a lightweight framework. Instead, enterprises have embraced the more modern concept of API's.

A modern API has taken on some characteristics that completely change the game:
o They adhere to standards (typically HTTP and REST), that are developer-friendly, easily accessible and understood broadly
o They are treated more like products than code. They are designed for consumption for specific audiences, they are documented, and they are versioned in a way that users can have certain expectations of its maintenance and lifecycle.
o Because they are much more standardized, they have a much stronger discipline for security and governance, as well as monitored and managed for performance and scale.
o As any other piece of software that is productized, the modern API has its own software development lifecycle (SDLC) of designing, testing, building, managing, and versioning.

An API-first approach depends on the modern API to act as the building block for streamlined business processes. With this approach, it is important to keep BPMN as business-oriented as possible, and IT should be focusing on providing building blocks accessible as APIs to support the business process. This is the only way to keep the business process model intact over subsequent changes.

While MuleSoft's Anypoint Platform does not include a BPM product, API-led connectivity using Anypoint Platform is a natural fit for any BPM initiative:
- Anypoint Platform provides connectivity to both legacy and SaaS systems with 150+ connectors
- It provides tried and tested interoperability with majority of BPM vendors

- Using an API/RAML as contract between business and IT allows clean and clear duty separation
- The API mocking capability allows business users to complete business process modeling and simulation, while IT implements the API and back-end capability in parallel
- Since Business Processes need to subscribe to APIs, it enables a mechanism for dependencies tracking

MuleSoft's Anypoint Platform can be the universal connectivity layer to support any BPM solution. This allows customers to leverage solutions like Activiti, Camunda, jBPM or new generation BPM PaaS (like AgilePoint NX), rather than a heavyweight BPM solution such as Oracle that comes with an unsuitable integration layer for Business Processes.

How to adopt BPM with Anypoint Platform

As mentioned above, BPM can leverage APIs exposed by Anypoint Platform to handle all complex system integration requirements and hence keep the Business Process "business-friendly". However, there are 2 key points to consider:

- **Business Process Readability**
  Organizations want to adopt BPM because it helps to formalize a business process description, via BPMN annotation, and the same description can be interpreted directly as an executable in the BPM Workflow engine. It helps to mitigate risk as we have a direct relationship between what we see and what actually gets executed.

  However, while BPMN annotation is an industry standard, the way a business process is modeled highly depends on the process architects. It isn't unusual for the same business requirement to end up with 2 completely different BPMN models, as the process architects will always apply his or her personal interpretation. Both processes can be accurate, but it will highly impact future enhancements, as the business process might be only readable by the process author.

- **Human/System tasks abstraction**
  As part of the Business Process readability, it is important to have a formal way to clearly identify and segment the tasks that are needed to support a business process. These tasks are either human-based or system-based. System-based tasks can be abstracted as an API. Inappropriate identification and segmentation will also impact the overall business process readability as well as the subsequent enhancement.

  To address these points, it is important to have some modeling principles, commonly shared across the organization in order empower the BPM and API benefits.

Example: API-led connectivity for BPM

The following example represents a travel request business process requirement, from which we need to model a BPMN based business process.

- Employee submits a business trip request
- If the submission doesn't comply to the corporate policy (booking period, destination, etc), send a notification to the CFO office
- In parallel, send the trip details automatically to the Travel Agent for a Quote
- Upon quote receipt, submit to Employee's Manager for approval
- If approved, send to Department VP for a 2nd level approval if required (based on trip duration, cost, etc), otherwise send confirmation to Travel Agent
- Travel Agent returns the final booking reference and the Employee receives the travel itinerary

The challenge now is in converting this requirement into a commonly readable business process across the whole organization, as well as providing clear segmentation between the Business and IT - so IT can build the appropriate APIs to support the process.

Typical Business Process Description	Actual BPMN Business Process
<ul><li>Employee submits a business trip request</li><li>If the submission doesn't comply to the corporate policy (booking period, destination, etc), send a notification to the CFO office</li><li>In parallel, send the trip details automatically to the Travel Agent for a Quote</li><li>Upon quote receipt, submit to Employee's Manager for approval</li><li>If approved, send to Dept VP for a 2nd level approval if required (based on trip duration, cost, etc), otherwise send confirmation to Travel Agent</li><li>Travel Agent returns the final booking reference and the Employee receives the travel itinerary</li></ul>	

Let's look at the details for this BPM rollout with Anypoint Platform.

Step 1: Identify the Roles, Verbs and Nouns to define a Task

Roles are denoted in orange, Verbs in green and Tasks in blue

- Employee submits a business trip request
- If the submission doesn't comply to the corporate policy (booking period, destination, etc), send a notification to the CFO office

- In parallel, send the trip details automatically to the Travel Agent for a Quote
- Upon quote receipt, submit to Employee's Manager for approval
- If approved, send to Department VP for a 2nd level approval if required (based on trip duration, cost, etc), otherwise send confirmation to Travel Agent
- Travel Agent returns the final booking reference and the Employee receives the travel itinerary

Step 2: Create and Order the Tasks in BPMN

- Describe your high level process by listing out the tasks
- A *Task* is a specific action within your process, that can be described as: [Role + Verb + Noun]
- Use your favorite modeling tool (Aris, Visio or any BPM designer tool) to draw an initial flow in its natural chronological order, from Left to Right
- Focus only on the Happy Path for the process

Step 3: Create Swimlanes for each Role

- Create swimlanes, one per Role defined previously
- Component names follow the nomenclature 【Verb+Noun】

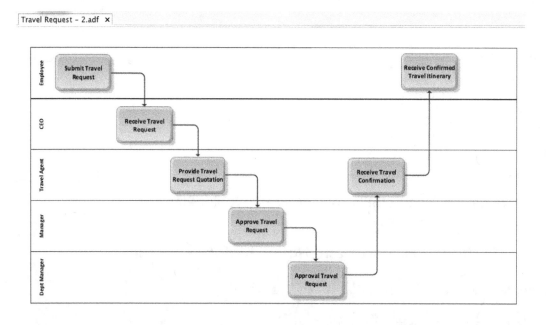

Step 4: Identify the Task type

- Identify which activities are Human Tasks and which ones are Service Calls
- In the diagram below, the green boxes represent Human Tasks and the blue boxes, Service Calls

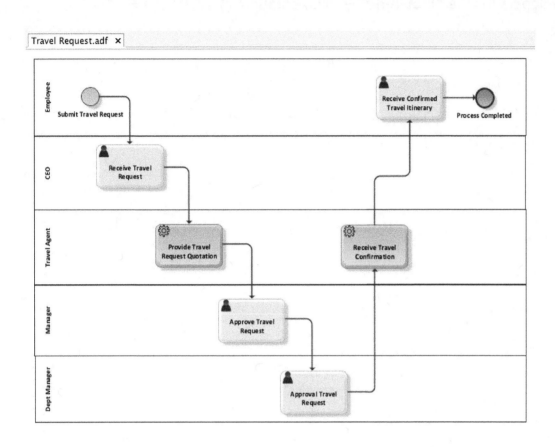

Step 5: Add Gateway or Business Rules to optimize the process aligned with the business practice

- Add Gateway to align the process with real-life conditions
- Run Simulation to fine-tune the process before handing over to process developers for the **"last-mile"** implementation

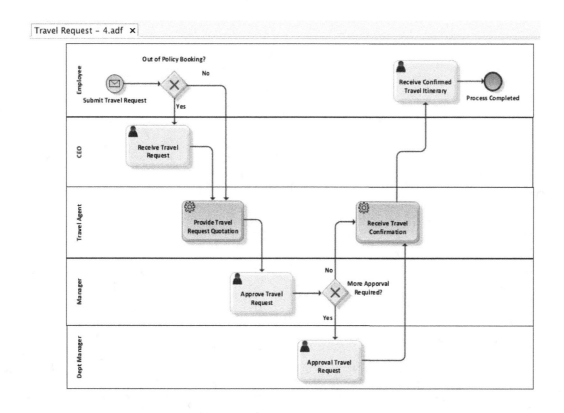

Step 6: Follow MuleSoft best practices and cover the entire lifecycle of the required System APIs

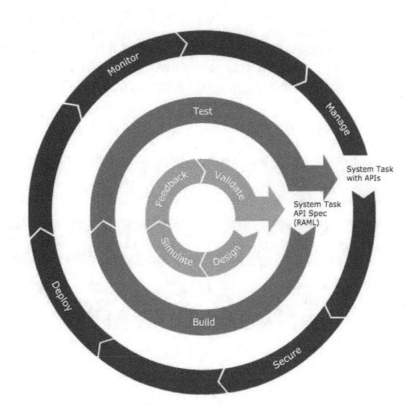

Start by defining the contract for the System Task API. We will call this a System API. The contract is defined in RAML. The business process can make the Service call using this API, which can initially be simulated (using the Mocking Service). The IT developer builds out the API implementation by connecting it to the respective back-end systems (using appropriate legacy or SaaS connectors). Tests for the implementation can be built using MUnit. Once deployed and ready for consumption from the Business Process, it can be secured using the appropriate API policies and monitored and managed with rich SLA analytics.

Step 7: Create a Process API for the Business Process

In this example, the Travel Request business process was event-driven and kicked off by an employee submitting a travel request. The same business process can be triggered programmatically, for instance by a mobile app for expense reports. For this, the business process we just modeled, should itself expose a well-defined API (also called Process API). Follow the same best practices with an API-first approach, starting from a RAML spec, to create process API's as well.

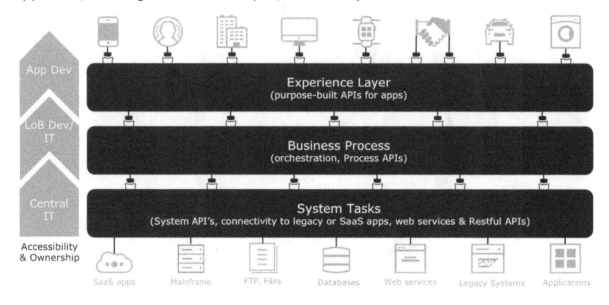

Following the steps documented above, a business requirement can be easily converted into a formal BPMN business process, while the system and human tasks can be extracted. System APIs within Anypoint Platform can now support each System Task.

Anypoint Platform covers the entire lifecycle of these System Tasks including documentation, governance, dependency analysis, usage analytics, reuse, collaboration, etc. Over time, a repository of System and Process API's can be built out that contributes to the corporate Application Network. These API's become relevant well beyond the realm of BPM, however the BPM delivery project is a great opportunity to API'fy assets. Each of these API's can be secured and governed using the industry-leading API Management capabilities of Anypoint Platform.

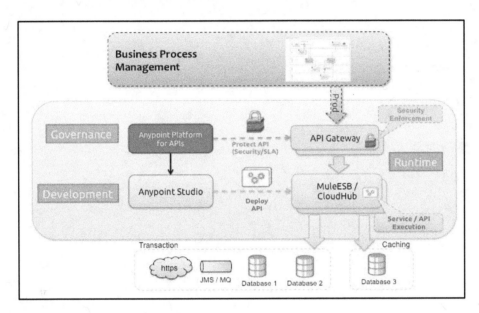

Summary

Exposing your apps and services as APIs can handle all your complex system integration requirements and hence keep the Business Processes "business-friendly."API-led connectivity enabled through Anypoint Platform can optimize your BPM rollout process. Following best practices can create positive outcomes in the function and management of your enterprise. Anypoint Platform is uniquely suited to implementing this approach, and as the real-world example of designing and implementing a business process demonstrated, this task can be made easier and more efficient through this strategy.

Take a look at more information and resources about how Anypoint Platform can help your business.

WHITEPAPER

CLOSING THE IT DELIVERY GAP

MAKE YOUR IT TEAM
MORE PRODUCTIVE
AND INNOVATIVE

Challenges

- Responding to technological change and digital disruption places a massive burden on enterprise IT teams, creating a gap between what the business needs and what the IT team can actually deliver.
- Resourcing for IT is expected to stay the same or rise very slightly, meaning the IT delivery gap cannot be solved through additional resourcing alone.
- If enterprises don't respond quickly to these changes, it is believed negative repercussions could occur in six months or fewer.

Recommendations

- Rethink IT's role in the enterprise from a sole deliverer of projects to a strategic partner and enabler of the rest of the business self-serving its own technology deliverables.
- Consider established business models, like franchising, when determining how IT can scale its delivery capacity.
- Establish both a strategic discipline of integration, led by APIs, and a capacity within the business to encourage and make visible reusable assets on which the entire organization can collaborate and utilize to deliver new products and services.

INTRODUCTION

Many business leaders think that we are currently going through the "fourth industrial revolution." Our current age, marked by a mix of technologies that are blurring the boundaries between the physical, digital, and biological, is considered to be just as disruptive — if not more so — as the agricultural, manufacturing, and electronic revolutions before it. Klaus Schwab, the founder of the World Economic Forum, outlined the hallmarks of this revolution:

"The possibilities of billions of people connected by mobile devices, with unprecedented processing power, storage capacity, and access to knowledge, are unlimited. And these possibilities will be multiplied by emerging technology breakthroughs in fields such as artificial intelligence, robotics, the Internet of Things, autonomous vehicles, 3-D printing, nanotechnology, biotechnology, materials science, energy storage, and quantum computing."

While these technological advantages have the potential to offer significant benefits to the world, they present extraordinary challenges as well. For the enterprise, the challenge of the emergence of all these technologies is particularly profound. These forces are not just a question of a seismic change in business model, like the way e-commerce disrupted the retail industry in the 1990s. The emergence of all of these forces at once is upending the way industries do business itself; it is starting to create a sea change in enterprise culture.

The qualities necessary to survive in today's enterprise environment are different from before. Organizations today have to contend with demanding stakeholders that engage through new channels, competition coming from everywhere due to lower barriers to entry, and a truly global marketplace. No longer does the big eat the small, as in years past; today, the fast eat the slow. The qualities that organizations need to succeed today are speed, agility, inventiveness and the ability to try many experiments rapidly and fail fast.

How can you make sure that your business has these necessary qualities to survive and thrive in today's competitive environment? How can you make sure that the IT delivery gap in your organization is as small as possible, enabling your technology team to step away from the reactive hamster wheel of projects and developing a truly nimble, innovative infrastructure for change?

The solution lies in our unique vision of enterprise architecture, the application network. An application network emerges from our approach to enterprise integration, called API-led connectivity, and our equally unique approach to organizational structure and application delivery, the Center for Enablement. The two go hand in hand. We will explore these concepts in further detail, and provide solutions to create a powerful capability for change in your organization that will close the IT delivery gap.

What is the IT delivery gap?

In January 2017 MuleSoft conducted a study of over 900 IT decision makers, and the trends they revealed were startling. Only half said that they were able to complete all the projects they were asked to do in the last 12 months. 60% said they were not adequately resourced to meet their company's digital goals. 60% also said that if digital transformation goals were not met, revenues would be negatively impacted in six months or less. And the single biggest obstacle to meeting those goals was time constraints.

It's not particularly difficult to understand why. As businesses are pivoting to respond to more and more changes in strategy and interaction forced by technological trends like cloud computing, mobile, and SaaS, IT has to shoulder the responsibility of implementing those responses. And because there are so many forces, and IT only has a finite amount of resources, what will ultimately occur is a gap between what IT needs to do and what it can do.

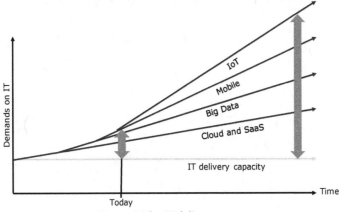

Figure 1: The IT delivery gap

With each new digital pressure coming on and with IT remaining unable to add any more resources or specialized capacity, the gap is widening exponentially and is accelerating. Moreover, under pressure, IT often will take short cuts and create technical debt, even while complexity is increasing, which compounds the problem. And this only addresses the technological change that businesses have to respond to today. IT decision makers believe that their businesses will change more in the next five years than they have in the last five. How will the IT team be able to accommodate changes that you may not be able to predict today?

Clearly a new approach to project delivery and technology strategy is required, one that can scale IT's capacity. It is clear that it would be impossible to keep adding resources to close the gap — what's needed is a way to exponentially increase the delivery capacity of existing resources. It seems like an impossible task, but it can be done through a rethink of IT's role in the business. In short, IT needs a new operating model.

The new IT operating model depends on established business principles

The new IT operating model employs an approach by which Central IT drives both the production of reusable assets and, importantly, enables the consumption of those assets by teams within the lines of business, to deliver digital initiatives. The model addresses production and consumption, but what is new is what is being produced as well as what is being consumed. This new IT operating model relies on business principles that have been around for decades, though they haven't often been applied to enterprise IT project delivery. And that model is franchising.

Think about a business like McDonald's, who, in many ways, were pioneers of the franchise business model. The central company has core assets such as recipes, retail layouts, and marketing offers which they package up for reuse by their franchisees, who execute to those plans in a self-service way. This encourages innovation at the edges by federating reusable assets and intellectual property for self-service and consumption by each individual franchisee. The company enables their franchisees or vendors by educating them with best practices and processes, and promotes quality both through established and exacting standards and through continual consumer feedback. Finally, the parent company retains control over the assets and has full visibility into the entire operation but federates work and innovation. This business model has two distinct advantages. First, the franchise model allowed McDonald's to scale and expand globally at a much faster pace than it would have otherwise. Secondly, even though every McDonald's all over the world recognizably belongs to the same business, franchisees in local markets can innovate according to their own business needs (e.g. localized items on the menu), increasing the chance of business success in markets in which it has expanded to based on local knowledge.

For IT organizations to scale to the level required by digital disruption, they must think about how they can adopt the principles of franchising. Franchise businesses have both core reusable assets (the what) and organizing principles (the how) that franchisers unlock and package for self-service consumption by their franchisees to drive scale and innovation, while maintaining quality and governance to exacting standards. In the new IT operating model, Central IT needs to morph its role into one that unlocks assets and enables consumption by lines of business and developers throughout the organization, to create scale, innovation, and speed, while retaining control.

How the new IT operating model should work inside the organization

The idea is that, much like a franchise business, Central IT should federate innovation across the organization by building reusable assets and enabling self-service rather than working on and delivering entire projects themselves. By leveraging the resources and capabilities outside of central IT, organizations can make a step change in delivery speed and capacity.

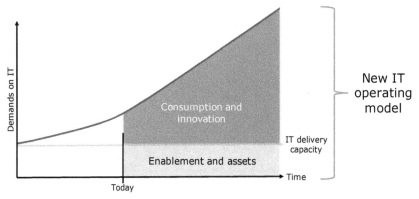

Figure 2. How IT scales with a new operating model

But what this actually means is that a change in the way that IT operates is necessary; rather than just delivering on projects, Central IT will spend its time creating reusable assets and enabling the rest of the organization to use them.

How does this actually happen in practice? There are three things that tech leaders have to consider as they work on scaling the IT organization. These seem like big changes, but the work done to put these initiatives in place will actually pay dividends in terms of increased productivity and innovation in the future.

- Changing your delivery model
- Changing your approach to integration
- Changing the way your IT team is organized

Changing the delivery model from production to production + consumption

As we now know, Central IT needs to move away from trying to deliver all IT projects themselves and start building reusable assets to enable the business to produce some of their own projects — to self-serve rather than waiting for IT to deliver. The key to this strategy is to emphasize consumption as much as production.

Traditional IT approaches (for example, SOA) focused exclusively on production for the delivery of projects. In the new IT operating model, IT will change its mindset to think about producing assets intended to be consumed by others throughout the business. The assets need to be discoverable, and developers need to be enabled to self-serve them in projects through a visible, usable repository and best practice documentation.

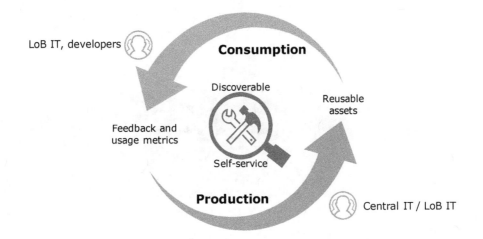

Figure 3. The production + consumption model

One of the best parts of this new operating model is that the most useful assets to the rest of the company will rise to the top thanks to active feedback from the consumption model along with usage metrics to inform the production model. The reusable assets that are most useful become the basis of numerous project deliverables that can be completed more quickly. Mike Hamilton, the director of IT at MuleSoft, explains how this works in practice:

> We took the entire project list of business processes that needed automation and decided to break each one down into pieces and then group the pieces into common services. What we found in doing this was that quite a lot of the projects had many needs in common. A key common microservice that came up was related to sending notifications via email, Slack, or SMS. Since most integrations had this requirement, the "notifications" microservice came up early as a quick win. The function of this microservice is to be able post information about who to notify, how to notify them, and the content to send in the notification and then have that delivered to the intended recipients. By creating this as a service, every project can leverage the capability of the microservice rather than implementing notifications as a part of each individual project. This saves development time on every project and provides us with a consistent way to implement notifications in all of our work.

By figuring out what all the delivery requests had in common, Mike and his team were able to develop a useful, reusable asset that will save both his team and any other team that has access to it time and effort in delivering any project necessitating notifications. The model has successfully been changed from pure production to consuming a reusable asset and then using that to speed production.

Changing your approach to integration

Julian Burnett, the CIO of House of Fraser, a premium department store in the UK, has noted that for many businesses, integration is not really a strategic discipline. "Most integrations between business systems, if I'm honest, occur point-to-point in a really rudimentary way. We hadn't really thought about integration as a capability." But as House of Fraser's technological capabilities needed to evolve in order to accommodate the massively changed and disrupted retail business, he realized that he would have to rethink his company's approach to integration beyond the usual point-to-point connections, in order to increase the speed of change and to de-risk the effect to current business operations.

What many businesses find, as they pivot to developing apps and other ways of responding to digital disruption, is that the point-to-point integrations required to make these apps work pile up over time, creating technical debt, a brittle architecture, and the inability to respond to changing business needs quickly.

Here's an example. You might wish to develop a web app to provide real-time order status and order history for sales teams to engage with customers. For this example, let's assume you have customer data in SAP and in Salesforce; inventory data in SAP; and order data in an ecommerce system. What might be commonly done at this point is that you would get your IT team to jump in and create aggregated customer data by wiring together customer data from both systems – with code. Then, the aggregated customer data is further combined with order data in the ecommerce system to produce both the order status and order history data – with more code. Now these two sources of data are hooked into a Web app API which can be leveraged by the web app.

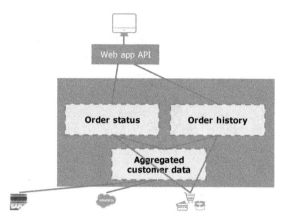

Figure 4. A project-based approach to IT delivery

This project might be considered a success; it was launched on time, on budget, and has the correct functionality. But then the sales team, who are often on the road, are demanding that this functionality be available on their mobile phones. So, the IT team is now tasked with building a mobile app. But the developers building the app aren't able to use any of the work that was done for previous projects. So they have to redo all the work, which in itself is not a great outcome.

Even though the developers know this is likely a short-sighted approach, they justify it given the typically intense time pressures. If there are consultants involved (as is typical), the problem gets worse, as they have little incentive to think about the long term. Over time, changes become very expensive or near impossible to make. But as change is constant, agility is now made very difficult. As you can see below, the familiar "spaghetti code" pattern begins to take shape.

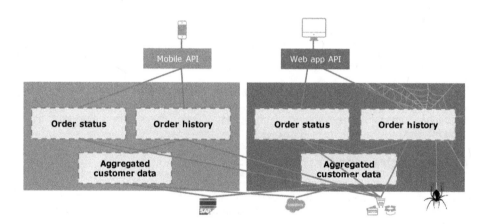

Figure 5. Too many shortcuts lead to the emergence of spaghetti code

With all subsequent projects, more non-reusable code is built anew. This deprecates all the learning and IP from the first project, demotivates developers, creates an unmanageable, duplicative, and expensive code base, and lays the foundation for strangling agility. The apps are now tightly coupled to the underlying endpoints; if anything changes with the endpoints or the business requirements, the entire app or major portions of the code need to be rewritten.

The next application to be built that uses similar data will have to be built from scratch, which means development teams will need the same system experts to get the data out of the source systems, which can add time to project delivery. And, as nothing is registered for security or governance or management, you have lost any visibility as to what is actually going on, which over time, can create security vulnerabilities.

A better way of going about this is through an strategy called API-led connectivity, which enables the new IT operating model. When we think about transitioning to a production + consumption model, core capabilities must be packaged up for consumption. Those core IT assets and capabilities are packaged in a well-designed API.

API-led connectivity is a methodical way to connect data to applications through a series of reusable and purposeful modern

API-led connectivity is a methodical way to connect data to applications through a series of reusable and purposeful modern APIs that are each developed to play a specific role – unlock data from systems, compose data into processes, or deliver an experience. With this approach, rather than connecting things point-to-point, every asset becomes a managed API – a modern API, which makes it discoverable through self-service without losing control.

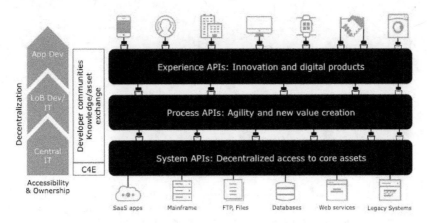

Figure 6. The API-led approach to connectivity

This approach to connectivity classifies APIs in three types:

Systems APIs: Your core systems of record (e.g. ERP, customer and billing systems, proprietary databases etc.) are often not easily accessible because they have proprietary connectivity interfaces and require highly specific skills, which are not readily available within the company (typically a major bottleneck). System APIs provide a means of insulating the user from the complexity or any changes to the underlying systems. Once built, many users, can access data without any need to learn the underlying systems and can reuse these APIs in multiple projects, such as a customer API to be leverage in a mobile app and a partner portal. System experts are not needed for every project that needs access to that system and central IT maintains and governs these APIs, given the importance of the underlying systems. The scope of a System API is to open up and provide consistent managed access to the underlying data. System APIs do not try to normalize the data too much or combine data from other sources.

Process APIs: Naturally, you would have a view of the customer, and order status, prescription status, etc. in this layer. These APIs interact with and shape data within a single system or across systems (breaking down data silos) and are created here without a dependence on the source systems from which that data originates, as well as the target channels through which that data is to be delivered. For example, customer information may be exposed across 2 or 3 system APIs, and you would create a view of the customer by composing fields from those 3 system APIs. This view of the customer might be a canonical model if you have one or it may be specific for the domain the API lives in. This customer API is more consumable because it narrows down all the possible information to just the things need for a set of applications. It's also easy to add new fields or create a different view of the customer for a different domain.

Experience APIs: Data is now consumed across a broad set of channels, each of which wants access to the same data but in a variety of different forms. For example, a retail branch POS system, eCommerce site, and mobile shopping application may all want to access the same customer information fields, but each will require that information in very different formats. Experience APIs are the means by which data can be reconfigured so that it is most easily consumed by its intended audience, all from a common data source, rather than setting up separate point-to-point integrations for each channel. An Experience API is usually created with API-first design principles where the API is designed for the specific use experience in mind.

With this approach, you have essentially "Lego-ified" your business, allowing you to compose, recompose and adapt these building blocks (APIs) to address the changing needs of the business.

So, with API-led connectivity, when your teams are tasked with building a new mobile app, you now have reusable assets to build from, eliminating all of the work needed to build them. And it is now much easier to innovate — in this case, adding shipment status information — in much the same way as you accessed order status and order history.

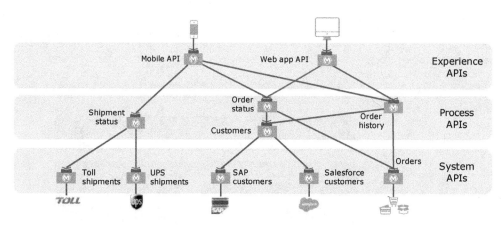

Figure 7. Web and mobile apps built with an API-led approach

An API-led connectivity approach to delivering IT projects ensures you are not only on time and budget with your first projects but you have created reusable assets that will save your company time and money, created an infrastructure which is designed for change, built in visibility, compliance and governance and, most importantly, met the needs of the business, which is long term sustained agility. It enables you to move fast on your first project, but then actually accelerate further from your second project onwards, due to reusable assets and a built-up organizational capability; API-led connectivity liberates resources, allowing you to innovate and to move quickly.

Changing the way your IT team is organized

We have discussed the delivery and technology infrastructure parts of the new IT operating model, but those on their own aren't enough. With a major culture shift that the new model requires, there needs to be a people and business process component as well. We suggest doing this by establishing a cross-functional team called a Center for Enablement, or C4E.

The Center for Enablement (C4E) is a team dedicated to enabling the organization to consume and get full value from the assets. It is typically staffed with members from Central IT, Line-of-business departments, and digital innovation teams and is charged with productizing, publishing and harvesting reusable assets and best practices. They promote consumption and collaboration, and help drives self-reliance while improving delivery through feedback and metrics. It captures the notion that there is balanced deployment approach to each project. The team decides if the project can use a reusable asset and if it should create reusable assets for future projects or if it is a one-off project.

The name might sound similar to an older concept — the Center of Excellence (CoE). However, C4E is a radically different idea. A traditional CoE would feature centralized expertise and knowledge, which would result in information being protected and rationed. CoEs often become bottlenecks which make developers and architects work around them. In contrast, the C4E model focuses on putting valuable assets in the hands of development teams across the organization, encouraging them to not only utilize the assets but add and improve assets as well.

As projects are initiated and developed, a core set of assets such as APIs, templates, common platform capabilities, like logging, caching and error handling as well as documentation, code samples, videos, become the initial asset base for the C4E. These assets must be productized for self-service consumption and published to a central repository like Anypoint Exchange so the assets can be discovered and utilized.

Then, as new projects come along (like the order status web application described earlier), the C4E will engage those project teams and encourage collaboration and reuse of existing assets. As the asset base grows, developers on the innovation teams throughout the organization can be self-reliant. They can find those assets, accelerate the development of their mobile app, add their own API assets for shipping information and feed that capability back to the C4E. This shows the multiplicative power of the community and its concomitant effect on IT delivery capacity.

Unilever, one of the world's largest CPG companies, has used a C4E and achieved great business outcomes. With its large and ever expanding portfolio of products, it was becoming an increasingly difficult process for Unilever to integrate systems across seamlessly for business needs like supply chain management and sale processes. During the last three years, the company started taking steps to decommission its legacy tools while speeding up its integration processes in parallel. Frank Brandes, Unilever's director of global enterprise business integration, started off by creating a Center of Excellence

it served as a bottleneck to business units. It came to be understood that Central IT would need to maintain a degree of control while giving business organizations enough freedom to innovate. The challenge here, Brandes said, is that "If you have too much control, you kill innovation. If you don't have enough control, you don't get the reuse, and you have people moving off in different directions."

Under those circumstances, an Adaptive Integration Capability team (a C4E) was created. It functioned like an internal integration consulting group, going around business units and solving their integration pain points. The team also aimed to provide reusable services on API platforms to shift the focus away from individual assignments to reusable platform capabilities. Not only do business groups have resources for API-led solutions in their possessions now, but the entire company also reaps the benefits of this flexible infrastructure. For example, after Brandes' Adaptive Integration Capability team was created, Unilever completed its SAP ERP integration project and reduced its cost by 26%.

The result is an application network

Making these three changes results in something very powerful emerging — an application network. An application network is a network of applications, data and devices connected with APIs to create reusable services and making them pluggable and unpluggable easily and as business needs require. APIs allow for any digital asset to be quickly and securely discovered and reused by consumers on the application network.
The salient features of an application network are that it:

• Emerges bottoms-up via self-service

• Creates visibility, security and governability at every API node

• Is composable and recomposable: it bends, not breaks. It is built for change.
Ultimately, an application network sets organizations up for speed, agility, and innovation.

Building an application network is not an activity that must take place outside of normal project delivery. Instead, it takes shape through adopting the API-led approach. From the very first project, the nodes of the network are built with all the intrinsic qualities of the network in them – secure, easy to change, discoverable, self-served, ready for reuse, modular, and composable.

Every new node in the network adds exponentially increasing value. Each node is secured by design, ready for self-service and discoverability. For your second project, and every subsequent project, you are delivering against project requirements while at the same time creating more of these reusable self-serve assets on the network.

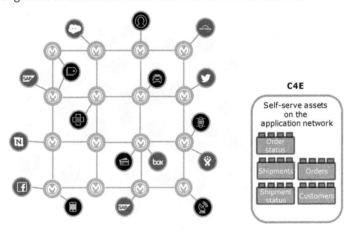

Figure 8. Emergence of an Application Network

These nodes get added from each new project and the value of your application network grows exponentially as more of your data is unlocked. What emerges now is your application network in which the nodes are inherently secure by design, they are easy to add and change. With this the speed with which every subsequent project is delivered begins to accelerate.

The application network is built as a natural yet powerful byproduct of day to day project work done using the API-led connectivity approach with an intention to expose assets that are discoverable, self-served, and consumable by the broader organization. The nodes are highly valuable pieces of a composable enterprise. They are like Lego blocks, which can be used to create an enterprise IT self-serve delivery model which drives speed and creates agility. Given that changes can be accommodated at the node level without breaking the entire architecture, the application network encourages innovation and a mentality to experiment and fail fast.

Why MuleSoft?

Many of these concepts are easy to imitate, and the messages are often repeated by other companies in the market, but MuleSoft is the only company that puts all these pieces together in a comprehensive and proven way. We are the only vendor in this space that offers the capabilities to achieve the new IT operating model that will allow our customers to achieve speed, agility, and innovation.

MuleSoft's Anypoint Platform is the only solution that enables end-to-end connectivity across API, service orchestration, and application integration needs through a single unified platform. This allows developers to rapidly connect, orchestrate and enable any internal or external endpoint. The result is a 2x to 5x faster time to launch new initiatives, connect systems, and unlock data across the enterprise and a 30% reduction in integration costs.

Furthermore, unlike alternatives, MuleSoft's Anypoint Platform can be rapidly deployed on-premises, or accessed as a cloud solution. Since MuleSoft's solutions are easy to use and understand, any developer can quickly become productive without lengthy training in vendor-specific technology resulting in 10% higher employee productivity and 70% higher productivity for app development teams.

Finally, MuleSoft's experience in partnering with our customers to drive digital transformation initiatives gives us unparalleled expertise in change management, organizational design and IT development best practices to complement our technology offerings and truly drive lasting success.

Conclusion

Our research reveals that the IT delivery gap is a real problem for every enterprise, and it isn't going away anytime soon. Yet if organizations don't figure out ways to respond to changing technologies, there will be consequences. Everyone knows they have to change, but the questions remain: What are the best practices? How do I get started?

Organizations ranging from Unilever to Coca-Cola to major banks have all used MuleSoft as a partner in their digital transformation journeys; MuleSoft enables the disciplines of reuse and the consumption model, allowing increased efficiency, productivity, and scalability at never-before-seen levels.

Contact us to find out how MuleSoft can help your company digitally transform.

Connectivity Benchmark Report

The Enterprise's Connected Future: APIs on the Rise

July 2015

Outline

(1) IT Priorities

(2) Integration Index

(3) IoT on the Horizon

(4) APIs Have Arrived

(5) Conclusion

About the survey

Between May 1 and May 6, 2015, MuleSoft surveyed 300 IT decision makers (ITDMs) to assess how organizations of all sizes are implementing and planning for APIs, the Internet of Things (IoT), microservices and other connected technologies.

The survey's overall margin of error is +/-4.17 percentage points at a 90 percent confidence interval.

Executive summary

- The digital era has created new opportunities for enterprises to connect the unconnected. The survey results point to a world that is rapidly embracing digital transformation.

- Traditional businesses are quickly evolving into "composable enterprises" built out of hundreds of connected software services, applications and devices.

- Most are adopting the Internet of Things (IoT) and microservices technologies like Docker. A large number of organizations are integrating wearables, like smart watches.

- APIs are at the center of this business transformation, which is driven by cloud, mobile and IoT. The data reveals that the majority are generating revenue or plan to generate revenue with APIs within the next year.

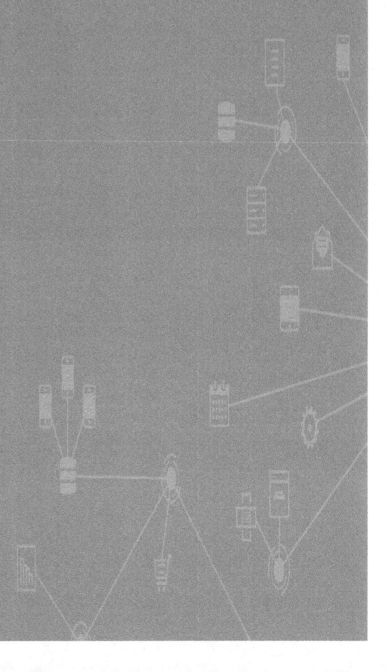

IT Priorities

Most ITDMs are under high pressure to deliver faster

How much pressure are you under currently to deliver IT services faster than last year?

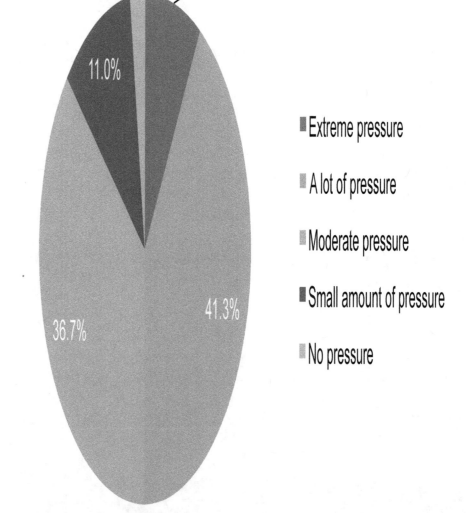

2.3%   8.7%

11.0%

36.7%   41.3%

- Extreme pressure
- A lot of pressure
- Moderate pressure
- Small amount of pressure
- No pressure

86 percent of IT respondents say they're under "moderate" to "extreme" pressure to deliver services faster than last year.

 MuleSoft

SaaS, data and APIs are at the center of business plans

Which will be the most important to your organization's business plans in the next 12 months?

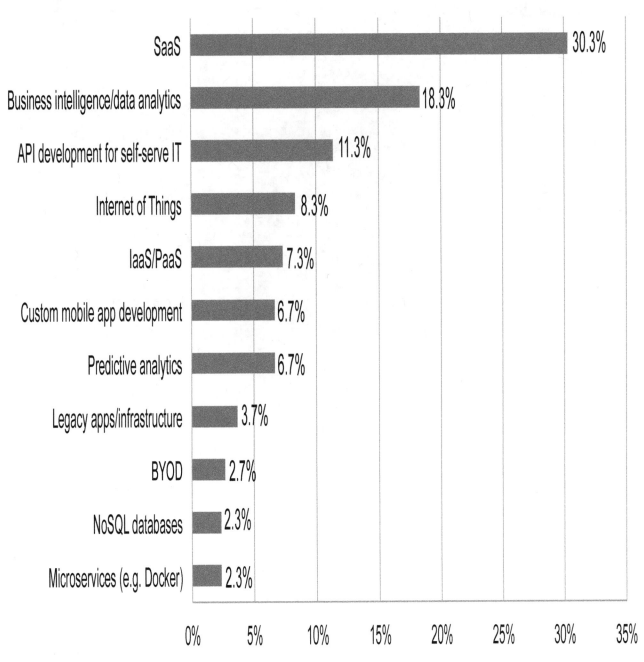

Category	Percentage
SaaS	30.3%
Business intelligence/data analytics	18.3%
API development for self-serve IT	11.3%
Internet of Things	8.3%
IaaS/PaaS	7.3%
Custom mobile app development	6.7%
Predictive analytics	6.7%
Legacy apps/infrastructure	3.7%
BYOD	2.7%
NoSQL databases	2.3%
Microservices (e.g. Docker)	2.3%

 MuleSoft

Microservices are more than a buzzword

How important are microservices (e.g. Docker) to your organization's business plans in the next 12 months?

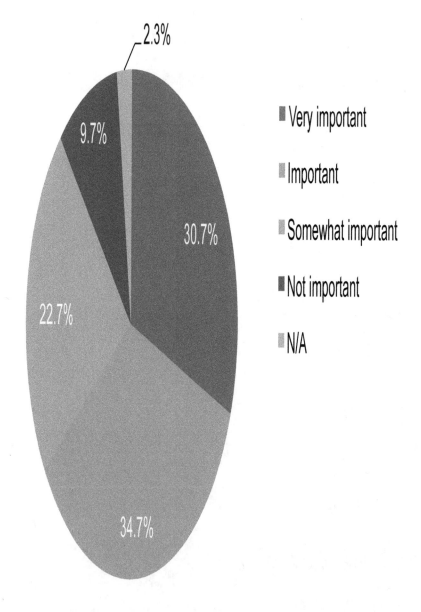

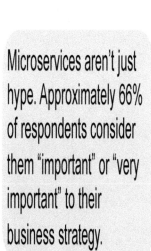

Microservices aren't just hype. Approximately 66% of respondents consider them "important" or "very important" to their business strategy.

- Very important
- Important
- Somewhat important
- Not important
- N/A

2.3%
9.7%
30.7%
22.7%
34.7%

 MuleSoft

Mobile is driving new investment

How do you characterize your organization's investment in mobile platforms and applications?

All ITDM respondents

Large enterprises (10,000 employees or more)

■ Investing more

■ Investing about the same

■ Divesting

■ N/A

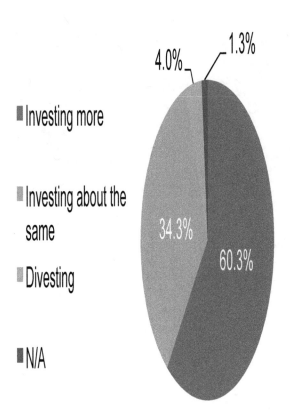

4.0%
1.3%
34.3%
60.3%

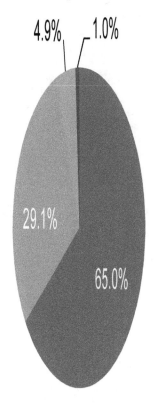

4.9%
1.0%
29.1%
65.0%

More ITDMs are increasing their investment in mobile. Approximately two-thirds of large enterprises (10,000 employees or more) will be investing more in mobile.

 MuleSoft

Integration Index

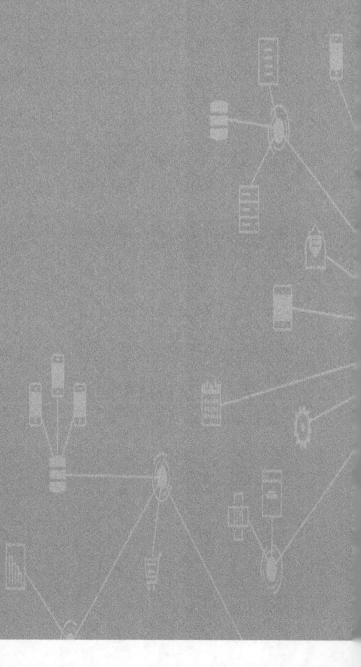

SaaS is the top integration priority

Which will be your top integration priority in the next 12 months?

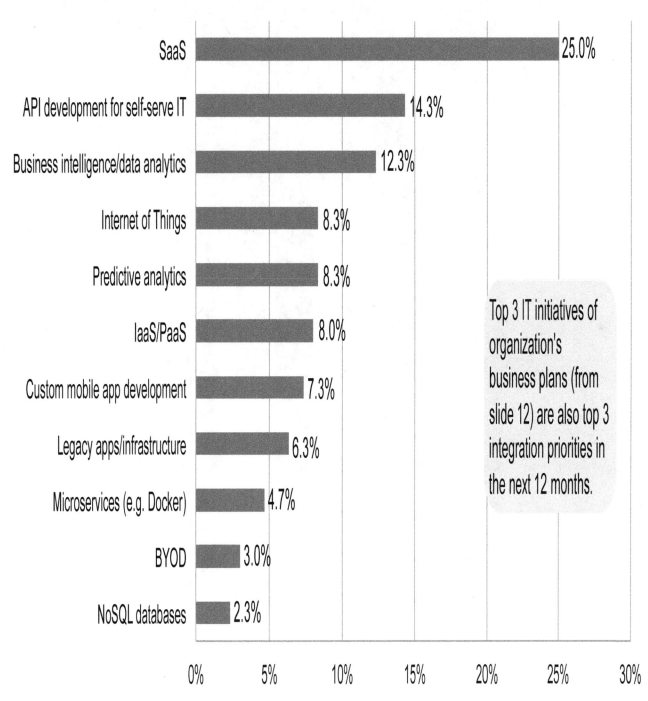

SaaS	25.0%
API development for self-serve IT	14.3%
Business intelligence/data analytics	12.3%
Internet of Things	8.3%
Predictive analytics	8.3%
IaaS/PaaS	8.0%
Custom mobile app development	7.3%
Legacy apps/infrastructure	6.3%
Microservices (e.g. Docker)	4.7%
BYOD	3.0%
NoSQL databases	2.3%

Top 3 IT initiatives of organization's business plans (from slide 12) are also top 3 integration priorities in the next 12 months.

 MuleSoft

73% of organizations integrate more than 20 apps

Approximately how many applications does your organization currently integrate?

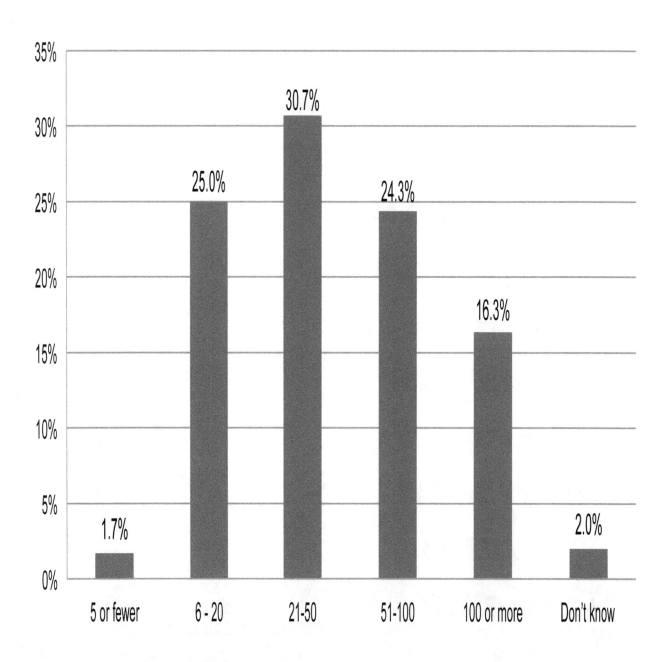

The largest organizations integrate 100+ apps

Approximately how many applications does your organization currently integrate?

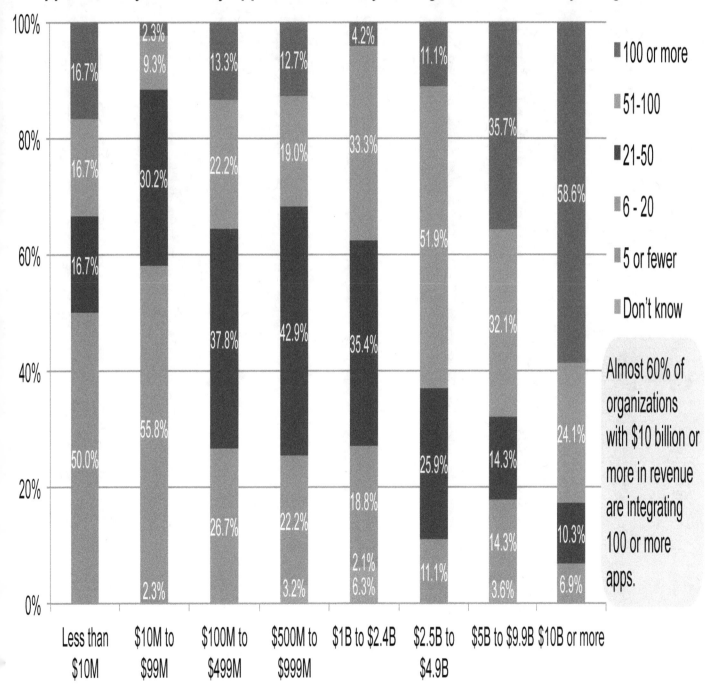

Almost 60% of organizations with $10 billion or more in revenue are integrating 100 or more apps.

 MuleSoft

Healthcare is the biggest integrator

Approximately how many applications does your organization currently integrate?

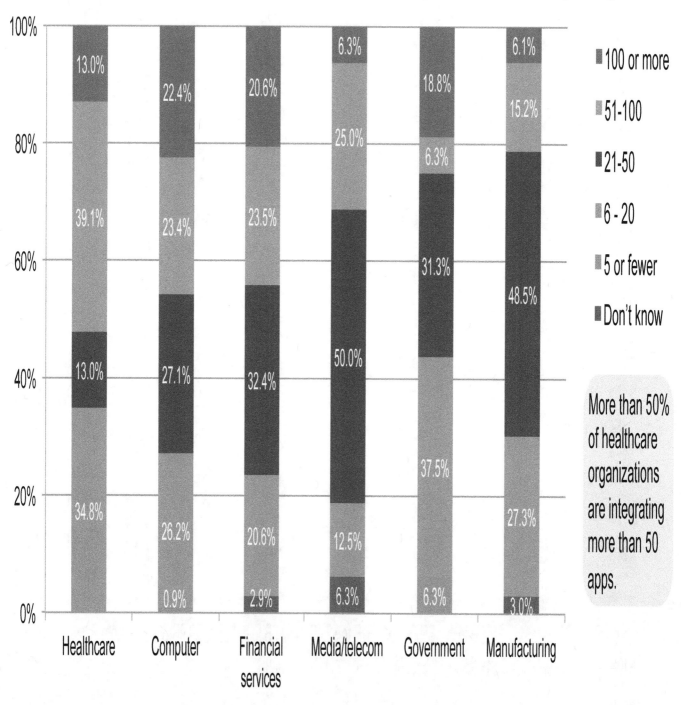

Legend:
- 100 or more
- 51-100
- 21-50
- 6 - 20
- 5 or fewer
- Don't know

More than 50% of healthcare organizations are integrating more than 50 apps.

MuleSoft

IoT on the Horizon

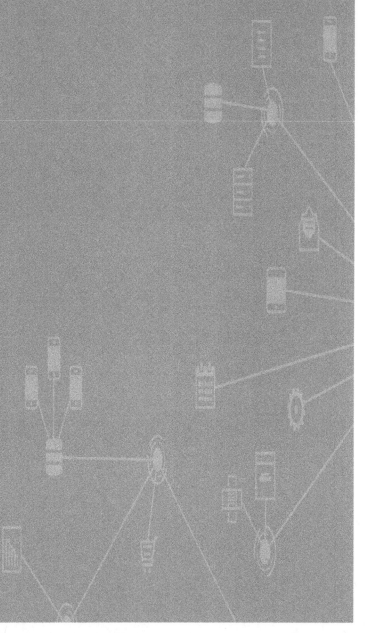

IoT may be coming sooner than we think

How important is the Internet of Things (IoT) to your organization's business plans in the next 12 months?

Approximately 75% of ITDMs ranked IoT as "very important" or "important" to their business plans over the next 12 months.

Top industries focusing on IoT this year include:
- Financial services (50%)
- Media/telecom (50%)
- Healthcare (44%)

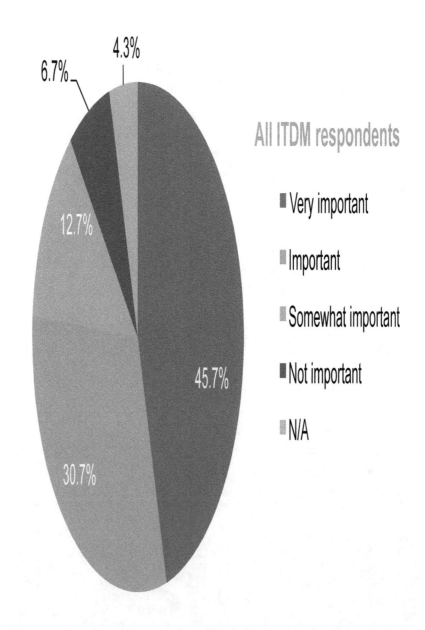

All ITDM respondents

- Very important
- Important
- Somewhat important
- Not important
- N/A

4.3%
6.7%
12.7%
45.7%
30.7%

 MuleSoft

IoT strategies are already in place

Does your organization have an Internet of Things (IoT) strategy?

77% of organizations say they already have an IoT strategy. Top industries reporting an IoT strategy are:

- Computer (84%)
- Healthcare (83%)
- Financial services (79%)

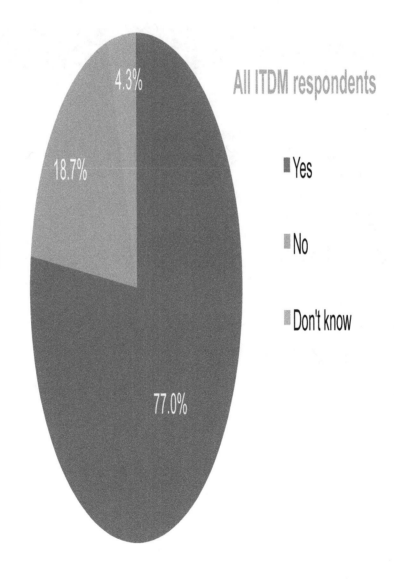

All ITDM respondents

- Yes
- No
- Don't know

17

 MuleSoft

Customer engagement is driving IoT strategy

What are the main drivers of your organization's IoT strategy?

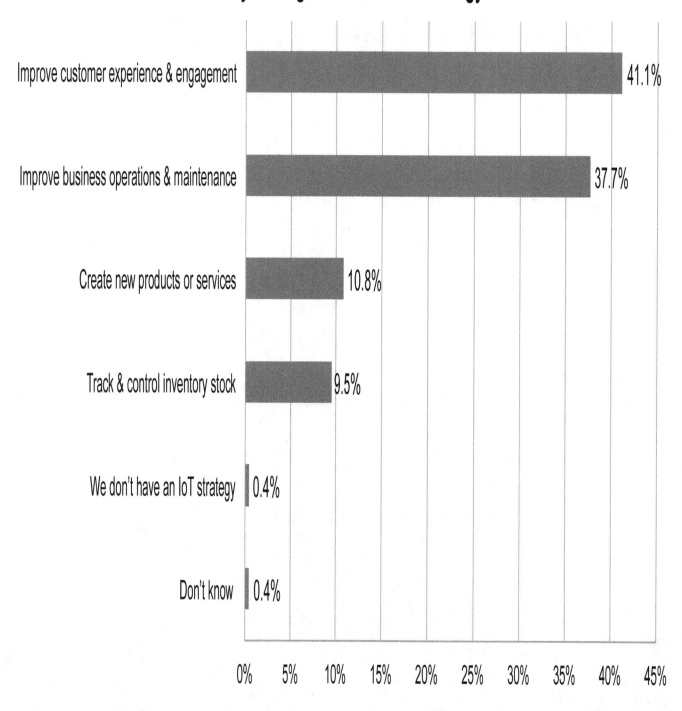

Driver	Percentage
Improve customer experience & engagement	41.1%
Improve business operations & maintenance	37.7%
Create new products or services	10.8%
Track & control inventory stock	9.5%
We don't have an IoT strategy	0.4%
Don't know	0.4%

 MuleSoft

Wearables are gaining momentum

Which of the following best describes how your company is currently connecting or integrating wearables (e.g. smart watch, smart glasses)?

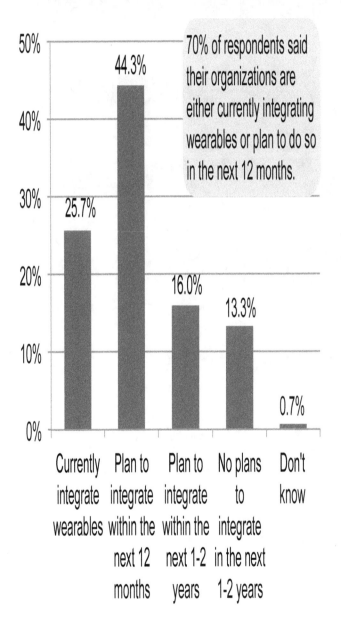

70% of respondents said their organizations are either currently integrating wearables or plan to do so in the next 12 months.

All ITDM respondents

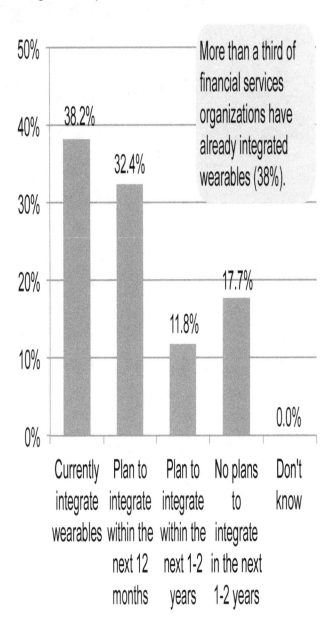

More than a third of financial services organizations have already integrated wearables (38%).

Financial services ITDM respondents

19

 MuleSoft

Top industries eyeing wearables in the next year

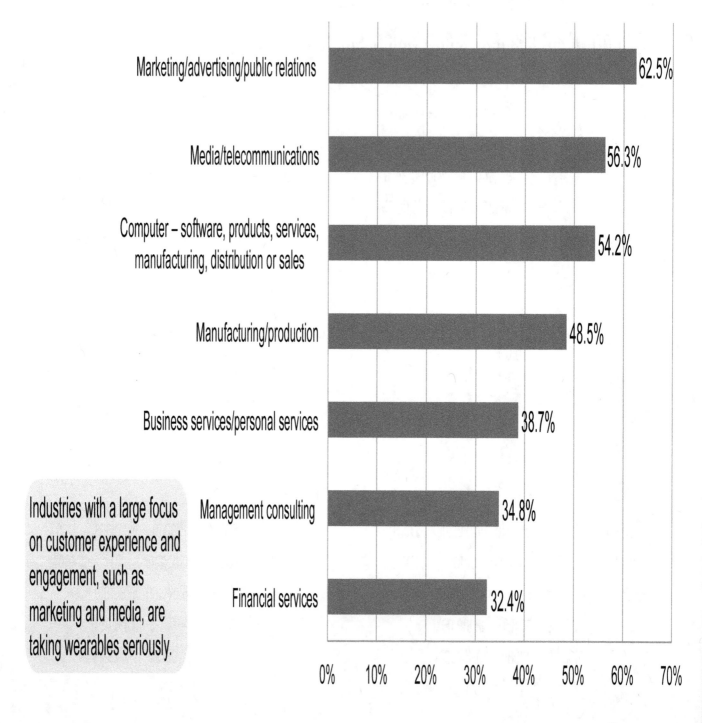

Industries with a large focus on customer experience and engagement, such as marketing and media, are taking wearables seriously.

Marketing/advertising/public relations — 62.5%
Media/telecommunications — 56.3%
Computer – software, products, services, manufacturing, distribution or sales — 54.2%
Manufacturing/production — 48.5%
Business services/personal services — 38.7%
Management consulting — 34.8%
Financial services — 32.4%

MuleSoft

APIs Have Arrived

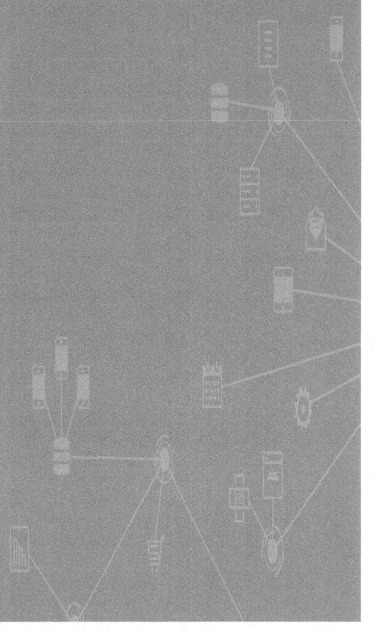

APIs are for everyone

Does your company have an API strategy?

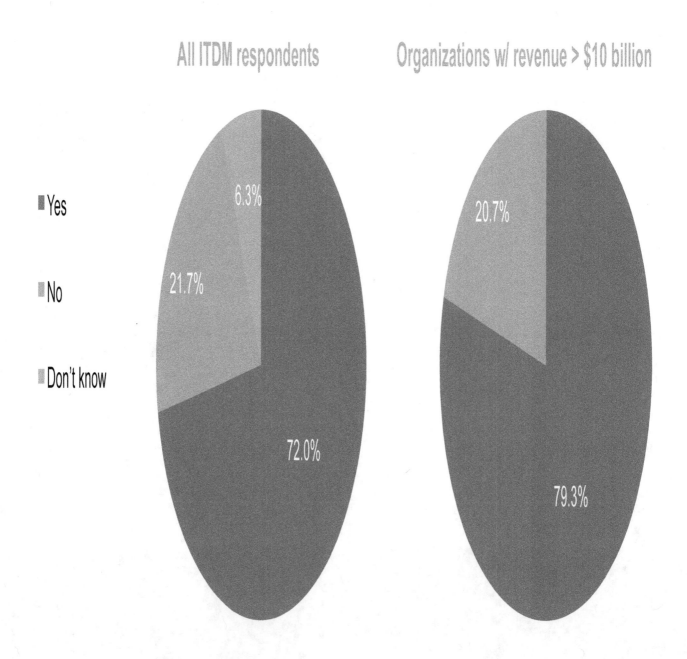

All ITDM respondents

Organizations w/ revenue > $10 billion

- Yes
- No
- Don't know

6.3%

21.7%

72.0%

20.7%

79.3%

MuleSoft

Software integration is a top driver of API strategies

What business needs are driving your organization's API strategy?

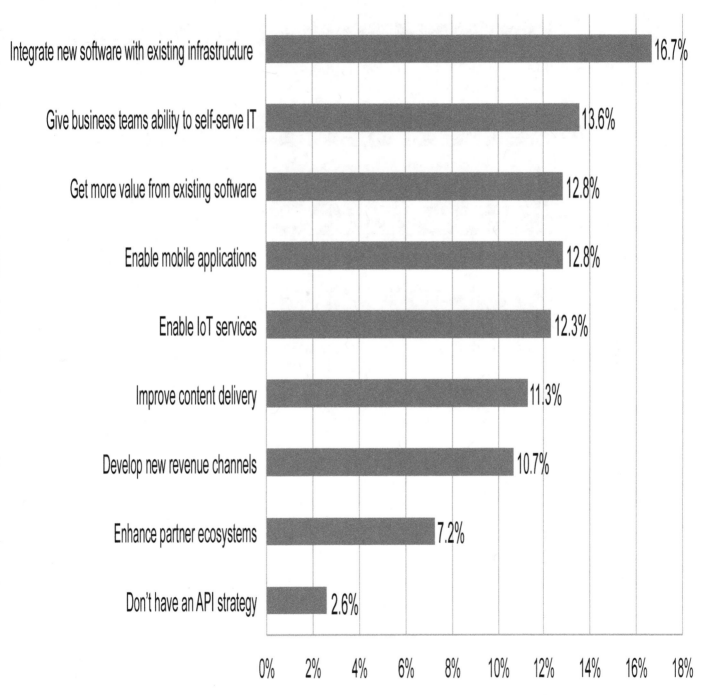

Business Need	Percentage
Integrate new software with existing infrastructure	16.7%
Give business teams ability to self-serve IT	13.6%
Get more value from existing software	12.8%
Enable mobile applications	12.8%
Enable IoT services	12.3%
Improve content delivery	11.3%
Develop new revenue channels	10.7%
Enhance partner ecosystems	7.2%
Don't have an API strategy	2.6%

 MuleSoft

Revenue is a top reason for having an API strategy

What is the most important value that APIs add to the business?

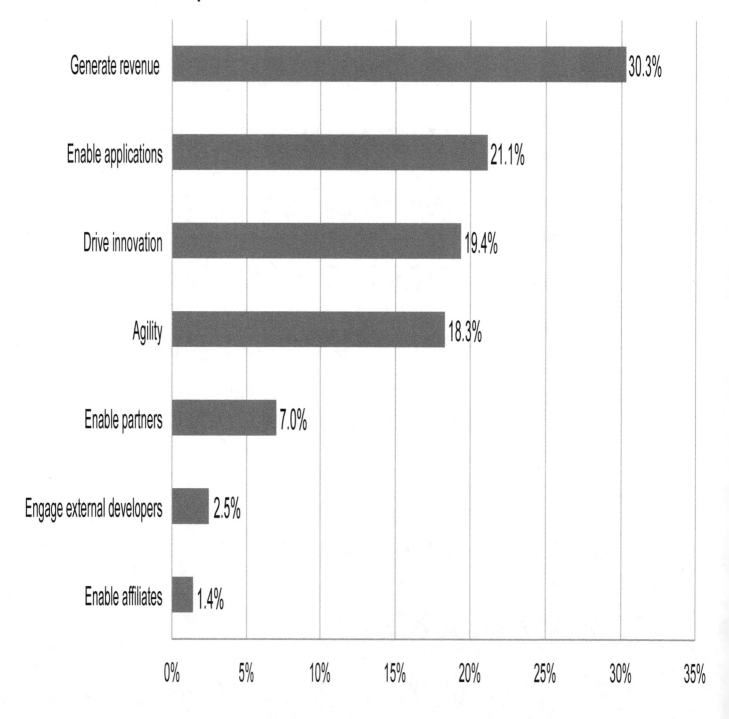

Generate revenue	30.3%
Enable applications	21.1%
Drive innovation	19.4%
Agility	18.3%
Enable partners	7.0%
Engage external developers	2.5%
Enable affiliates	1.4%

MuleSoft

Most generating revenue from APIs (or will be)

What's your company's timeline for generating revenue through APIs?

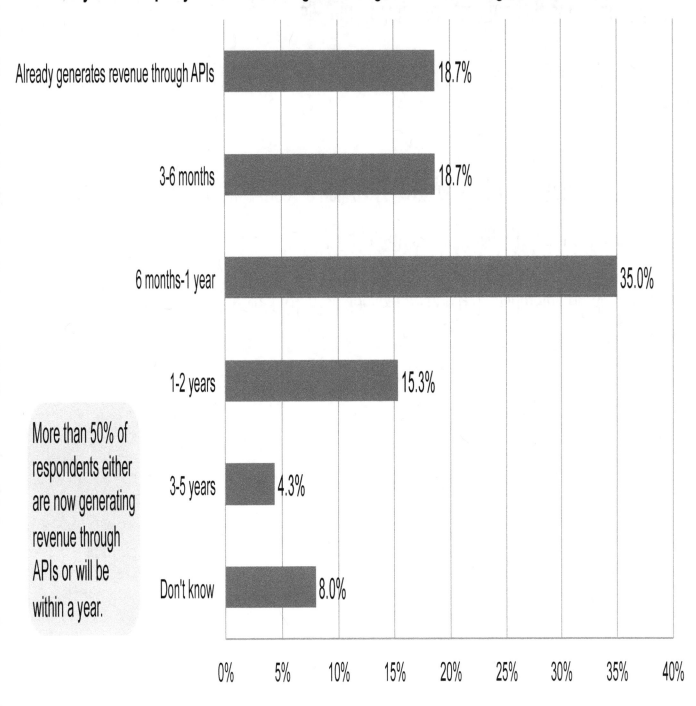

Already generates revenue through APIs — 18.7%

3-6 months — 18.7%

6 months-1 year — 35.0%

1-2 years — 15.3%

3-5 years — 4.3%

Don't know — 8.0%

More than 50% of respondents either are now generating revenue through APIs or will be within a year.

0% 5% 10% 15% 20% 25% 30% 35% 40%

25

 MuleSoft

Making millions with APIs

Of organizations that generate revenue from APIs:

- 73% indicated that their company makes more than $500,000 a year from APIs.

- 72% of organizations with revenue of $10 billion or more indicated that their company makes more than $10 million a year from APIs.

- 80% of large enterprises (10,000 employees or more) say that their company makes more than $5 million a year from APIs.

  - 30% say $5-10 million a year

  - 50% say $10 million or more a year

- 50% of media/telecom and 33% of financial services organizations indicated their company makes more than $10 million a year from APIs.

Conclusion

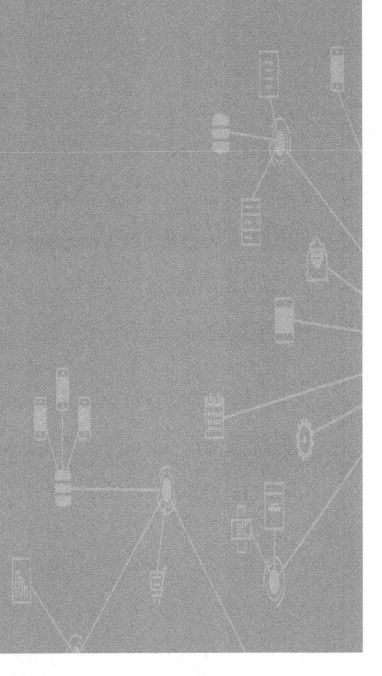

CIO takeaways

- **Organizations are adopting new technologies fast:** CIOs will be under pressure to enable and accelerate innovation across the enterprise. They will hold a significant role to connect the unconnected, delivering real-time information across current and new systems, applications and devices, to enable new products and services or improve what they already have.

- **The new role of connectivity goes beyond integrating back office systems**: There is a shift in the CIO mindset from project to project delivery inside the organization to opening up the value of the organization. CIOs will need to find ways to unlock this value and allow the business to actually take part in creating new digital experiences, services and products.

- **APIs are driving business strategy**: Many organizations are already realizing business impact from APIs. CIOs will play an increasingly strategic role in creating and supporting new lines of business that sell services through APIs.

For any questions or sales inquires, contact MuleSoft at info@mulesoft.com or 1-415-229-2009.

Deliver zero message loss environments that scale
A guide to cloud messaging with Anypoint MQ and Anypoint Platform

Introduction

Most enterprises need to change the way they operate, which is driven by two challenges. First, consumers are demanding that everything be always on and always mobile. This puts the enterprise under tremendous pressure to unlock their data and processes to deliver new consumer apps and open new digital channels. Second, technology is now adopted by every corner of the enterprise. This means the demand for connectivity between technology investments within and outside the enterprise keeps growing rapidly. It also means the cost of building and maintaining connections the old way has become unsustainable.

Many IT organizations have tried to address these challenges by taking old operating models for IT and pushing them harder and faster. As those approaches weren't designed for automation and agility, they aren't working. Instead, MuleSoft recommends a modern IT operating model to better align IT outcomes with those of the business, an approach we call API-led connectivity. By adopting API-led connectivity, the most successful enterprises are creating outcomes alignment across the business, delivering on IT and business initiatives quickly through an application network that unlocks critical assets and ensures information flows between systems reliably and securely on a platform built to scale. This whitepaper will focus on how organizations can use messaging, specifically Anypoint MQ and Anypoint Platform, to provide reliable, zero message loss environments, decouple applications to enable scale, and to unlock data for broader distribution.

How messaging can solve enterprise IT challenges

Increasingly, organizations must act in real time to connect with employees, partners, and customers. Messaging plays a critical role in making these connections and has become a critical pattern in most enterprise architectures. In healthcare, for example, a messaging pattern might be used to create a buffer between the electronic medical records system and any number of consuming applications who need to know when a patient record has been updated. Or in retail, a messaging pattern might be used to ensure a customer can have a seamless experience as they modify their shopping cart across, in-store, web, and mobile channels. Or in IoT applications, a thermostat can use a message queue to perform an over-the-air firmware update to numerous devices distributed across the world to roll out a security fix or an application enhancement.

Generally, messaging enables four core architectural outcomes:

Scalability
By decoupling applications with a traditional asynchronous publish/subscribe messaging pattern, applications that publish messages to a large number of consumers can be scaled without spinning up new servers or infrastructure. Asynchronous processing also enables receiving applications to operate at their individual peak capability without affecting other applications.

Reliability
By enabling both the sender and receiver of a message to provide acknowledgement of delivery and receipt, messaging patterns enable zero message loss reliability. A common pattern is to persist a message in a queue until the receiving application has acknowledged receipt as both successful and complete. Similarly, if a message queue supports idempotency, the receiver can block duplicate messages to avoid creating problems in the receiving application.

Durability
A highly available message queue enables architects to provide guaranteed delivery either at least once or only once depending on the desired outcome. These fail safes enhance the durability of an architecture. If, for example, a receiver fails in processing a message or is disconnected while processing the message, the message can be stored and played back

by the sender after the receiver is restarted.

Data consistency
Sharing data between applications to ensure data consistency across the enterprise is becoming a top-level concern for many enterprise architects. With a messaging layer in place, enterprises can send information to multiple receivers that need to be kept in sync regardless of where they are located -- on-premises or in the cloud.

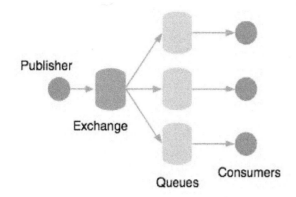

Figure 1. A typical publish/subscribe pattern with multiple queues and an exchange

Delivering messaging in the cloud

Until now, most messaging has been driven by on-premises technology requirements. As connectivity moves more to the cloud, the ability to deliver messaging patterns in the cloud and connect services and applications located globally with zero message loss reliability becomes increasingly important. That's why MuleSoft created Anypoint MQ.

In addition to the four outcomes outlined above, Anypoint MQ provides:

Hybrid connectivity
With Anypoint MQ, queues and exchanges live in the cloud, receive messages from cloud and on-premises systems and send messages to cloud and on-premises systems, increasing both operational efficiency and architectural agility.

Global connectivity
On-premise technology cannot keep up with the information generated globally from proliferation of mobile devices, wearables, and multitude of purchasing channels. Anypoint MQ is available in multiple regions across the world and supports deployment of the same application across multiple global datacenters.

Flexibility
Different types of applications have different processing times. Anypoint MQ enables throttling through which individual applications can operate at their peak throughput without affecting other applications. This creates flexibility in planning infrastructure upgrades instead of requiring computing infrastructure to be well-matched across applications.

Security
Anypoint MQ provides out of the box industry standard passphrase based encryption at rest for messages that traverse through the queue. As a service of Anypoint Platform, Anypoint MQ delivers comprehensive queue and client management from the same pane of glass used to manage APIs, applications and other Anypoint Platform resources.

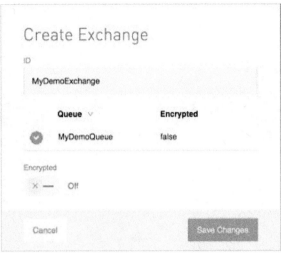

Figure 2. Secure queues and exchanges by enabling the 'Encrypted' option

Anypoint MQ: a next generation messaging solution

With Anypoint MQ, Anypoint Platform users can perform advanced asynchronous messaging scenarios such as queueing and pub/sub with fully hosted and managed cloud message queues and exchanges. A service of Anypoint Platform, Anypoint MQ supports environments, business groups, and role-based access control (RBAC) to help you deliver seamless customer experiences across channels and integrate devices reliably for Internet of Things (IoT) applications with enterprise-class functionality.

Specifically, Anypoint MQ includes:

Queues and Exchanges: send messages to queues, pull messages from queues, or create a message exchange to perform pub/sub scenarios and send a message to multiple queues, decoupling applications and enabling scale.
Easy connectivity: send/receive messages from any Mule application running in the cloud or on-premises. MuleSoft's REST API allows easy interface with non-Mule applications.
Secure, reliable message delivery: persistent data storage across multiple data centers, ensuring that it can handle data center outages and have full disaster recovery. Queues can also be encrypted so data at rest is secured.
Unified management: fully integrated with Anypoint Platform, offering role-based access control, client application management, queue statistics and status monitoring, queue management and environment management

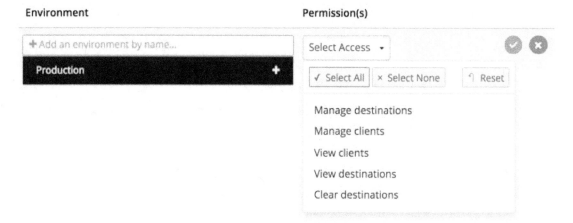

Figure 3. Define user permissions by environment

NOTE: Anypoint MQ is not currently available for deployment on-premises. For customers with cloud restrictions, MuleSoft provides pre-built connectivity to a number of proprietary and legacy messaging on-premises messaging solutions, including MSMQ and IBM Websphere MQ as well as common messaging protocols like AMQP and JMS. For customers who wish to have a fully supported on-premises messaging deployment, MuleSoft provides support for ActiveMQ when used in conjunction with the Mule runtime engine in a predefined set of use cases. For more information on our supported ActiveMQ offering, please contact your account team.

Using Anypoint MQ

With Anypoint MQ, MuleSoft enables customers to deliver messaging on a solution designed in the cloud, making it fully elastic and multi-tenanted out of the box. Below, we've provided a few examples of how Anypoint MQ could be used.

Routing messages to cloud and on-premises systems

Many organizations have processes in place for updating customer records in their cloud CRM -- updates that on-premises customer DBs and ERPs need to consume to keep data consistent. Rather than sending customer updates individually, an unreliable and error prone pattern, with Anypoint MQ one could set up a cloud exchange with hybrid connectivity. Through this exchange, the on-premises systems could subscribe to any published updates from the cloud application, pull these messages down into their respective consumer queues, and process messages at their own pace. By putting acknowledgements in place to ensure the messages are received and processed successfully, this would provide a highly reliable delivery system.

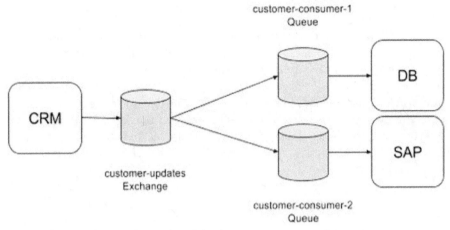

Figure 4. A diagram showing the routing of cloud messages to on-premises systems

Competing consumers
Frequently in messaging scenarios, there are multiple consumers vying to receive messages from a single point-to-point channel. When the channel delivers a message, consumers can compete with each other to be the receiver. Once a consumer receives a message, the message will be locked, preventing other from receiving it unless the lock is released. This pattern allows tasks to be efficiently distributed across multiple competing workers without losing tasks. This pattern is used when balancing the processing load at the receiver endpoints or to optimize throughput. With the global connectivity available with Anypoint MQ, throughput can be further optimized by delivering messages in the datacenter closest to the receiving application.

Processing peak e-commerce traffic around Black Friday
E-commerce applications running in the cloud typically process large numbers of requests from multiple distributed clients. Processing these requests synchronously as they arrive works during off-peak hours, but won't scale to handle peak demand. By pushing requests into a cloud-based messaging queue and then allowing other services to process these requests asynchronously, applications won't block requests from multiple clients, allowing more clients to connect to the application and place orders, providing a better customer experience and making the application scalable without requiring massive investment in servers and infrastructure.

Supporting microservices and service oriented architectures
With the advent of microservices architecture, many cloud applications involve tasks that invoke shared services such as a query service or storage service. When multiple applications invoke these shared services, it may overload the system and result in the service failing altogether. A message queue can act as a buffer or enabling loose coupling between the application and shared services. Delivering this queue in the cloud provides the flexibility to scale up and down in line with the needs of the respective microservice.

Compensating transactions
One of the classic cases for messaging is the use of a single booking web service to book a flight, hotel room, and rental car at the same time. The booking web service invokes services of the flight booking system, the hotel booking system and the rental car booking system, each of which is developed and architected in a different manner. If the user books through the service, the flight and rental cars get confirmed, but the hotel room is no longer available at the original price, the transaction would be incomplete. Without a compensating transaction roll back, either the consumer of the booking service or booking service could suffer financial loss. Anypoint MQ provides a 2 phase commit model with the ability to rollback transactions if an abort response is ever received to avoid this problem.

IoT applications

As consumers become more tech savvy and comfortable using connected devices, they expect their home security systems to talk to their home energy management systems such as thermostat, HVAC and lighting controls. For example, a user could arm their security system while leaving for work and expect the security system to set back the thermostat temperature setting and turn off lights to save energy. These IoT devices have serious interoperability issues and rarely communicate with each other at the physical layers; instead many of these devices stream data to device clouds managed by different vendors which are part of different ecosystems such as Google's Brillo, Apple's Homekit or Samsung's Smartthings. To get these devices working together, the device clouds could use Anypoint MQ to publish and subscribe encrypted data streams of interest, thus allowing the different devices to communicate with each other in a highly scalable, distributed, protocol agnostic, and secure manner.

Case study

One of the world's leading independent biotechnology companies needed a reliable way of sharing patient enrollment and clinical trial assignment details coming from a newly purchased third party system across a number of cloud and on-premises systems. Familiar with ActiveMQ and needing to host the solution in the cloud to reduce operational overhead and ensure scalability, this MuleSoft customer was planning to purchase and manage their own AWS instance with ActiveMQ installed when they discovered Anypoint MQ. With Anypoint MQ, they were able to deliver a cloud-based exchange with cloud and on-premises subscribers and establish receipt criteria to ensure each subscriber could acknowledge message delivery and receipt. As use of the third party system grows, the firm is confident they'll be able quickly scale their implementation and manage the complex messaging use cases with Anypoint MQ. By removing the burden of configuring and managing their own cloud ActiveMQ deployment, building out encryption policies, and delivering highly available queues, the firm is able to instead focus on the intended outcome -- ensuring a reliable consumer experience.

Conclusion

With Anypoint MQ, users of Anypoint Platform can perform advanced asynchronous messaging scenarios such as queueing and pub/sub with fully hosted and managed cloud message queues and exchanges. A service of Anypoint Platform, Anypoint MQ supports environments, business groups, and role-based access control (RBAC) providing simplified management. Finally, Anypoint MQ helps organizations power APIs that better connect assets to audiences, create compelling customer, employee and partner experiences, and allow the business to transform and succeed in today's digital world.

To access Anypoint MQ, sign up for a trial of <u>Anypoint Platform</u> and contact your account team to ensure the trial Anypoint MQ entitlement is available within your account.

Digital Transformation in Higher Education
How to increase the clock speed of IT delivery

Executive Summary

Institutions of higher education are under pressure from demographic and technological changes. The pool of potential students in North America is shrinking due to demographic changes, resulting in more institutions competing over the same pool of students. Globally, the number of students enrolling in tertiary education is expanding; as an example, the population of OECD countries aged 25-34 with higher education degrees exceed that of older generations by 16 percentage points.[1] Many of those students want to go to the world's elite institutions, particularly those in the US; the number of international students in American universities has doubled in the last 20 years.[2] The globalization of higher education further increases competition at top universities worldwide and provides an impetus for universities to competitively differentiate from their peers. As Chris Wessells, the Vice Provost and Chief Information Officer of the University of San Diego points out, "With the rapid innovation and intense competition between top private universities today, the experience has to be exceptional."[3]

Today's students are exceptionally well-versed in technology and it has shaped their lives; they want the same consumer technology experiences at their universities that they experience in other aspects of their daily routine. In addition, as university IT departments field requests to develop technological solutions for their stakeholders - students, faculty, administrators, etc., demands on their time are growing at a rapid rate. With a limited number of resources, it becomes difficult to cope with the requests. Finally, as online learning and MOOC providers like Khan Academy and Coursera are becoming an increasingly important part of the educational experience, universities want to re-imagine learning as something that occurs outside of the traditional bounds of the lecture hall.

Satisfying these demands using traditional IT delivery methods is beyond the capacity of any IT team in any industry, but perhaps especially so at an institution of higher learning. There is a cap on what IT can deliver with a certain amount of resources, and with the need for technology solutions from every part of the institution growing exponentially, the university's central IT department will need to find another way to increase capacity.

This whitepaper will delve into how institutions like MIT, the University of San Diego, and the University of Oklahoma are using MuleSoft's approach to enterprise integration, called API-led connectivity, to create an application network that seamlessly delivers applications, data, and devices and increases IT delivery capacity through composable, reusable services. An application network increases the clock speed of technology at these universities, makes technology delivery more efficient, and lowers operational costs.

> "With the rapid innovation and intense competition between top universities today, the experience has to be exceptional...we are always looking for something new and innovative to enhance the student experience."
>
> -Chris Wessells, Vice Provost and Chief Information Officer, University of San Diego

Introduction

It's said that we are in the "fourth industrial revolution,"[4] and the forces of digital disruption have deeply affected businesses of every size and in every industry. Those forces are affecting the higher education industry like every other, but there are also prevailing winds unique to colleges and universities that are causing profound disruption. There are

---

[1] OECD Publishing, Education at a Glance 2015.

[2] Tyce, Henry, Pagano, Ernesto, Puckett, J., and Wilson, Joanne. "Five Trends to Watch in Higher Education." Boston Consulting Group, April 10, 2014.

[3] LePoideven, Sylvia. "University of San Diego Revolutionizes Study Abroad with WISE Built on Google Maps and Google Cloud Platform." Sadasystems.com, February 10, 2015.

[4] Wladawsky-Berger, Irving. "Preparing for the Fourth Industrial Revolution." The Wall Street Journal, February 26, 2016.

several major trends - demographic, technological, and cultural - that are creating challenges and opportunities for higher education leaders and driving technological change at nearly all institutions.

One key differentiator from most industries is that its most visible and prestigious members are non-profits; for these institutions, their competitive threats do not usually culminate in obsolescence, decreased revenue or new entrants to the market, but rather constitute a battle to attract the most talented students who want personalized communications from the university throughout their lifecycle from applicant to student to alumnus. In addition, these students are the most digitally savvy consumers on earth, and expect the higher education product they purchase to have the same amount of constant availability and convenience as all other aspects of their lives. Their demand for always-on, always-connected services is changing the educational market and driving demand for new experiences in the most important investment of their lives to date.

According to the National Center of Education Statistics, there are over 4,600 degree-granting institutions in the United States as of 2015, and they each are under pressure to attract students, produce scholarly output, and raise funds for their operations. While the competitive forces at work in higher education do not have quite the same effects as those affecting other industries, these global trends are still driving change and modernization, and creating challenges and opportunities for which universities are seeking solutions.

Three Trends Driving Change in Higher Education IT

I. Business Drivers

There are inexorable demographic trends that are problematic for American universities. According to the Boston Consulting Group, "as a result of a bubble made up of the children of baby boomers, the number of high-school graduates peaked in 2011 and is projected to continue falling or to stay the same until 2024," creating a smaller pool of applicants from which to choose. Since colleges derive most of their revenue from tuition and fees, declining enrollment could put institutions at financial risk.[5]

As a result, budgets are under pressure. It is possible to reduce administrative overhead, and processes, but technology expectations are growing year over year, and they're not just coming from the students. There are numerous stakeholders wanting technology throughout universities, whether it's researchers needing the latest technology or admissions officers needing better CRM solutions.

Case Study: Massachusetts Institute of Technology

MIT is one of the most prestigious institutions in the world; their head of IT, John Charles, has a vision and a plan to bring their IT systems in line with the cutting-edge research the university is doing. Called the 20/20 Plan, the idea, as John Charles puts it, is to "modernize the systems that widely support MIT's administrative services and educational enterprise, we also want to enable the MIT community to innovate IT services in response to its diverse and specialized needs. I believe these two complementary approaches will allow IS&T to better meet the needs of our community."

Stephen Turner, an enterprise architect tasked with carrying out the 20/20 plan, noted the challenges that his staff had to overcome.

"We have to modernize our legacy services. A an example is our SAP platform, which we've had in-house for 20 years. We also have to enable the MIT community to serve themselves and do things for themselves by giving them better data--better access to data that we have locked away in our backend systems and our services. Web APIs are the key here.

The use of AnyPoint Platform has made it easier for us to provide these APIs. We feel that developing integrations is made relatively easy by the tooling that the AnyPoint Platform gives us.

We find that deploying our applications that we build -- the integration applications and APIs--is very, very easy using CloudHub."

---

[5] Ibid.

Every IT department is facing the following dilemma - the demands on them to deliver technology are growing exponentially, but their capacity to deliver remains the same:

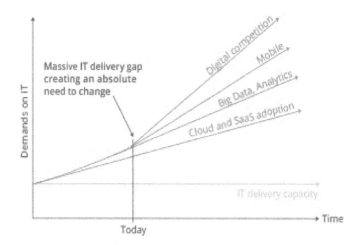

University central IT departments face a challenge for their resources due to the external nature of their budgets, competitive pressures, and the demands of multiple stakeholders with multiple and multi-faceted technological needs. A solution is needed urgently.

II. Student Engagement

The current cohort of American college students are famously some of the most technology savvy in the world. 85% of Americans aged 18-24 own a smartphone[6] and spend a third of their time on their devices using social networking apps, the most common of which are Facebook, Instagram, and Snapchat.[7]

But in addition to spending their free time on their devices, this group wants to learn using mobile technology as well. 81% of students use devices like smartphones and tablets to study, 77% say mobile technology has improved their grades, and 62% say that mobile technology leaves them better prepared for classes. This emphasis on mobile is changing the way students learn. Sharon Loeb, vice president of marketing for McGraw-Hill Education Higher Ed, the sponsor of the research, points out that "mobile suit[s] the way students study now. The feedback we've received from students and instructors suggests that today's students tend toward shorter, more concentrated bursts of studying anywhere they're able, rather than waiting for several hours to hunker down in the library...institutions will need to adapt their infrastructure and faculty will want to consider ways to incorporate mobile learning into their courses."[8]

[6] Nielsen. "Mobile millenials: over 85% of Generation Y owns smartphones." September 5, 2014.

[7] Comscore. The 2015 Mobile App report. September 20, 2015.

[8] McGraw-Hill Education. New McGraw-Hill Education Research Finds More than 80 Percent of Students Use Mobile Technology to Study. March 9, 2015.

This means that IT staffs are going to have to figure out ways to deliver mobile capability to students, faculty, and administrators. Chris Wessells, the Vice Provost and Chief Information Officer at the University of San Diego says, "We are always looking for something new and innovative to enhance the student experience. As the CIO, I feel that giving students applications that are personal and effective, in the palm of their hand, is a key strategy for the university and for the central IT organization that I run."[9]

In order to create those mobile experiences, IT teams are in demand from many different areas of the institution - faculty departments, the registrar's office, financial aid, etc. - to orchestrate that data and make it available on mobile devices. To do that, data currently housed in various databases and departmental siloes needs to be exposed and transformed to make it easily readable by many different systems. IT needs a way of unlocking that data and making it freely available to everyone who needs it in order to create the experience that students, faculty, and other parties expect.

III. Reframing Learning and Educational Content

Technology has brought with it the chance for the democratization and greater accessibility to higher education through MOOCs. MOOCs are not restricted to online education providers like Khan Academy and Coursera; traditional institutions of higher learning are experimenting with them as a way to broaden their educational communities and add additional dynamism to the classroom experience.

Case Study: The University of San Diego

The University of San Diego has over 8000 students, 50 applications in use, and hundreds of integrations. Their goal as a university is to provide better customer experiences, so the supporting IT initiative needed to provide the infrastructure to make that happen. This meant integration of their CRM, ERP and other systems that contain customer data so that they have a single view of the customer, in this case their students, granting USD the ability to better cater to their needs based on their history.

USD has begun their journey into the digital revolution by making a number of new mobile apps available for their students. Students can buy books via their mobile phone, obtain sports tickets, and check their dining account balance from their phones. USD IT staff estimate that with MuleSoft, they are building new apps in a fourth of the time, and on-ramping new developers in a third of the time. "Before MuleSoft, we didn't engage in conversations about connectivity because we didn't think it was possible," said one IT manager. "Now that we have Anypoint Platform with an application network that allows us to connect anything, we are not only thinking about what is possible, but we are also making it a reality."

The venerable lecture has been characterized by educational theorist Ludy Benjamin as "like Velveeta cheese - something lots of people consume but no one considers delicious."[10] Even though there hasn't been much pedagogical evidence that lectures are particularly engaging or effective, they are the way 80% of college classes are delivered. With online learning, universities have a chance to develop more dynamic educational experiences, if they can provide the technology.

The technology enablement to create these new experiences generally runs through central IT departments. Stephen Turner from MIT cites the edX example: "we have the edX learning platform which is a tremendously successfully initiative driven by MIT and Harvard and other institutions. Some portions of this online learning experience may actually come to supplement the traditional on-campus ways of learning, the traditional lectures, so there's going to be demands at touch points between those kinds of services and the service my own department provides." Again, this creates more demand on IT than current resourcing is able to provide.

---

[9] Grush, Mary." Once More with Insight: USD Students Get a Personal Assistant Mobile App." A Q and A with Chris Wessells. Campus Technology, March 15, 2016.
[10] Wood, Graeme. "The Future of College?" The Atlantic, September 2014.

The Solution: API-led connectivity

The sheer amount of applications, data, and devices in use or needed at universities means IT can no longer own everything. Rather than being in charge of every piece of the application stack, how does IT unlock the value of that data so that other people in the organization can build those applications without compromising security and performance? When one considers who is actually building applications in universities today, there are designers, business developers, mobile app developers, and development partners, and they're all going to build new applications and new experience for consumers with or without IT involvement. To succeed in provisioning technology to everyone who needs it in the right way, IT needs to think less about controlling the data and more about governing and providing self-serve access to it.

Central IT departments can make their current resources more efficient by removing technical debt and enabling IT departments outside central IT to self-serve their own technology needs. This is done through a concept called **API-led connectivity**, which leads to a delivery method of applications, data, and devices called an **application network**. These two concepts go hand in hand to reduce IT delivery time, make IT teams more efficient, and create ways to allow IT departments anywhere in the university to set up their own technology solutions quickly and easily.

The API-led connectivity approach provides a view of the organization based on reusable capabilities and who should own and access those capabilities. The ownership and accessibility of technology assets shifts in this model, because IT is unlocking the value of the data inside various departmental silos by decentralizing both access and value creation throughout the institution, rather than controlling that data themselves. The API-led connectivity approach takes a three-layered model with a System layer, Process layer and Experience layer. These layers open up data, model processes, orchestrate and augment data, and help define innovative experiences.

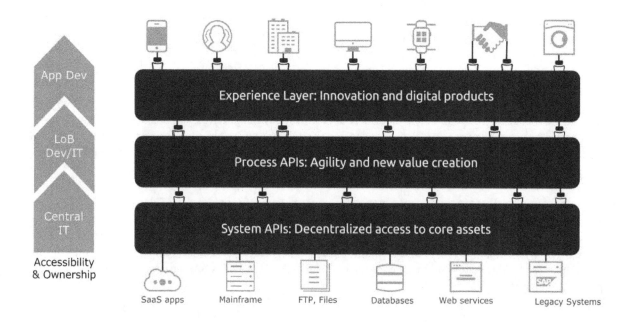

The role of each layer is to provide access and governance to the assets below. Each layer can deliver a different consumer experience so that people with different skillsets and requirements can access and leverage capabilities. API-led connectivity isn't just an architecture, it's a cultural shift -- a mode of operation. In this model, IT delivers capabilities to the university that support a broader range of needs and experiences and in turn the university learns to self-serve and not work around IT. The three API layers relieve tension, allow IT to retain control and permit other areas of the institution to be successful, autonomous, and drive new technology solutions.

Using the approach of API-led connectivity, central IT can create an application network, which is the means by which data, devices, and applications are simply connected to each other. Instead of spending time devising custom code for every new experience an IT team wants to add, using a central IT-supplied store of APIs, any developer or IT department can get their technology solution up and running without having to be supported by central IT or even having to do custom development work. This saves time, money and hassle.

Three Key Benefits of API-led Connectivity and the Application Network

I. Integrated

As universities move to cloud-based SaaS applications to save money and increase agility like Salesforce, Servicenow, and Coupa, integration becomes a key strategic challenge to make sure value is unlocked from these applications and that they work well and provide their benefits from the get-go.

Ross Mason, MuleSoft's founder and VP of Product Strategy points out, "More connectivity always leads to more innovation. We're about to move from a merely connected world to a hyperconnected one. if you can find a way to simplify and fast-track integration—among devices, applications, clouds, and networks—you can boost innovation and create new opportunities. The core technology trend enabling this shift is the API,which enables organizations to provide their ecosystems with standardized access to data and application functionality previously only available internally."[11]

The application network allows integration to happen quickly and easily through APIs; instead of doing endless custom point-to-point integrations, IT departments throughout the university can simply use an API to connect one system to

Case Study: University of Oklahoma

The University of Oklahoma has 30,000 students and has more National Merit Scholars than any other public university. With a newly appointed provost leading the charge, OU IT was challenged with reinventing itself to help drive better business intelligence; digital citizenship for students, faculty, alumni and partners; and a transition to real-time student services via mobile.

OU acknowledged the old way via batch file processing was non-sustainable. MuleSoft established a vision focused on both the digital experience and expectations of students and faculty; if OU wanted to remain competitive and retain its extremely high-performing student body, it would need to provide the technology experiences students wanted and the engaging educational experiences the faculty desired to provide.

MuleSoft offered an approach for OU to adopt an agile and repeatable path to market for disparate organizations within IT. MuleSoft also created a framework for their IT organizations to come together as a single unit.

After consulting with MuleSoft's other customers, including the University of Texas, OU decided that API-led connectivity was the right approach to modernize their IT architecture. They felt that API-led connectivity was the best way for IT to interact with its disparate stakeholders (students, faculty, and third parties), provided speed and repeatability, and gave OU the ability to meet future demands.

---

[11] Mason, Ross. "Connectivity: The Backbone of Innovation." Wired. March 9, 2015.

another, increasing productivity. API-led connectivity also provides room for future development, as APIs can be built to accommodate new technology quite easily.

II. Reusable

With this approach to connectivity, IT departments don't have to create bespoke new services and custom connections anymore. All data resources on the application network are made available through reusable interfaces, meaning that any application on the network can be a modular service that, like LEGO building blocks, connects to everything else very easily. New applications can be plugged into the application network as easily as one can plug in a printer.

The US State of Colorado demonstrated just how important reusability is in increasing IT efficiency. Like many public sector organizations, Colorado had an increased number of citizens needing public services, and a demand to make those services available online. Deputy CTO Michael Brown notes, "We are a cloud first, mobile first and API first state. We are constantly looking for opportunities where we can use technology to provide enterprise level services to our citizens."[12] By utilizing reusable integration templates, developers could connect its existing database systems and its citizen engagement platform to a CRM system almost immediately, doubling productivity. Colorado officials estimate that If they hadn't modernized their engagement platform, they would have had to increase staff and budget to be able to perform the same tasks.

Using an application network that provides an integration platform, and a central store of reusable APIs and integration templates, an IT department within a university can create any kind of application that they need without having to wait for IT to create the connections. This enables the technology that students, faculty, and administration want without creating undue burdens on IT to deliver it.

III. Self-Service

Partnering with the previous two concepts is the ability of any university IT department to self-serve their own technology solutions. This notion is absolutely key to expanding the footprint and the ability to deliver technology throughout the institution. If there is a limited amount of resourcing and time, the only way to increase central IT's output is by allowing other IT departments to create their own solutions.

The secret sauce to making this happen is the API. APIs form the glue that sticks together the various application components and other services, including the small, modular components called microservices. And now that APIs leverage REST, JSON, and other easy-to-use protocols, there's no excuse for developers not to get them right.

Stephen Turner from MIT explains how this works at his university: "The Math Department used to get a feed of data from our registrar's office information about the Math students and their academic record. This used to be a custom extract from a student system that the registrar's office would run. They'd put all this data in a spreadsheet, put it on a thumb drive and walk it over to the Math Department, and the Math Department would have to interpret the spreadsheet and load it up into their system to do whatever they needed to do with it. We've eliminated the thumb drive. We've created an API, so Math can just get this data directly from the API whenever they want it. It's not a special request to the registrar's office, waiting several days for somebody to run the extract and walk over the thumb drive. Now they have an API and they can get the data immediately."[13]

It's extraordinary to think that a necessary application needed to depend on someone putting data into a spreadsheet,

---

[12] Mulesoft.com. "State of Colorado: Elevating complex customer engagements."

[13] Mulesoft.com. "How MIT is increasing its clock speed." April 7, 2016.

dumping it on a thumb drive, and physically walking that data to where it needs to go. In an API-led connected world, this simply doesn't have to happen anymore - the data is simply where it needs to be for whoever needs and is authorized to use it.

Conclusion

Like many industries, universities are under pressure to provide new and innovative digital experiences for their students, faculty, administrators, and other stakeholders. Universities like MIT, the University of Pennsylvania, and and the University of Texas are turning to MuleSoft's vision of integration and IT delivery because of its ease of use, reusability, and its ability to lower operational cost and speed the completion of IT projects.

For more about MuleSoft's vision of how colleges and universities can take advantage of the opportunities that digital transformation affords, take a look at our book on how IT leaders can use the application network to harness business trends and make digital transformation possible. In addition, take an in-depth look at API-led connectivity to understand how it can benefit your institution from both a technical and an enterprise perspective.

Increasing E-Commerce Agility

The role of integration in staying ahead of the curve in a changing e-commerce environment

Abstract: In the fast-moving e-commerce marketplace firms are increasingly participating in more complex multi-partner value chains. As they do so they must build the agility to adapt to ever-changing market conditions, new entrants and emerging business models while maintaining cost competitiveness and reacting to high levels of staffing churn. To deliver on this imperative, firms must continuously build, maintain and update complex integration applications that pull together CRM, ERP, custom apps, partners and suppliers amongst others. Learn how a lightweight, standalone Enterprise Service Bus (ESB) lays the foundation for e-commerce software infrastructure and a series of best practices from market leaders who have built such infrastructures.

1 Maintaining velocity in a changing e-commerce landscape

While the hype of the late 90s dot-com boom may have faded, electronic commerce continues to be one of the fastest growing and most dynamic industries in the world. According to a recent report by Forrester Research, the overall e-commerce market in the United States alone is growing at a rate of around 10% per year and will reach nearly $300 billion by 2015. Forrester estimates growth rates in Europe to be slightly faster at 13% and emerging market growth rates at still higher rates.

Figure 1 Forecast: US Online Retail Forecast, 2010 To 2015

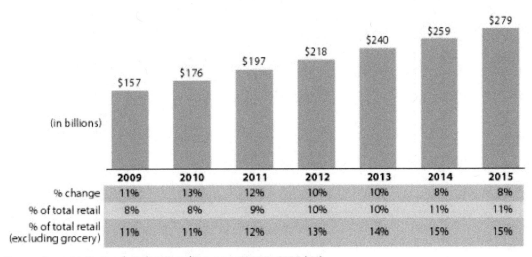

	2009	2010	2011	2012	2013	2014	2015
% change	11%	13%	12%	10%	10%	8%	8%
% of total retail	8%	8%	9%	10%	10%	11%	11%
% of total retail (excluding grocery)	11%	11%	12%	13%	14%	15%	15%

Source: Forrester Research Online Retail Forecast, 2010 To 2015 (US)

58596   Source: Forrester Research, Inc.

As e-commerce continues to grow worldwide, the marketplace is constantly undergoing transformation. The relatively simple online retailers of days gone by are increasingly being replaced by emerging vendors, retail ecosystems, more complex value chains, and other seismic shifts in the marketplace. E-commerce firms need to quickly pivot to respond to these market conditions.

Some key challenges faced by firms include:

- Enabling partner ecosystems and dynamic business relationships to exploit short market windows
- Maintaining cost leadership and margins without sacrificing innovation
- Managing the inherent high employee turnover in many technical roles to minimize business impact

While perhaps not immediately obvious, the choice of application integration technologies directly impacts each of these challenges. Integration is core to the entirety of an e-commerce transaction. For example, a fairly simple web order may entail interactions with web services, CRM applications, billing systems, ERP for

manufacturing and supply chain management, and/or external suppliers. On top of these common business systems, e-commerce applications often include unique e-commerce packages, for example shopping cart systems such as Magento or Shopify. Orchestrating between these different systems is core to a successful e-commerce infrastructure. For this reason integration can have far-reaching implications.

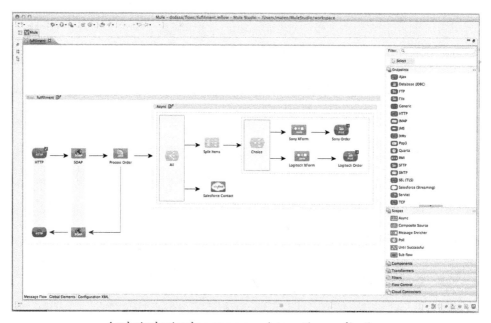

A relatively simple e-commerce integration application

2 Enabling Partner Ecosystems

In the early days of e-commerce, firms were fairly vertically integrated. Amazon.com, for example, established a reference model of a firm that provided a soup-to-nuts approach from ordering to warehousing to fulfillment of the entire order. However, Amazon quickly discovered the true power of e-commerce was in building an ecosystem around its core and forming a network of affiliates. Today, 40% of Amazon's sales derive from its affiliate program.

Amazon is not alone in its shift from a solely direct model to one of a complex ecosystem. The most successful e-commerce firms in recent years have adopted this type of model, focusing on specific portions of the value chain. In this sort of model, application integration becomes integral to success. Whereas monolithic systems were suitable for vertically integrated businesses, applications must be decomposed into services that can be utilized by different ecosystem partners in order to enable the new types of models.

In order to exploit new business opportunities, firms need to onboard partners quickly without negatively impacting the services of their existing lines of business and partners. For example, a new partner may utilize

---

new and idiosyncratic protocols, data formats or other technologies for communications. Fulfillment may differ between different lines of business, with some being internally fulfilled while others are sent back to a partner for fulfillment. The key to success for an e-commerce firm is building the flexibility to bring these new partners on-board quickly and in a repeatable manner.

E-commerce firms often, however, fall into pitfalls in their quest for rapid growth. E-commerce firms typically have substantial in-house development knowledge and try to design fully in-house solutions. Very often development teams believe the most expedient approach is a custom point-to-point integration with a large new partner. These approaches, however well suited to the first partner, fail to scale when partners need to be onboarded repeatedly and rapidly. Over time they become increasingly brittle and the velocity of the organization slows, allowing competitors to gain traction.

One of the largest ecosystem e-commerce players is Ebay. Ebay maintains multiple lines of businesses serving everyone from individual buyers and sellers to large companies. Ebay, of course, was an early leader in creating a marketplace for the exchange of goods that it did not directly deliver.

Ebay's GSI Commerce division largely delivers its business offerings. GSI delivers e-commerce, multichannel retailing and interactive marketing for large, business-to-consumer (b2c) enterprises in the U.S. and internationally.

GSI Commerce serves dozens of large enterprises and constantly onboards new firms. While doing so, GSI/Ebay must maintain complete reliability for its existing clients. To do so, GSI built its architecture as a series of services integrated using Mule ESB. By doing so, GSI is more able to quickly respond to the needs of clients, both new and old.

Learn more about how eBay's GSI Commerce division built their architecture to support a wide ecosystem of clients.

http://www.mulesoft.com/case-study-gsi

While Ebay is of course a huge organization and one of the dominant players in the e-commerce space, smaller e-commerce firms arguably have even more to gain by building a strong partner ecosystem. For smaller firms to keep pace with larger competitors they must adopt the right architecture to enable rapid partner onboarding.

MashON provides an example of how a smaller firm can build an ecosystem. While Ebay focuses on brokering e-commerce transactions, MashON's focus is on the customization and fulfillment of products. Its business model centers on creating customized or personalized versions of standard products.

Due to its focus on customization and personalization, developing an ecosystem around MashON is absolutely paramount to its business. MashON customizes products for other firms and thus its ability to gain share is gated by the speed at which it can onboard new partners. Before adopting a standard integration framework, MashON struggled with its growth. Like many firms, it had initially attempted to build a platform entirely in-house. The result was every new partner required a substantial custom integration effort. Typically, this took 3-6 months to complete.

Facing the challenges of growth, MashON adopted Mule ESB as their integration framework. Mule reduced MashON's partner onboarding to less than 3 days. MashON was, therefore, able to more quickly exploit new business opportunities and accelerate their growth rate.

Learn more about how MashON reduced their partner onboarding time from 3-6 months to less than 72 hours.

http://www.mulesoft.com/case-study-mashon

When evaluating how to best enable partner ecosystems, the top questions to ask include:

- What are the time-to-market considerations I must consider? How fast must I onboard my partners?
- If I needed to substantially increase the number of partners over my current plan to support growth, how would I scale my efforts?
- Will my choice of integration solution impact partner onboarding?

3 Maintaining Cost Leadership without Sacrificing Innovation

A productive partner ecosystem can be a significant source of competitive advantage in the fast-evolving e-commerce marketplace. However, fundamentally, e-commerce is an industry characterized by price transparency and cost competition coupled with product innovation. Even miniscule differences in cost overhead can determine success or failure for e-commerce firms. For this reason e-commerce firms have

been leaders in managing determinants such as their supply chain and cash conversion cycles. However, software integration choices can also be major determinants in the cost structure of firms.

As was previously discussed, many firms initially try to build their entire platform in house. From an application integration perspective, this takes the form of developing a series of point-to-point integrations for each component of an e-commerce application. Many firms find this initially expedient when faced with getting their core engine up and running. The problems arise over time. These approaches entail significant maintenance costs as applications are modified to changing business needs. In an industry as fast moving as e-commerce, this transition from creation to maintenance and modification happens virtually immediately. Firms that take this approach often fail to react to changing market conditions and suffer from a high cost structure over the long term, render them uncompetitive.

Large software vendors often responded to this common pain point for e-commerce firms by offering service oriented architecture (SOA) stacks. These large stacks were primarily designed for usage by the financial services industry during its most flush period and proved ill-suited to the needs of e-commerce. They were designed for projects that had long delivery timeframes where scale was important but speed was of limited interest. Furthermore, they were designed for large, monolithic development processes and data center architectures rather than the more agile approaches required in the e-commerce space. The implementation costs and up front investment proved far too great for firms engaged in cost competition. As a result, these SOA stacks proved ill suited to e-commerce, and were often abandoned.

An integration architecture for e-commerce needs to be lightweight, flexible and deliver low total cost of ownership both at deployment time and in the long term. It must conform to the modern data center architecture used by e-commerce firms as well the agile development methodologies necessary to stay ahead of the curve. Finally, the integration architecture must ease, not hinder the embrace of new technologies such as cloud services, mobile devices and open APIs, each of which holds the prospect of future business growth.

One of the United States' largest low-cost airlines provides an excellent example of how to use integration to maintain cost leadership. While one might not think of an airline as an e-commerce case, this airline handles 75% of all bookings through its own branded website and hence, can reasonably be counted as one of the largest e-commerce firms in the world. By using Mule ESB as the core of the integration between its front end e-commerce and back end systems, it has lowered the cost of development and reduced developer training costs while increasing its ability to grow and expand. The airline has managed to maintain cost leadership in its space and impressive growth in a competitive environment, consistently outpacing its peers.

Another example of cost reductions in e-commerce lies in the non-profit part of the e-commerce sector. Again this might not be the most frequently considered part of e-commerce, but it is one where cost leadership is most important because any extra costs detract from the core mission of the organization.

By using Mule ESB, the Leukemia & Lymphoma Society reduced its overhead for online fundraising from 7% to 2% of revenue collected.

Learn more about how the Leukemia & Lymphoma Society reduced the cost of their e-commerce transactions.

http://www.mulesoft.com/case-study-leukemia-lymphoma-society

Similarly an e-commerce vendor focused on college textbooks adopted Mule ESB for the integration of their e-commerce application to an ERP system. By doing so the firm substantially reduced the cost of developing applications, improving both their cost structure and ability to develop new applications.

When evaluating how to maintain cost leadership without sacrificing innovation, the top questions to ask are:

- How much up front investment will this approach require? Consider both hard hardware and software costs and softer costs around implementation time.
- What is the long-term cost of my solution? Will this solution prove easy or hard to maintain?
- As my needs change and the market evolves will my choice help or hinder my ability to adapt?
- Is my cost-reducing choice hindering my ability to innovate or embrace emerging technologies in the future or is it, in fact, enabling me to do so?

4 Managing the inherent high employee turnover in many technical roles to minimize business impact

A final challenge facing all e-commerce firms is the high turnover rate in their development teams. Compared to other industries e-commerce firms have far above average levels of employee churn. This creates a number of challenges. When employees, particularly "superstar" employees, leave the firm they often take key knowledge of applications with them. New staff often struggle to maintain the applications these employees initially built. On the flip side, new employees present their own challenges. While the new employees may be quite capable they often are unfamiliar with some of the key technologies used by the firm.

To solve the first challenge—departing employees leaving the organization with applications that are difficult to maintain—there are a number of solutions. In addition to those deriving from good software development methodologies, the choice of integration approach can have a substantial impact. Using an integration platform like an ESB can separate business logic from protocols and data formats, making maintenance easier regardless of the developer tasked with the job. When a key developer leaves, this platform facilitates the migration of maintenance to new staff.

In terms of new staff, the choice of integration platform can have a substantial impact here as well. Organizations adopting SOA stacks from vendors such as IBM and Oracle often struggle to find talent with specific skillsets. E-commerce firms are most appealing to generalists rather than "integration specialists." Furthermore, these specialists typically command salary premiums of 30% or more and require substantial additional training, impacting the bottom line of the hiring company. In contrast, Mule ESB is designed to be used by any Java developer with limited additional training. This makes staffing and onboarding new employees much easier for e-commerce firms.

When evaluating how to manage employee turnover, the top questions to ask include:

- How will I transition integration projects when staff changes?
- Do I want a set of "integration specialists" or would I prefer technology generalists?
- What level of salary will I expect to pay for future staff?
- How quickly can new employees become productive and what level of training is required?

5 The Software Architecture for E-Commerce

Integration is an often-overlooked area within the field of e-commerce. However, it is absolutely core to the success or failure of e-commerce firms. As e-commerce moves increasingly towards more complicated ecosystems and value chains, integration is the determinant of whether a firm can exploit new partner

opportunities or whether the firm will fall victim to industry change. Integration can enable a firm to create or maintain cost leadership or it can be a burden on the balance sheet. Finally, given high employee turnover amongst developers in e-commerce, integration can either enable firms to deal with this reality or exacerbate the challenges it creates.

The most successful firms in the e-commerce industry utilize integration middleware that enables rapid deployment, quick developer onboarding and faster integration. Selecting the right integration strategy and supporting architecture is one of the most important decisions firms make. MuleSoft has extensive experience in delivering solutions tailored to the needs of e-commerce firms. Many of the largest and most successful e-commerce firms rely on a Mule ESB backbone.

MuleSoft can help you evaluate your key challenges and objectives and develop the key integration applications that will help you grow in coming years.

To learn more and contact an expert visit http://www.mulesoft.com/mulesoft-e-commerce

About MuleSoft

MuleSoft delivers the world's #1 integration platform for the cloud and enterprise. Built on the most widely used open source application infrastructure products, Mule ESB, iON integration platform as a service (iPaaS), and Tcat (enterprise Tomcat server) provide an ideal combination of simplicity and power to today's web applications. The company's offerings boast more than 2 million downloads and over 3,200 organizations in production, including leading companies such as Walmart.com, MasterCard, Nokia, Nestlé, Honeywell and DHL, as well as 5 of the world's top 10 banks and over 35% of the Global 500. MuleSoft is headquartered in San Francisco with offices worldwide.

For more information: www.mulesoft.com, or email info@mulesoft.com.

Download Mule ESB: http://www.mulesoft.com/download/

www.ingramcontent.com/pod-product-compliance
Lightning Source LLC
LaVergne TN
LVHW060133070326

832902LV00018B/2781